majority of the board will be comprised of women; including seated board member Melissa Patla.

With Ms. Thomas the board would have six of nine board members female. What a story! My proposal is a token award for the leader in the political challenge for women, in our community. On my own I purchased this cup for Missi, a heroine by all standards.

Stated on this cup: ONLY THOSE WHO WILL RISK GOING TO FAR CAN POSSIBLY FIND OUT HOW FAR ONE CAN GO. Followed by; "I am only one; but still I am one. I cannot do everything, but still I can do something. I will not refuse do the something I can do.

This is what is written & pictured on the cup. It is my conclusion that Melissa believes and practices the Helen Keller philosophy.

We have a handicapped female, financially challenged, like many of us, driving an old van that breaks down weekly, single, been there, raising her daughter's children. When SOS was having so much trouble the last election getting people to run, who steps up to the

plate, Grandma. Then in the spirit of the Energizer Bunny

emphasis added, emphasis added again, she hit the road, holding meet & greets, fund raisers, and hand outs.

Except for Caffery tiny emphasis, she was the top vote getter.

Melissa stands well among those who wield power in Wilkes-Barre. Never came naturally. She is a tuffy!

Mike Belusko City Council, Tom Teletz WBA business manager, Mike, Christine Solomon, Beth Gilbert, City Council, Missi, Tony Brooks City council, Mr. Maher, Kanjorski's chief of staff.

On May 4, 2019 a forum was held at St. Stephen's Church where each candidate gave a briefing on his or her platform.

In the last election Missi went to an event with me [Dr. Holodick] and sat on the dais actually physically shaking, but handled it like a pro.

Actual picture of her on the dais. proud emphasis!

Now we move to her experience on the board. But before we discuss it; be it known that Missi is also the board's rep on the WB Career & Technology Center's Joint operating committee, and has been the recording secretary for Save Our Schools. The school board experience for her has not been fun. The world leaders in intimidation, intimidated her, sometimes there were actual put-downs. But she stood her ground.

How about Rev. Walker who supported the neighborhood schools, but changed and actually told me that because he was in the minority, "he went along to get a long." How's that working for our kids & taxpayers? As a coach in the district he knows full well the value of neighborhood schools for the economically challenge students and their families.

Not Missi, she has held stead fast voting NO every time anything came up relating to the consolidation of the high schools destroying the neighborhood schools concept. She has been intimidated behind closed doors and in public meetings because of her stance for the education and safety of children and taxpayers. The following photo taken at the ground breaking is perhaps the most bold and courageous stand. She is dressed all in black to make a statement, she backs it up with refusing to wear the hard hat, and she refused to accept the shovel with her name engraved on it.

The solicitor, first on left with head bowed, stated to Missi, that is your constitutional right, and should OSHA fine you I will pay your fine; very symbolic of WBASD's intimidation tactics.

To[photo is Ray, Brian, Melissa, Rev Shawn & Denise.

If we equate that line up in the bottom photo above—of administrators, solicitor(s), architects, construction management firm personnel, board members and legislators, who 15 minutes prior praised the site and the consolidation to high hell, Board Member Patla stands head and shoulders over the entire group.

Having 50 years in the private and public sector, I can't name very many people would do what she has done; it took commitment and bravery.

Thank you Missi. You are Special!

Preface

Please don't forget that first and foremost nearly all evidence says don't consolidate schools because it harms academics, student sense of well-being, student participation, and that it increases costs. Having said that, the site is receiving such attention because outside of perhaps Chernobyl, it would be difficult to find a worse spot to build a school.

It's Time to Replace the Tyrannical Leaders of the Wilkes-Barre Area School Board (WBASB)?   It is not too late!

FYI: What is tyranny?

We are all interested in knowing or being reminded. The Wilkes-Barre School Board is practicing tyranny as we speak and so let's define it for neophytes and for oldsters who need to be reminded.

Tyranny is cruel and oppressive government or rule. Who feels tyranny? Especially people who survive war – they most often escape tyranny. There are many synonyms for tyranny which will help us all put this nasty word in perspective. They include:

despotism · absolutism · absolute power · autocracy · dictatorship · undemocratic rule · reign of terror · totalitarianism · Fascism · oppression · suppression · repression.

There are more as in "a nation under cruel and oppressive government...cruel, unreasonable, or arbitrary use of power or control..."the tyranny of the nine-to-five day" ·

Those in ancient Greece saw tyranny as a rule by one who has absolute power without a legal right.

A number of these definitions fit the acts perpetrated by the Wilkes-Barre Area School Board. Hopefully, though this book, we will be able to change the complexion of the board for the future.

We are citizens of a truly exceptional country and a fine city and county and school district. Regarding our school district, it is like a train that has temporarily gone off the track. In order to put it back on the right track, the people of the Area need to remove all of the incumbents running for the board this year. They are cluttering up the tracks with bad ideas and a disdain for the people of the area.

Jody Busch, Debra Formola, Terry Schiowitz, Beth-Ann Owens Harris, and Robin Shudak, are at the ready to serve on the board to represent the people. All they need is our vote.

America, of course, is the exception to all rules for forming governments. Our country is founded on principles of liberty and freedom. It is the first government ever to elect officials who are subject to the will of the people and not vice versa, no matter how this board practices its official role.

The rule is to be of, by, and for the people, not of, by and for the government. The people matter. The school board does not matter unless they are doing the work of the people. All of the very powerful officials in all forms of governments—local, state, and national, and even school boards—work for the people.

Unfortunately for the citizens of Wilkes-Barre Area, our school board, which was elected in good faith by the citizens, believes it was elected to office to serve their own selfish agenda. They have chosen to disregard the will of the people. They do not believe in the precepts brought forth by the founders. Instead they have made their governance all powerful instead of being subservient to the people as it is written in law.

The Founders knew that even the great Constitution they wrote might not be enough to keep knaves and scoundrels from subverting their work. We see the personification of everything the bad notions from which the Founders attempted to protect us in the current Wilkes-Barre Area School Board. I wish it were different but what is, is.

Quite frankly, they are bad! bad! bad! The people must therefore be strong and forget about friends on the board. This is not a beauty contest but those who follow the will of the people are beautiful in spirit and those who do not are simply ugly. For the good of all the people of the area, this board must be voted out of office They have broken their bond of trust with the people. There is no other solution that can be effective.

And so, today, 230+ years after the Constitution was ratified, all is not perfect in America, nor is it perfect in the burgs and cities and towns that make up the individual parts of America. Nonetheless, the principles of the Constitution are so sound and so powerful that even a knave politician cannot bring our country or any municipality down—even though they may try.

Our tyrannical school board will not stand. The people will prevail. Voting on November 5, 2019, the people have another opportunity to win back control of their school board. Vote in the SOS slate of candidates who are in place for the people—and that says it all.

We have all learned from our recent experience that there are far too many politicians who today control the Wilkes-Barre Area School Board. Their mission is to overthrow the will of the people and impose their will upon us. The big concern in Wilkes-Barre Area, of course is that if we don't smarten up, things can and will get a lot worse. Nobody expects a school board dictatorship amidst a democracy / republic. I suspect that is why you are reading this book.

The people in our area and beyond have reason not to trust politicians as our recent history shows that the people are often considered last. Remember the Judge's scandal with Judge Ciavarella and Judge Conahan now doing time in the Big House. They let the people down. This does nothing to make anybody believe that the politicians are on the side of the people.

Then, of course we have more recent bad news with Mayor Courtright in Scranton, just up the road from Wilkes-Barre Area, resigning in the midst of a major scandal of graft, bribery, and poor governance for the people. Many, right now, are not sure that our current school board could withstand such scrutiny.

Members of the boards from the past had a tough time staying out of trouble and some could not stay out of the Big House. Somehow their fingers got really sticky when they reached the positions in which cash and perquisites were close by. Former board members Pizzella, Dunn, & Elmy and other officials, are three reasons why

Wilkes-Barre Area regular people do not trust their school board to do the right thing most of the time. There are even more but in recent times, these three have been convicted of corruption from their activities on the Wilkes-Barre Area School Board and other public jobs. Here are a few examples, the full facts of which are easy to find in news archives.

Former Wilkes-Barre Area School Board President Frank Pizzella Jr. remained silent as he walked out of federal court after his sentencing on a corruption charge. The people did not do this and did not falsely accuse. Mr. Pizzella was found guilty of passing a bribe to help secure a teaching job for his nephew. Nobody said that's all he did but it was enough to change his life.

Former Wilkes-Barre Area School Board member Brian F. Dunn conceded he "made a mistake" when he pocketed a $5,000 reward for helping a prospective teacher secure a job in the district. Some believe that Dunn found a way to make his unpaid position pay off.

The most recent corruption in the news was Louis Elmy who everybody I know liked. It must be so easy to get extra stuff that everybody on the board seems to have their hand out and they expect no bad results. Yet, three at the top at one time are still paying the price.

Now, the current board has this school they want to build. Humph! The former president of the Wilkes-Barre Area School Board, Elmy, plead guilty to federal extortion and weapons charges that could send him to prison for life, according to the U.S. Department of Justice. He was recently charged with drug trafficking and a weapons offense. He reached a plea deal agreement with federal prosecutors.

Elmy's charges are from alleged actions while working as a counselor in the work release program at Luzerne County Correctional Facility. How did they get him? Elmy extorted money and other items of value from work release inmates in exchange for giving them special privileges and unauthorized furloughs, according to charging documents. Just the guy you want in charge of prisoners Right?

He accepted cash, liquor and assistance in obtaining crack cocaine from work release inmates, in return for granting those inmates special privileges and perks, prosecutors allege. He also created fake documents to further the extortion scheme, by cutting and pasting the signatures of county judges from legitimate court orders, the charging documents state. He is in big trouble.

Elmy's illegal activities took place from November 2013 until his arrest in February 2016, prosecutors allege.

It begs the question "will anybody from the current board be found guilty of anything regarding the hurried up acquisition of Plains property and the building of a school on top of a toxic mine dump? Who knows? Maybe they did nothing wrong? Maybe Pizzella, Dunn, and Elmy did nothing wrong and it's just a mistake. Maybe snow is made from boiling water? Maybe the people are the bad guys because we voted them in and let them do what they did for way too long.

Go a bit north and it gets worse. Mayor Courtright of Scranton, just twenty-miles north from Wilkes-Barre became the third Democrat mayor in eastern Pennsylvania to be convicted of public corruption in about 16 months. These criminals all engaged in similar schemes believing they were more powerful than the people they served and who they can dupe into reelecting them—even when they serve poorly. The former mayors of Allentown and Reading are already serving their prison sentences.

US Attorney David Freed commented that: ""I think the citizens of Northeastern Pennsylvania could be forgiven for feeling like they've been down this road before," adding that the investigation continues. "I think what this shows is we will work as hard as it takes, where we have credible evidence of wrongdoing." Thank you, Sir!

Residents of Wilke-Barre Area who are now learning that a tyrannical school board has its own agenda to follow and the agenda does not include what is best for the people need to take heart. These crooks eventually will go to jail. With prosecutors such as Attorney Freed on our team, the reign of terror of the Wilkes-Barre Area School Board may itself find an inglorious and ignominious end. Hopefully soon!

Federal prosecutors made their case against Courtright, 61, who first took the office of Scranton Mayor in 2014. He collected tens of thousands of dollars in bribes by pressuring people who needed city permits or contracts. He also got use of a beach property, carpentry at a karate club he owns, and landscaping at his home. He was so brazen, before being caught, he thought it was OK.

With what our own school board has brought to Wilkes-Barre Area residents, can we not envision a scenario where the greed and selfishness of these know-it-alls comes back to bite them? Nobody would cry if it did! We await their trials if they come.

It serves us well to ask how such wise men from the founding of the country could have created a system in a representative republic in which the knaves who are elected can choose to direct the good of the area to serve themselves and not the people. With a decision to build a massive and expensive consolidated school on top of toxic mine waste, risking children who will breathe in the mine-shaft coal ash poison every day, how is it that this elected board could not have done better. What is it they hope to achieve by putting citizens in peril?

Our area's ailments are large and growing. Taxes are too high; elected officials are out of touch; government has become too big and powerful for the people, local spending is out of control; and the people seem to have no voice in government at any level. Look at the dirt on the major streets and the uncut weeds, the potholes on avenues, and the disrespect the public is given in public meetings and it is easy to conclude that whatever decisions are made in this area, they do not address the problems or the immediate needs of the public. It should be different. It will never be different, however, by voting in the bad guys back for another go at the public treasury.

How about Wilkes-Barre city which put its hands up in the air when the big bad Wilkes-Barre Area School Board said they were closing down all the high schools in the city. How will that affect the people of Wilkes-Barre. WB officials never asked. They simply let this powerful board of directors have their way. Even the newly nominated Mayor of the Democrat party has not suggested once of which I am aware that moving all the high schools in WB to Plains is a bad idea for Wilkes-Barre.

Our SOS group is sponsoring replacement board directors for the school district. I hope you vote for them. Perhaps the group should have found a few write-ins for WB officials who offer nothing regarding the Mine Shaft High debacle. At least Beth Gilbert, the strongest council member in a poor lot, offered that she would like to do something but…Sorry to say nobody else even offered that we might even hear their whimpers before the more powerful WBASD board.

The school board is so powerful, all WB City officials are afraid to offer even a word of caution to the people. Maybe we could have found a better group to represent Wilkes-Barre. Just Maybe! Why is Wilkes-Barre the city that always draws the short straw. Well, folks, maybe we are electing the wrong cowards? Maybe?

Looking across the country we find that too many people are too lazy to hold government accountable, too many politicians are on the take, and worse than that, the list of ailments is growing, not shortening. The losers in every election cry foul even when the Constitution is followed. Some are willing to cast the Constitution, our guarantee from tyranny, aside so that their guy can win an election. Then what?

Well, when a school board like ours chooses not to represent the people of Northeastern PA, what choices do the people have? The simplest way to solve a problem of poor leadership is to replace the leaders. I am pleased that the Save Our Schools group is sponsoring five candidates for the school board to do just that. In addition to getting better leadership, at the same time, we also get to throw the bums out, and they well deserve the boot even if the door is not wide open.

Your intention no doubt in learning about the issues of the people v the WBASD board has to do with how the people who knowingly voted in these candidates and officials, who now rule by tyranny, can come up with a solution to minimize the great power that they gave away to these knaves in past elections. We can do it unless we give up! Let's not give up!

One would think that an elected member of the school board in the WBASD, would recognize the desires of the people and would do their best. But it has not happened and it looks like it will not happen.

The current board has known during their term that the fundamental laws of America place the people first in the hierarchy. Yet, for their own reasons, they have not decided to do the right thing for the people of this area of Pennsylvania. They care only about being reelected by chicanery.

For their glory and perhaps their pocketbooks, they take the risks expecting the people will not fight their rewards. We must deny them the privilege of serving us. Vote in the five SOS candidates who promise to be servants of the people who elect them.

By choosing to read this book, you have decided that you want to understand why what is happening regarding this area of the country is happening. Thank you. That is why Brian Kelly wrote the book and why the members of the SOS team are so glad that it is out here now for all of us to read.

The Founders saw it as a civic duty for Americans to pay attention to our government so that we could avoid being chumps and being snookered by crooked professional politicians. That is why you are reading this book. The board team from the WBASD do not think you matter. They are sure you are worthless. You are nothing. If you think they are right, vote their pretty faces back in to mess with the people another day. I hope you don't. Please talk to your God before you cast your ballot.

The board would like it if we all sat back and simply took it on the chin and we forgot that we have been and are harmed by the government policies enacted by WBASD officials. They may seem constitutional but they are selfish and corrupt edicts that are anti-people. That is why the dedicated SOS group fights the tyrannical leadership of the WBASD. Maybe if the board chose to represent the people according to their oath of office, we could all be in synch. But, the verdict is in. This board has got to go and the sooner the better.

Your author continually monitors what is happening to our government, including our school board. He has written extensively on the major problems our country and all our institutions of government face. He knows that regardless of problems in government, the people's issues must always be number one.

Brian Kelly is one of America's most forthright and eloquent nationalist spokesmen, always ready to bite back after being bitten. This school board has bitten us all and we do not have to take it anymore. Kelly has written over 200 books in his quest to make America better. He is committed to see Coughlin, GAR, and Meyers survive and thrive for many more generations.

When Philadelphia thinks it is time to rip down Independence Hall after almost 300 years, maybe we in Wilkes-Barre Area should inquire about "why." ? Then we should figure out how many years we really have left in our own well-built facilities. More and more state and national advisory groups think our buildings—Coughlin (Wilkes-Barre High), GAR (Grand Army of the Republic) and Meyers, named after a great City Patriot Elmer L. Meyers, can last forever. I do also once we find a school board that promises to keep them properly maintained. They are what the state of PA calls forever schools because, "unless crooked school boards choose to kill them, they will never die."

Brian W. Kelly characterizes himself as a nobody from Wilkes-Barre PA. He is the author of America 4 Dummmies, The Bill of Rights 4 Dummmies, The Annual Guest Plan, Saving America, Taxation Without Representation, Millennials are People Too! Jobs! Jobs! Jobs! The Federalist Papers by the Framers, and many other patriotic books. All books are available at www.amazon.com/author/brianwkelly.

Kelly wrote this book so that the people of Wilkes-Barre Area can know the stakes of having an incompetent and incorrigible board in office and so that the people will always make the right decisions on representation in the future. Thank you for reading this book.

You are going to love the rest of this book since it is designed by an American for the Americans who are living in the Wilkes-Barre Area. Few books are a must-read but *The Big Toxic School! Wilkes-Barre Area's Tale of Corruption, Deception, Taxation & Tyranny* is destined to quickly appear at the top of Northeastern Pennsylvania's most read list.

Sincerely,

Brian P. Kelly, Editor in Chief

Table of Contents

About the Author

Brian W. Kelly retired as an Assistant Professor in the Business Information Technology (BIT) program at Marywood University, where he also served as the IBM i and midrange systems technical advisor to the IT faculty. Kelly designed, developed, and taught many college and professional courses. He is a contributing technical editor to a number of IT industry magazines. On the patriotic side, you can find many of Kelly's articles on www.brianwkelly.com. He is the major author for Lets Go Publish – www.letsgopublish.com

Kelly is a former IBM Senior Systems Engineer and in his post technical career, he has been a candidate for US Congress and the US Senate from Pennsylvania. He also ran for Mayor of Wilkes-Barre. Not being a politician, Brian learned in his losses that it is very difficult to fight the machine,

Kelly has an active information technology consultancy. He is the author of 201 books and numerous articles. Ask Brian to speak at your next rally! You would enjoy his frank perspectives!

Over the past twenty five years, Brian Kelly has become one of America's most outspoken and eloquent conservative / nationalist protagonists. Brian loves America. Besides *The Electoral College 4 Dummmies*, Kelly is also the author of many other patriotic books. Check them out at www.Amazon.com /author/brianwkelly, Kindle, Barnes & Noble and other fine online booksellers.

Chapter 1 The Wilkes-Barre Area School District & the Board

Please don't forget that first and foremost nearly all evidence says don't consolidate schools because it harms academics, student sense of well-being, student participation, and that it increases costs. Having said that, the site is receiving such attention because outside of perhaps Chernobyl, it would be difficult to find a worse spot to build a school.

The Wilkes-Barre Area School Board. The villains in this story

The first part of the story sets the stage for the rest of the story. The current board has had a number of prior boards to teach them their tricks.

The Culture of Cooperation

What is it that the people Wilkes-Barre Area will have to deal with if the board has its way and the Big Toxic School is built on the Big Toxic Mountain in Plains Twp. Health, poor education results, big time taxation and a special burning when and Bill # 76 ever passes. See Chapter 21.

Will it be the culture of corruption or the culture of cooperation or both and more. The checkered past of the board is something we all need to remember when we try to sort out the movements of the current board of directors. Let's review some of the big time board "heroes" of this storied past.

Board members like to cooperate with each other, perhaps just a little more than they should. Does their culture of cooperation raise to the level of "Kids for Cash?" Consider this: "If seven thousand students are not meeting their potential, and 2400 are placed in harms way, it's damn close." There is only one group to blame—the Wilkes-Barre Area School Board. No doubt about it. Top secret sources provided much of the information for this section--NATO, SEATO, CRYPTO!

The first :hero" on the left top above is Frank Pizzella, listed as "board president." The story and the facts coincide on this one as this board member was not elected to the lofty position of Board President until **after** the FBI indicted him. Yes, after he was indicted, his peers believed that he had become worthy of the board presidency.

As we move on to another infamous "board president," of the past, we find Lou Elmy, not shown. Some were quite concerned when they saw him at a board meeting held in the gym at Solomon Elementary. For everybody to see, there was a sign in the upper left corner of the gym that clearly said soft drinks were not allowed in the gym. To set the example, Elmy had a soda right in front of him as shown below:

This was clearly violating the board's own law—breaking the law? Then a while later, the headline was out that stated, "Former board president faces life in prison." Possession of weapons, drugs with the intent to distribute, and forging the signatures of sitting judges. The stories can't get better for the reader. But these were the characters that once ran this board.

Then we have some sitting board members who are active in the fray. We can start with Ned Evans, a board member with credentials as a retired principal. He has what the folks have heard is "an almost doctorate." He got very publicly arrested for a DUI not too long ago but did not believe he should be charged. He told the officers he was a WBA school board member in a plea for exoneration.

The hospital personal, security et al said he was a belligerent drunk. Done? We would think! Not enough to stop this member of the board cooperative. Ned later posted on social media that a teacher raping a student can be seen as "humorous." It was reported as oral sex, Ned wrote," I hope she didn't break her teeth." Whew!

For the first time in the 100-year history of the district, the eight remaining board members and the superintendent requested the resignation of a board member. What do you think happened? Here is the result in a newspaper picture. Result?

66 My votes are for the children of the
district and the taxpayers of the district. 99

Evans insists he won't go

2nd WBA director in hot water

By Mark Guydish
mguydish@timesleader.com

WILKES-BARRE — Denise Thomas
became the second Wilkes-Barre Area
School Board member this week grap-
pling with calls for her resignation thanks
to Facebook posts.

Denise Thomas

Current board member, Denise Thomas is the second board member
who made the papers as you can see. She held a district position as a
clerk at GAR high school. There were many (16 purported) copies of

e-mails found that were extremely racist, and there were put downs of poor minority test scores.

Denise defended herself and said someone else was on her computer and they posted the suspicious e-mails while she was on break. Also her face book posts were considered questionable. Her sister supposedly posted derogatory statements about Mexicans and Methodists. The word is that Denise gave her approval or agreement. Though the FBI had nothing to do with her promotion, her stellar behavior in this instance earned her the board presidency.

Next is Jim Geiger, the third compromised board member of nine. He is a retired Pa. Corrections Office, SCI Retreat. Jim did not run this time for the board. Maybe he was tired from so many public jobs. Who know?. No paper photos; these came from the candid camera.

Jim's first notoriety of which the public is aware was at a board meeting when a citizen caught him snoozing – below pic…Honk!

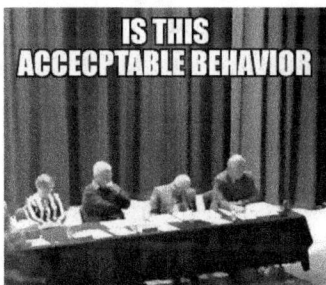

The second incident was caught clandestinely by a passer-by who noticed something racy on his phone screen during a meeting. Though some may not find it funny at all, it was a quiet gaff in which he was caught on video watching some stuff that was "inappropriate" on his smart phone while Joe Caffrey was reaching crescendo. If Caffrey ran more exciting meetings perhaps the board would be able to nap someplace else and not need such diversions. As Paul Harvey said, the Rest of The Story to Follow—some day!

Pennsylvania	**Third-degree felonies: malfeasance or misfeasance in office, or for any misdemeanor in office shall forfeit his office. 65 Pa. Stat. Ann. §121.** Misfeasance definition is – trespass; specifically: the performance of a lawful action in an illegal or **improper manner.** Misfeasance definition, which is an act that is not illegal but is improperly performed. It is also distinct from Nonfeasance, which is a failure to act that results in injury. **Would the following constitute meeting the state statue, 121?**

There are even more difficult to believe tales of board members with significant evidence of illegal, unethical, and heartless actions by this board. For example, there was a board meeting held in the auditorium of GAR High School. The reason for the meeting was to gain board approval for a plan to submit to the Pa. Department of Education, Plan Con Division.

The board plan was ill-conceived from the beginning. The essence was to consolidate a state of the art new high school for the Coughlin and Meyers High School; heartlessly intentionally segregating the GAR students from the new school.

Sixty people spoke to the board requesting that the discriminatory plan be tabled, while concurrently, the students in attendance were singing the GAR alma mater. In a zoning hearing, under oath, the superintendent stated that the GAR students would not be included in the new school. The idea was taken to a zoning hearing where it failed.

Had the board listened to the 60 people the taxpayers would not have lost $4.9 million dollars. GAR still needed a better plan than nothing. The High School has the highest percentage of minority students and economically disadvantaged students in the district. The NAACP Executive Director gave her opinion on the plan. It was a combination of malfeasance and misfeasance. Most people understand the meaning of malfeasance.

'RACISM IS ALIVE AND WELL'

NAACP leader blasts W-B Area consolidation plan

Misfeasance is defined as an act that is not illegal but is improperly performed. It begins with the board not waiting for zoning approvals and spending $4.9 million on the Washington Street project, and it failed. The act of authorizing the work was not illegal but certainly improperly preformed.

Next was the purchase of the Pagnotti site where the solicitor and superintendent had the board sign a sales agreement at a cost of $4.2 million dollars, justifying the over payment ($250,000 to $800,000 appraisal) stating the deed contained mineral rights at $3.2 million. However, the deed did not list mineral rights.

Then there was payment of 4 times the lowest assessed value for the toxic site. They then awarded a $763,000 contract for site work before the sales agreement was even signed.

Worth re-stating: "There is a wider lesson here also for the voting public: character matters when placing people in office and choosing un-trust worthy leaders at any level of government can have dire, real-life consequences." Citizens Voice

Here are some pictures of the board's handiwork at Meyers. Why not just fix the buildings rather than contract with an out of the area company to build the menagerie you see on the next page. Why not just have a few custodians build the temporary covering that in the end was unneeded anyway. Was the board trying to prove that Meyers was bad, bad, bad. How is it they could not find any craftsman in the area could build this "shed."

The "sheds" at Meyers and Coughlin, placed to catch falling bricks, cost the taxpayers $243,000 and did not include painting. They have been up for nearly 5 years and not a pebble on top. Some refer to them as costly theatrical props.

  k W

Many communities form Wilkes-Barre Area School District

When the price must be paid by Wilkes-Barre Area taxpayers for the boondoggle consolidated school that is planned to be built over a toxic mine dump, there will be a lot of weeping and gnashing of teeth as the board has consistently misrepresented the truth about the real cost to the taxpayers. When the new school was supposed to be in Wilkes-Barre, the cost was in the neighborhood of $75 million.

When the Plains site was selected, the people then learned that the new cost would be about $100,000,000. Now with very little work done, as more truth comes in and more problems arise with building on top of toxic ash are discovered, the cost has already risen to an estimated $121 million dollars. But do not worry, this cost will be borne by the taxpayers (not the board) as the board extracts the largest tax increases allowed by law every year forever from now forward. What if I said the cost to the taxpayers will be lots more than $121 M. Would you believe me?

Outside experts having looked at the project closely have a more accurate estimate that suggests that the real cost ultimately brought forth by the double-dealers on the board is more than four times the current $121 million estimate. Folks, that is about a half billion dollars over forty years.

Last time I checked, there are no billionaires contacting the Chamber of Commerce looking for property in our area. Even if they were looking, would they continue their search when they found out that they would be asked to pick up the tab for our ill-advised consolidated school – Mine Shaft High?. Of course not. We get to pay it ourselves. Nobody will be moving to this area for an awful long time as the over-taxation will be way too stiff for any normal human being to afford.

The consolidated school impacts all of the communities in the Wilkes-Barre Area. There are a number of people who think this is just about Wilkes-Barre City because it is losing its three high schools. It is much more than that. The School District tax burden for the Area will not be paid just by Wilkes-Barre as well as Plains where the new school is to be built. Everybody in each of the communities will get a big kick in the wallet from the action of the tyrannical board. It is not just Wilkes-Barre and Plains.

To remind us all what is at stake for whom, it helps to remember that the Wilkes–Barre Area School District is a suburban public school district located in Luzerne County, Pennsylvania, which of course is in the United States. The District itself encompasses about 123 square miles. The communities within the district besides the city of Wilkes-Barre and Plains Township, includes a number of even smaller surrounding municipalities. It serves Bear Creek Township, Borough of Bear Creek Village, Borough of Laflin, Buck Township, City of Wilkes-Barre, Laurel Run Borough, and Wilkes-Barre Township.

We should have the 2010 census data available but not all that should be in government ever is. So, according to the best data we have, the 2000 federal census data, the complete district serves a resident population of 62,749. In 2009, the residents' per capita income was $16,751, while the median family income was $40,336. Though probably slightly higher in 2019, none of the communities in our Area are very well to do and most people are in the poverty category. Consequently, this extra-large tax albatross is expected to be a major burden causing many seniors to have to give up their homes by selling or have them taken by the school district tax man.

School District official figures released in school year 2007-2008 show the District provided basic educational services to 6,696 pupils through the employment of 524 teachers, 244 full-time and part-time support personnel, and 33 administrators. Mr. Brian Costello recently became the district superintendent.

The district operates 5 elementary schools, one junior high school and 3 high schools. James M. Coughlin Junior-Senior High School is the largest school in the district, housing more than 1,050 students (2010–11). Meyers High School houses 949 students (2010) and G.A.R has 1134 students (2011).

Richard Holodick, President of the Save Our Schools Group offered the following in a post on July 2, 2019: As you will see, not only has the Wilkes-Barre Area School Board performed poorly in the protection of valuable assets from neglect, it does not do even an adequate job of teaching and preparing students for the real world.

Richard Holodick: Five districts-Greater Nanticoke Area, Hanover Area, Hazleton Area, Scranton and Wilkes-Barre Area-PERFORMED THE WORST, missing state averages on all 18 tests. I am not an advocate of testing due to many possible variables that test validity. But when you are at the bottom, labeled the worst, a validity test is not needed to draw realistic conclusions.

It's a fact we have serious academic achievement problems; what is our board's "master plan?" The first priority, consolidate all sports reducing student's opportunities to participate; activities are known to keep students in school and maintain passing grades. Move all high schools out of the city's neighborhoods to an isolated potentially toxic site, adding to the burden of economically disadvantaged parents and students to be active in school events.

Convert GAR High School to a middle school, where our own studies and the research say contributes to academic decline and attendance problems. Build a consolidated school that our own study and PFM list as a "disadvantage," and research established is not conducive to low achieving students, adds to discipline and attendance problems.

We are number one in the state for truancy and the number of students fleeing the district. Oh, then we bus 2400 students adding hours to some student's day, a haven for bullying, and then getting 58 buses in and out of the isolated site; pick-up of 2400 students at 7 am, over a 117 square miles will be a real challenge.

What sane school board would foist such misery on the people they serve. Nobody has an answer for that. That is why folks, we cannot afford to give the incumbents another shot at putting our area further behind the eight ball.

More information about the schools and the school board follow:

The Board of Education

There are nine current members of the Board of Education
* Up for reelection in November

Joseph A. Caffrey	Board President
* Rev. Shawn Walker	Board Vice President
* Mark D. Atherton	Board Member
Ned J. Evans	Board Member
** James Geiger	Board Member
Melissa Patla	Board Member
* John R. Quinn	Board Member
* Dr. James F. Susek	Board Member – lost in primary
Denise T. Thomas	Board Member

* Five posts are up for reelection in November 2019
** Did not run for reelection

Other Board Officials

Brian J. Costello	Superintendent
Thomas F. Telesz	Board Secretary
Suzanne Saporito	Assistant Board Secretary
Raymond P. Wendoloski, Esq.	Solicitor

WBA has 117 sq. miles and district owned property to select a site. They select a coal-mine, coal ash toxic dump. Little concern for the safety of the children and staff. They pay 5 x the lowest assessed value, & $3.2 M for un-assesed mineral rights that could be worth zero. They purchased un-reclaimed land and are building on un-reclaimed land. No concern for the taxpayers and so irresponsible there needs to be an investigation.

Richard Holodick, president of the SOS group offered the following information about the potential for some other reasons than excellence (perhaps long time nepotism or cronyism) being the determinant in the hiring of the young Superintendent of Schools:

> Never in the history of the district (100 years) has a board hired a superintendent with zero experience as an assistant super or superintendent. Never has a super been hired at the top salary, with the traditional three-year trial contract ignored and a five-year contract awarded. Here is a man with 4 years' experience as an assistant principal, and four years' experience as director of curriculum in central office, responsible for student achievement.

> How did that work? Dr. Prev, retiring super had experience as a principal, assistant principal, acting superintendent and superintendent retiring at $148,000; Costello's starting salary. This miracle man salary doubling in less than six years, going from vice principal to superintendent, had nothing to do with his late Dad serving on the board and his father-in-law a state representative [Eddie Day Pashinski]. Is this nepotism/cronyism or both?

> In the balance was three historic high schools and due to a deplorable fiscal picture, a need existed to use all available resources. The board throws fiscal condition out the window and didn't hire one architect/engineering firm—they hired three architects and one engineering firm. Not one had large school restoration experience and only sparse large school construction experience. Cronyism?

Is there any reason why Wilkes-Barre and the surrounding areas never get the best? Why is there always somebody who already has the good government jobs even before they are posted. We can stop this by electing the five candidates sworn to support the people's needs, not the current school board's dreams.

Buildings and school complexes

The prominent schools / buildings in the Wilkes-Barre School District include the following:

- Coughlin High School
- G.A.R. High School
- Meyers High School
- Solomon/Plains Complex / Elementary
- Dodson Elementary:
- Flood Elementary
- Heights Elementary
- Kistler Elementary
- Mackin School Building
- WBASD Administration Building

Coughlin High School:

Address
80 N Washington St
Wilkes Barre, PA 18701

James M. Coughlin Junior/Senior High School is a public school located in Wilkes Barre, PA. It has 906 students in grades 9-12 with a student-teacher ratio of 15 to 1. According to state test scores, 42% of students are at least proficient in math and 57% in reading.

G.A.R. High School

Address
Grant & Lehigh Streets
Wilkes-Barre, PA 18702

GAR Memorial Junior/Senior High School is a public school located in Wilkes-Barre, PA. It has 911 students in grades 7-12 with a student-teacher ratio of 15 to 1. According to state test scores, 14% of students are at least proficient in math and 25% in reading.

Meyers High School

Address
341 Carey Ave
Wilkes Barre, PA 18702

Elmer L. Meyers Junior/Senior High School is a public school located in Wilkes Barre, PA. It has 900 students in grades 7-12 with a student-teacher ratio of 13 to 1. According to state test scores, 24% of students are at least proficient in math and 40% in reading.

Solomon/Plains Elementary

Address
43 Abbott St
Plains, PA 18705

Solomon Elementary School is a public school located in Plains, PA. It has 835 students in grades K-6 with a student-teacher ratio of 15 to 1. According to state test scores, 45% of students are at least proficient in math and 58% in reading.

Dodson Elementary

Address
80 Jones St
Wilkes Barre, PA 18702

Dodson Elementary School is a public school located in Wilkes Barre, PA. It has 562 students in grades K-6 with a student-teacher ratio of 16 to 1. According to state test scores, 12% of students are at least proficient in math and 29% in reading.

Flood Elementary

Address
565 N Washington St
Wilkes Barre, PA 18705

Daniel J. Flood Elementary School is a public school located in Wilkes Barre, PA. It has 660 students in grades K-6 with a student-teacher ratio of 17 to 1. According to state test scores, 19% of students are at least proficient in math and 35% in reading.

Heights Elementary

Address
1 S Sherman St
Wilkes Barre, PA 18702

Heights Murray Elementary School is a public school located in Wilkes Barre, PA. It has 793 students in grades K-6 with a student-teacher ratio of 16 to 1.

According to state test scores, 15% of students are at least proficient in math and 28% in reading.

Kistler Elementary

Address
301 Old River Rd
Wilkes Barre, PA 18702
Dr. David W. Kistler Elementary School is a public school located in Wilkes Barre, PA. It has 938 students in grades K-6 with a student-teacher ratio of 16 to 1. According to state test scores, 27% of students are at least proficient in math and 41% in reading.

Mackin School Building

Address
13 Hillard Street
Wilkes-Barre, PA 18702
Edward Mackin Elementary School was an elementary school in Wilkes-Barre's East End neighborhood that closed down in 2005 in disrepair. After extensive renovations it reopened Jan. 4, 2017 for Coughlin High School's ninth and 10th grades as part of the Consolidation of Schools. The Wilkes-Barre Area School District had closed Mackin a decade ago.

WBASD Administration Building

Address
730 South Main Street
Wilkes Barre, PA 18702
The WBASD Administration Building houses the major administrative offices of the School District including the office of the Superintendent. It is one of a number of major building complexes in the District which adds to its $300 million dollars in real estate assets.

6/30/2019 Plains TWP wants own school district

Here is a little piece of news. Even Plains wants no part of the WBASD.

Who can blame them. Even they think building a school on top of a "get you sick" toxic mine dump is an idea not to be considered.

One of the major disadvantages of having the fight between Wilkes-Barre Area and the school board so public is that everybody is learning what a terrible school board WBA is stuck with for now. Just today I discovered a new web site on Facebook –

https://www.facebook.com/plains.township.area.school.district

You got it. Plains wants its own school district. The more you know about WBASD, the less it is appealing—even for the Plains Twp contingent. More than likely, Plains as a municipality would not have cared if it were not always for the 500 pound gorilla in the room. I mean that the plans to put the three Wilkes-Barre High Schools together in Plains did not materialize as the greatest news for Plains residents. The zillion dollar increase in taxes did not sit well eather. A Plains school district fits in nicely as both a neighborhood school and a neighborhood school district.

Here is the first post on this Facebook site as of today, July 9, 2019
/

Plains Township Wants Its Own School District
June 30 at 3:07 PM ·

A perfect ZERO for the Wilkes-Barre Area School District, which finished below all 17 state averages! One of the many reasons Plains Township would be better off with our own school district. Please build the new school in Wilkes-Barre City. And please get away from those old social/economic excuses!

Here is another not too positive comment on the Plains Facebook page

Robert M. Dohman: This is the death of the valley, and will cause death in the long run, it's not a question of if it will happen, but when and how severe it'll be in addition to it sinking into the mines, it's already damaging houses and creating sink holes on adjacent properties, your property values plummeted already when ground was broke and will continue to plummet as the construction continues, and that is all properties not only in Wilkes-Barre city, but all property in the whole Wilkes-Barre area school district. It's still amazing to me how so many people don't care about the safety of the students, faculty, and teachers by not voting them out. Just proves the money is so much more important than an education and proper treatment and learning environment for the students.

Here is some artwork from the new site:

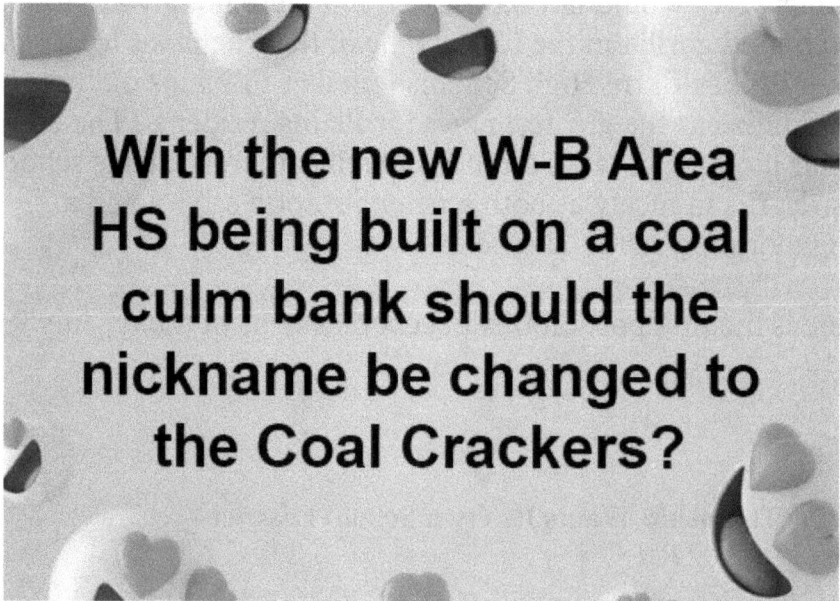

With the new W-B Area HS being built on a coal culm bank should the nickname be changed to the Coal Crackers?

It makes more sense than the Wolf Pack?

Chapter 2 The Wilkes-Barre Area School Board Does Not Hear the People

Please don't forget that first and foremost nearly all evidence says don't consolidate schools because it harms academics, student sense of well-being, student participation, and that it increases costs. Having said that, the site is receiving such attention because outside of perhaps Chernobyl, it would be difficult to find a worse spot to build a school.

Just like our board hears nothing

A group called Save Our Schools is comprised of citizens who pay attention to the corrupt board and who care. They also are interested in saving Wilkes-Barre from its certain demise as the proposed Mine Shaft High in Plains TWP, will be the last nail needed to sink Wilkes-Barre City into oblivion. How could the officials of Wilkes-Barre City permit the school board from making its three high schools irrelevant.? The people have not been paying attention but we must. That's why I wrote this book. Please pay attention and vote for what is best for Wilkes-Barre and surrounds.

The following article from the Citizens Voice from May 2017 by SOS Officers nets out the school consolidation issue and tells the folks in Wilkes-Barre and surrounds that with this current board, the public does not matter and the public has no chance of surviving the taxes coming our way.

Time to end W-B Area board's intimidation

CITIZENS VOICE

BRACKETS [ ] INDICATE TEXT WAS ADDED IN 2019 BY EDITOR

LETTER TO THE EDITOR / PUBLISHED: MAY 5, 2017

To CV: What do outdated, scarce textbooks and supply shortages have in common with big administrative raises, cavalier hiring, crumbling buildings, nepotism, crippling debt and misspent funds? It's their home at the Wilkes-Barre Area School District.

Three incumbent board members are seeking reelection [back in 2017] despite a gruesome record of achievement: Student performance is abysmal, taxes, the highest allowed by law, and nearly every facility fails state standards. One historic high school is unusable and abandoned. Two others have been systemically neglected and may meet the same fate. The board's remedy, which has yet to be fleshed out, could cost a quarter of a billion dollars.

While not all these problems are attributable to these three board members, in their first facility foray, these incumbents spent $4.9 million on a consolidated school site without zoning approval which ultimately was denied. Under this board, a surplus has rapidly approached a $70 million deficit. The fiscal response was "Pathway to the Future" which cut 37 teachers who served the very programs which keep some of our students in school. Further teacher and program cuts are to follow.

In the meantime, administrators have been getting raises and buyout incentives. [Life was very good in 2017 for those big shots in control of the people's tax money.] A proposed high school consolidation does not include GAR, which is the high school with the largest number of impoverished children. Candidates Thomas, Caffrey and Evans approved this plan. While GAR students keep their neighborhood schools, they will not share in state-of-the-art technology. A more recent iteration of the "plan" leaves the City without a high school, altogether, which will be a death knell for our neighborhoods.

These same board members refused to hear from school restoration experts, Bancroft Construction, which has restored historic schools with remarkable outcomes. The board has dismissed the research, opinions and involvement of community members and faculty. The board believes that consolidation will save the district money, despite quite the opposite outcome in Hazleton and Williamsport and the overwhelming conclusion of the educational literature.

They ignore the consensus that larger schools are particularly detrimental to academically challenged students. At the April board meeting it was stated that the extra cost in busing would be offset by three less administrators. Williamsport with 1,400 students has a head principal and four vice principals; Hazleton with 2,200 students also has the same set up with five administrators. This board is not doing their homework.

The time is now for WBASD stakeholders [We the People] to end this board's intimidation, arrogance and bullying. Instead of the public being treated like children being told what is to be done, we need meaningful community dialog and collaboration to reach a mutually acceptable solution. Community input is a Pennsylvania Department of Education requirement. The district has a neighborhood school system, which is the envy of many districts, as well as many who are trying to emulate it. This board would destroy its major advantage. To quote Joni Mitchell, " You don't know what you got 'till it's gone."

Urban consolidation in disadvantaged communities makes no sense. Read the scholarly articles published by Dr. Mark Schiowitz. You can't read the board's response to his articles because there is none.

The recently retired superintendent said in a public meeting, "We can't do it alone we need your help." They have proceeded to do it alone; how has that worked? A second headline stated that a total of

$6 million dollars has been spent, "with nothing physical to show for it." Demand more, you are paying for it.

Richard A. Holodick, President
Bob Holden, Vice President
Jack Nolan, Treasurer
Melissa Etzle Patla, Recording Secretary
Dave Wilson, Board Member
Save Our Schools
WILKES-BARRE, PA

WBA School Board Hammers Nails in the Coffin of Common Sense

Written by Brian Kelly and the London Times

An Obituary printed in the London Times.....Absolutely Brilliant!! Postscript uses poetic license.

Many in Wilkes-Barre and surrounds are mourning the demise of the three City schools that have been doomed to the axe man as the school board cannot find a way to save our schools. It would be as if all common sense was stripped by Martians in their last journey to planet earth. How else can we explain it.

Today we mourn the passing of a beloved old friend, Common Sense, who has been with us for many years.

No one knows for sure how old he was, since his birth records were long ago lost in bureaucratic red tape. He will be remembered as having cultivated such valuable lessons as:

- Knowing when to come in out of the rain;
- Why the early bird gets the worm;
- Life isn't always fair;
- And maybe it was my fault.

Common Sense lived by simple, sound financial policies (don't spend more than you can earn) and reliable strategies (adults, not children, are in charge).

His health began to deteriorate rapidly when well-intentioned but overbearing regulations were set in place. Reports of a 6-year-old boy charged with sexual harassment for kissing a classmate; teens suspended from school for using mouthwash after lunch; and a teacher fired for reprimanding an unruly student, only worsened his condition.

Common Sense lost ground when parents attacked teachers for doing the job that they themselves had failed to do in disciplining their unruly children.

It declined even further when schools were required to get parental consent to administer sun lotion or an aspirin to a student; but could not inform parents when a student became pregnant and wanted to have an abortion

Common Sense lost the will to live as the churches became businesses; and criminals received better treatment than their victims.

Common Sense took a beating when you couldn't defend yourself from a burglar in your own home and the burglar could sue you for assault.

Common Sense finally gave up the will to live, after a woman failed to realize that a steaming cup of coffee was hot. She spilled a little in her lap, and was promptly awarded a huge settlement.

Common Sense was preceded in death;

- by his parents, Truth and Trust,
- by his wife, Discretion,
- by his daughter, Responsibility,
- and by his son, Reason.

He is survived by his 5 stepbrothers;

They are listed on the next page:

- I Know My Rights
- I Want It Now
- Someone Else Is To Blame
- I'm A Victim
- Pay me for Doing Nothing

At his funeral to assure Common Sense would never return to disrupt plans to rip down the three long-serving high schools in Wilkes-Barre, the following seven of nine Board members showed up with nails and hammers:

- Louis M. Elmy
- Joseph A. Caffrey
- Ned J. Evans
- Dino L. Galella
- John R. Quinn
- Dr. James F. Susek
- Denise T. Thomas

Christine A. Katsock and Reverend Shawn Walker [A one-time ally of the people] came to aid Common Sense but were bullied and overpowered by a majority of the School Board, who still believe the WB Area voters will not throw them out of office for malfeasance and tyranny

I can see voters bringing multiple Stanley Claw Nail Pullers to the first Board Meeting after the November Election to remove the nails from the Coffin of Common Sense.

[Though 2017 did not work, Common Sense is alive and well in 2019 and all members of SOS are for its re-adoption. The people simply have to vote for the SOS candidates featured in this book. It's just Common Sense.]

As a side note, not many attended the funeral of COMMON Sense because so few realized he was gone. Find Common Sense at the Save our Schools forum. We'd love to show him to you.

If you still remember him, pass this on and tell others.

...If not, join the majority of the world and do nothing.

Thank You Lisa Barth and Hundreds of Meyers Supporters

All of these supporters are for doing what is right for Wilkes-Barre and Plains.

This piece was written by Brian Kelly. At the time of being copied into this book, after being published on 28 June, 2015, there had been 2243 hits. That's enough to win an election but we know we need more to really win.

Thank you

At 2PM on one of the most dismal days of this new summer, Saturday, June 17, 2015, thanks to organizer Lisa Barth, hundreds of Meyers High School supporters joined together to send a loud and clear message to the Wilkes-Barre Area School Board. "End your foolishness before it goes any further."

Meyers High School, Wilkes-Barre, Pa.

Meyers High School is still a beautiful school under the artwork approved by the board.

See the next two pictures of this once magnificent high school. Our school board is OK with this new look

Meyers as of July 2019 with attractive board provided gutter add-ons. Picture by Kate Kelly

The board

Thousands and thousands of Wilkes-Barre City residents and others from the WB Area affected by the change oppose the board's foolhardy plan requiring $100 million in new taxes from an overtaxed, beleaguered and struggling population. Considering there was no time invested in gaining an exact estimate, taxpayers can expect to pay double for this board boondoggle. The good news is that there is an election coming in November [this year it is 2019] and this whole process can be reversed simply by voting out the board members who have chosen not to listen to the voice of reason or the voice of the people.

In 2017, I suggested two nominations for write-in candidates for the Wilkes-Barre Area School Board. The first was Lisa Barth, and the second was MARK F. SHIOWITZ, M.D. Please check out Dr. Schiowitz's editorials to the Citizens Voice by typing his name and Citizens Voice. With a determined populace, this oppressive decision foist upon Wilkes-Barre taxpayers will not stand.

Big thank you's to the Citizens Voice for being the voice of the Citizens in this important matter. It would be nice if the Times Leader joined the management of the Citizens Voice in helping citizens in our community battle against School Board tyranny. We can replace four members of the Board in November and undo this tragedy. We sure could use the help of the two major newspaper media outlets, and the Radio and TV media outlets, WILK, and WBRE . Let's see how community oriented the media really is in our home town.

Now, here we are in 2019 and guess what? We have five candidates for the board. They are all great. There is so much power for incumbents in Wilkes-Barre that it will be tough to get all 5 elected. But who wants to pay taxes that are unaffordable. Vote this board out and vote for the following. Busch and Formola need you to learn how to write-in votes. The other three are already on the ballot because in some cases, they already beat incumbents. Let's put them all in so Wilkes-Barre keeps its three high schools and gets a school board that cares about student achievement.

Save Our Schools Candidates for WB Area School Board. Formola & Busch are write-ins

Brian Kelly wrote this article on June 18, 2015 as the fight for the schools was heating up. Its title is

Will Times Leader Approve this Comment?

Kelly says who knows… they did print it. Here it is

I saw a good article today about nepotism in the WBASD. I was surprised that the Times Leader would risk its neutral stance on everything to offer a bone to citizens of Wilkes-Barre. Yet, they did.

http://www.timesleader.com/news/editorial/154085479/OUR-VIEW-Nepotism-sinks-trust-in-schools

This is disgusting as is all of Wilkes-Barre politics.

At the big board meeting, Dr. Bernard Prevuznak, a good person but in a situation that was well over his head and the head of all board members meekly offered his assessment: "Both James M. Coughlin and E. L. Meyers High Schools were showing signs of years of deterioration and neglect."

That's it -- so spend $100 million and solve the problem. Easy! Then what? Where is the Operations Manager for the District or the Operations Engineer who would have been on this like a hawk. Where are the building engineers? Why so many maintenance (custodial) people when nobody is doing any maintenance? Check out the new site www.savewbschools.com. It is just being formed but it is there and will grow and it will help us overthrow the gestapo in charge of the school district.

Dr. Prevuznak is not an engineer, nor are any board members. So, who represented the school district when they hired contractor engineers? How could the School District agree to adopt the recommendation of outsiders when none of them really know anything (crap) about engineering?

What's a hundred million among friends when the taxpayers will have no choice but to take on the heavy lifting? Would anybody (engineering firm) that is hired for a small job ever recommend a solution that would give them a favored position for lucrative contract for a big job? If there is no corruption going on as in the many Dunn Deals of not too many years ago, then why is the web site so sparse?

Who is on the building maintenance staff? Does the Building and Grounds Supervisor serve as the only in-house counsel for board decisions? Can you trust greedy engineering firms on contract to represent the district when even on this small matter of nepotism, the district fails? What about a $100 million? Should we trust these buffoons? Where is the line item budget? What is the budget for each department? Why is everything a secret? If outside interest such as the State or the Feds do not intervene, do the people have a prayer?

It's always been this way… But bot for long

If you take the PFM review, the facility 1/2 million dollar study, and the $25,000 study, analyze the recommendations and the percentage of adoptions is correlated with the academic achievement percentages. The following is 2006; chump change compared to nearly $20 million spent to date. Notice in the lower-left corner, "Former W-B board president faces life in prison." This was the time period when there was $10 million spent over the approved budget. Ray Wendowloski said it was an error the funds were for facility improvements and it should have come from the capital category.

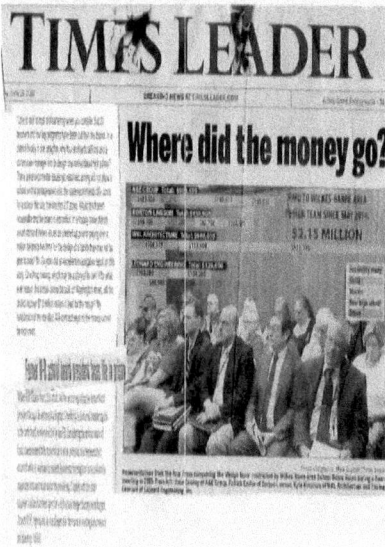

Yes, the people get to vote in November and we can and will vote out the corrupt Wilkes-Barre Area Board of Directors. And the crowds will cheer!

Government of the people, for the people, and by the people will prevail in Wilkes-Barre Area once again!

Chapter 3 How School Buildings Should Be Maintained.

Please don't forget that first and foremost nearly all evidence says don't consolidate schools because it harms academics, student sense of well-being, student participation, and that it increases costs. Having said that, the site is receiving such attention because outside of perhaps Chernobyl, it would be difficult to find a worse spot to build a school.

Wilkes-Barre High School – later Coughlin – A one-time handsome building
Later circa 1950 and Annex was built to its left.
In 2017 the school was closed and a big ugly fence built in front of it.
This building can be restored and History would love it. My dad went to this school.
Graduated Circa 1930

Here it is in its patented school board ugly filthy regalia
Picture by Kathleen Kelly

By the way, looking at the Coughlin building today, you can tell there is no building maintenance plan whatsoever for Wilkes-Barre Area School District. And, that is not funny!

There is no maintenance plan and there never was in the Wilkes-Barre Area School District. It's hard to believe. That is the cause of so many school buildings being in a dilapidated state. With a plan, all buildings would be in ship shape and there would be no need for building a new school anywhere, especially not over a toxic mine shaft.

Is Good Maintenance an Essential Need?

Absolutely yes!

Well operated school districts operate with a maintenance plan so that District buildings last as long as possible and they do not have to replaced prematurely.

The fact is that without a reliable routine planned maintenance program and a scheduled preventive maintenance plan, a school district cannot effectively maintain its facilities. The Wilkes-Barre Area School District can serve as the "poster boy" for what happens when there is no policy other than neglect.

A top-flight program cannot be a short-term commitment. Instead, it must be an ongoing continued work task, assessment of conditions, and the development and implementation of preventive and corrective measures. The results of such a program can affect the District's facilities by a reduction of overall costs, lessening impacts on the educational process, providing stable conditions, increased years of reliable service, and the ability to adequately budget.

The advantages add up as students get a non-disruptive education and the District is never surprised by facilities down situations that cost many dollars to bring back on-line.

Communication:

Having a well-oiled maintenance plan helps all aspects of the District. The prime uses of such a program /plan are the development of adequate communication to assess each school and the condition of facilities on an ongoing basis. If the District officials are not checking the condition of the buildings regularly, how can they determine what is needed to keep them properly functioning?

A well-developed program brings the schools' staffs and the districts' maintenance department together to find and resolve maintenance problems and to have a record of what has happened and needs to happen to make things better. It is very important that ongoing schools' staff and new employees understand how the system works and what part they play in its continuing operations..

Exceptional:

Those in the WBASD understand that the many schools are unique and they are exceptional from other building types since they encounter intense use and the daily abuse of young occupants, who often do not necessarily care how they treat District assets. Thus, the schools deserve special design requirements and special monitoring. With such human high traffic in schools, there is more of a need for facilities to be up at all times than in a typical business.

Consequently, rigid standards and extra precautions are required to be taken to ensure life, safety, and building continuance. All buildings are seasonal but with long periods of use and short periods of limited occupancy though exceptions always do occur—and at the worst times—making backup plans even more important.

All of these factors make school maintenance difficult to do without interfering with the educational process and therefore maintenance must often be done after school hours or during vacations periods.

Districts that ignore these requirements end up like the Wilkes-Barre Area School District. Over time school buildings become so out-of-repair that they need to be replaced as the neglect catches up with what a normal maintenance plan would provide. Simple repairs that are ignored can add up to a school needing to be replaced because of official negligence, which is often called deferred maintenance and the deferral is often permanent until a big issue arises.

Training and Development

Nobody seems to know anything about construction or building maintenance at Wilkes-Barre Area School District. The board for years has opted to "get by" without the right team of knowledgeable experts and craftsmen. The fact is a District such as ours with over $300 million in real estate assets needs to be led by skilled professionals such as school district Architects or competent Engineers and this is just the first phase of assuring building assets last for their entire expected life.

Consequently, building maintenance in school districts has grown to become a sophisticated process with new equipment, materials, and maintenance personnel required to have more technical skills to keep the major systems -- electrical, mechanical, and special systems in operation. To do this, nothing happens overnight. Instead, formal career path training must be offered and motivated individuals must be selected and the selected individuals must attend courses to increase their skills. Continual education on the latest and evolving technical issues is as base requirement. A District that uses its skilled Academic personnel including its Superintendent to perform such maintenance work is doomed to failure in both the Academic side and the facilities side. It's like lighting a candle at both ends. It only seems brighter for a short while before it burns you.

One of this board's greatest faults is that when they took the oath to serve the people of WBASD, they promised to care for the $300 million in district building assets. However, they reneged on their oath and instead neglected all maintenance. When the buildings begin to crumble as expected, they cried for help from the people to bail them out.

It is hard to believe that this same untrustworthy board actually want the people to trust them again with a new building expected to cost a $HALF BILLION over 40 years. They hope to build something new—which of course will also have no plan for reaching its expected life. Yes, folks it is a shame. It is a sin. But, it is the way the board operates. They think we are all dummies. We are for sure if we do not vote them out on November5.

They never created a maintenance plan. It is hard to imagine until you see Coughlin and Meyers after their neglect.

There was no plan and there still is no plan. Moreover, there is no plan for the new building. If anything ever gets fixed today in the Wilkes-Barre Area School District, it is not part of an overall plan. It may not be an accident but it sure is not part of a major plan that would have been built to assurc buildings last a long time.

Historically, our school district takes action only when absolutely necessary and never by plan. As witnessed recently with Mackin

School, Meyers, and Coughlin nothing happens until the disrepair reaches a point where a major renovation or a replacement project is the only option. You would not hire anybody from the WBASB to make sure your house is kept in good repair.

Think about your own home for a minute. Say your only toilet breaks. When this happens, you fix it or have it fixed post haste. When your roof has a leak, you fix it. When the porch has a rotted plank, you fix it. When there is a hole in a plaster or sheet-rock wall, you fix it. You do not wait until you have to replace the whole house after ignoring small repairs brings your home to a beyond repair condition. Why should citizens of WBASD trust this board with new property worth well in excess of $100 million? .

The school board for many, many years chose to operate without an appropriate qualified maintenance staff headed by somebody who understands all aspects of the building trades. I am talking about a competent architect or engineer such as those employed by Scranton University or Misericordia University and the other colleges in this area. The school superintendent, though perhaps a gritty and feisty administrator is not competent in the trades, nor should he or she have to be competent in the skills of building and grounds maintenance. Actually, with our school district last in testing, perhaps this Super should not even be in charge of academic achievement.

From all observations of the WBASB, the Superintendent himself uses his cronies in the trades industry without first having long-term maintenance contracts to solve issues as they arise. Whether plumbing, carpentry, electrical or other emergencies that the custodial staff is not prepared to handle, the superintendent is forced to get involved to contract with a favored cadre of cronies or perhaps relatives to get a problem resolved. Otherwise, the problem will be neglected, get worse, and be unsolved and more serious when the next emergency comes around.

Since calling in outside help, even if part of a friend or crony team, puts stress on the budget (if there is one), it is likely that the superintendent might choose to postpone actual repairs. The Wilkes-Barre Area super uses that approach. More than likely, like, me, you have gone into a district school, and found a sign on the restroom door asking you to find another toilet someplace else in the building. It is a common occurrence.

A sign can be reused and is lots cheaper than fixing a problem when it occurs. I bet you have found signs calling out other issues and perhaps dangers in our schools. Signs are cheaper than repairs but using signs v repairs is not a good business practice.

You might have gone into Meyers High school over the last several years underneath a maze of particle board built to protect passersby from falling building material. For a school board hell-bent on making Meyers look like a school needing to be torn down, adorning the entrances with cheap blue painted particle board surely does the trick. The intricate PVC pipe maze adds an additional aura of incompetence to the overall picture of the front of what otherwise would be a beautiful school entrance. The temporary fix must have become permanent recently but it sure is ugly.

If the board wants Meyers to look bad, shoddy work like this is a sure way to do it. It makes the school look to be in worse shape than it really is. It is the product of a patchwork quilt maintenance philosophy that no competent craftsman would recommend.

Why would the superintendent spend the money to fix something needing the proper expertise—such as say a plumbing issue, when he or she has a private Water Closet tucked handily away in his or her own comfortable and private office. The point in this chapter is simply that without a well-conceived, written maintenance plan available, nobody can ascertain problems of any nature. How could they ever be fixed with no system in place. We have demonstrated that the Wilkes-Barre Area School District uses neglect as its only maintenance philosophy. That is very obvious.

This is how buildings, including school buildings, without a plan for their ongoing regular maintenance eventually fall into a state of complete disrepair and begin to look so shabby that inspectors might suggest ripping them down and building new buildings rather than investing in significant repair work.

Toilets are a good example of which we can all relate. Neglect causes one broken toilet on one floor to become two broken toilets on two floors until there is only one functional toilet in the building. Then what? Well, then the wise men in charge declare the problem unsolvable and decide to move all school operations to another building with functional latrines.

Whether the issue is broken toilets, weak beams, leaky roofs, falling plaster, exposed asbestos, missing floor sections, eventually, the list of *to-be-fixed* items becomes so great that the superintendent decides to punt rather than deal with an area outside his or her expertise. Punting is a regular occurrence in the superintendent's office.

In school districts that have spent the time to construct a maintenance plan and have hired an in-house staff with expertise to use the preventive maintenance plan, as a rule, holes do not appear in floors and toilets do not break all of a sudden. Instead, buildings last and do not need replacing after a few maintenance incidents.

Deferred repairs quickly can turn into replacement events. Colleges with many buildings on campus have the same issues as school districts. Stanford University recently published a report titled "Guidelines for Life Cycle Cost Analysis," which explains how as a building or campus ages, the cumulative cost of operating and maintaining facilities significantly impacts the overall budget — not just the maintenance budget. Even when funds are set aside to construct new buildings, they rarely extend to the ongoing operational costs vital to maintaining the facility and slowing the decline of building utility and performance.

In other words deferred maintenance is a sure way of increasing long-term building costs. The best approach is to fix it before it is broken through preventive maintenance. But, you need a team of artisans to do that. The team costs lots less in the long run, however, than not having the team.

The greater issue with deferred maintenance is that it grows in scope — and cost — the longer it is prolonged. *Don't put off 'til tomorrow what you can do today*. This is a lesson still unlearned by the Wilkes-Barre Area School Board.

When a repair is delayed, it is still subject to the daily use and abuse of school occupants. Students do not stop coming to school because a toilet is down or a light is out or a floor is overly slippery. In fact, it's not uncommon for a "repair" to turn into a "replacement" because, in the process of being deferred, it becomes completely broken.

Replacing a door, lock, window, etc., is much more costly than simply repairing it in a timely manner. But not only is the expense higher, there is also a frequently overlooked cost in staff productivity as replacements typically take much longer to complete than repairs. When whole buildings need to be replaced because of excessive neglect, the costs grow out of the affordability range of most taxpayer bases.

On the other hand, buildings and facilities that have implemented comprehensive preventive maintenance programs have found that the operation of their systems is more reliable, and those systems also last longer and cost less in the long run.

Preventative maintenance measures

Projects that are put on hold, repair that is neglected, or maintenance that is ignored adds up to a costly and complex problem. The cost of deferred maintenance could potentially be 30 times that of the early intervention cost. From what we have seen with the notion of a new consolidated high school in Plains Twp., there is still no overall plan nor a preventive maintenance plan in place and unless it is a secret, the board has not discussed increases in the quality and quantity of maintenance personnel. There are no architects or engineers in the hiring pipeline to make sure construction and maintenance is performed safely and appropriately. The superintendent appears to be the only one checking out the construction site. And, that is not good. When the superintendent is in the field checking construction is someone from the custodial staff doing his superintendent job?

And, so, what can we expect long after the current board is out of office *say in* twenty or thirty years? Will their new consolidated Taj Mahal on a mine shaft be ready to be replaced because with no assigned maintenance personnel and no plan, it will have been neglected? For the current board it may not even matter. Nobody will be around for the folks of 2050 to blame for their continued imprudent maintenance philosophy. This board has no plans to make maintenance better so they must be fired. It is that simple.

What I am saying is that the importance of preventative maintenance cannot be overstated. If this current board were better caretakers of the real estate assets of the District, there would be no need for a major repair project and certainly no need for a huge high school consolidation project designed to bankrupt a community.

Experts estimate that between two and six percent of an annual operating budget should be spent on preventative maintenance in order to effectively minimize a facility's rate of decay. Quality building materials such as granite as was used in proper high school buildings before 1950, is hard to come by within budget but the buildings would surely last longer with top-grade materials. Besides materials, prevention not only saves money, but it helps facilities avoid replacement — which requires capital assets and often creates an extensive process from evaluation and design to funding and implementation.

By nature, preventive maintenance is the least disruptive, singular in resolution, planned for in advance alternative and often includes training for future maintenance. Most of all, it helps reduce building failure and poor conditions that can negatively impact mission critical building operations, a school district's image, student results and retention, energy efficiency and even employee morale.

Nobody would expect a school district to operate without a boss. In other words it goes without saying that a person schooled in curricula and the proper ways of running a school's academic programs, most often called a superintendent is an obvious necessity in order to operate a school. A multi-school menagerie of buildings at various grade levels called a school district is even more of a challenge. The board would without question be fired if it chose not to hire a superintendent.

Yet, somehow, the same board would permit a superintendent with no expertise in toilets or leaky roofs, or structural issues or electrical or flooring to be the top maintenance person serving as the facility engineer or architect. How can that be? If the superintendent is serving as the maintenance director then there is no superintendent when the top academic boss available is not wearing his superintendent hat.

The superintendent, brilliant though she or he may be, cannot be an expert in all things. A board in fact that permits dual roles is itself incompetent. How can they permit the extremely high paid superintendent to perform maintenance decision making and the hiring of contractors and subcontractors and the monitoring of large multi-year projects?

Brian Costello (by title, superintendent) in his work as WBASD Architect/Engineer

How many pictures do we need to see of superintendent Brian Costello checking out the Plains work site? By the way, what an ugly site! Is the academic record of the District so high that a superintendent doing Superintendent work is not necessary? No, WBASD is ranked 444th out of 500. How can the Superintendent know the construction or repair work is done properly when it is commissioned and finished? Answer. They cannot. That's why buildings enter a state of disrepair far too often when nobody with knowledge is taking care of them.

By the way, at 444th, the Wilkes-Barre Area School District is a lot closer to the bottom of the pack academically than the top. Perhaps the super serving as the only architect/engineer on maintenance projects has already taken its toll.

Universities / colleges similar to school districts

When I was with IBM, one of my roles was to serve as the Higher Education Coordinator for IBM working with the ten colleges/universities in Northeastern PA. In this role I was trained to understand how academic institutions were structured and how they operated. I had to know what made them tick to help them choose IBM equipment over Brand X. In my own technical consulting business after I retired from IBM, I had the pleasure of directly supporting Marywood University and College Misericordia and occasionally I would perform technical consulting work for other NEPA academic institutions.

Marywood had an outstanding in-house maintenance team. You can still see the results of their fine work all over the campus. They not only did the normal construction monitoring and facilities job, they also employed craftsmen who remodeled and repurposed facilities for new uses.

For example, this team took the one room Information Technology Department of 1970 and over forty-plus years, I watched them build several new data centers and a new state of the art department with private offices for their analysts, programmers et al. This team was led by a lead Architect/Engineer. When the cost of furniture was high or did not fit the room space, the craftsmen designed and built their own furniture and the result was always first-class. Besides being a great university, I was very impressed with the results of their maintenance team

College Misericordia's facilities maintenance crew were also under the control of an architect when I was the chief computer technology officer on campus. They had a maintenance plan and were always painting or refurbishing a given area on campus. To save dollars, as the college became a university and expanded their academic programs, they chose to subcontract out their maintenance department while keeping the in-house architect, who reported to the President. The preventive maintenance plan was even more important when the department was outsourced.

Scranton University was not an IBM customer but I had a friend who happened to live in South Wilkes-Barre who at one time served as the

Architect on the University's many projects. Scranton U was always building something and everything that they built needed a maintenance plan.

On the University's web site, they tell something about their current team.

"Our Design and Construction department is a service organization responsible for the engineering, planning, documentation, construction, renovation, repair, and maintenance of all University buildings and facilities."

So, why did I just go through the similar methods three different educational institutions use to assure their buildings and facilities are all operational all the time? I have never seen an organization in higher education that did not have an Architect or a maintenance plan. Like the colleges, with $300 million in real-estate assets WBASD cannot function without the expertise of an architect and a well-orchestrated maintenance plan and a staff of building artisans. They kid themselves to think they can.

Moreover, I recall no buildings ever being ripped down on a local college campus because of their maintenance team's neglect. The Wilkes-Barre Area School Board should have employed these same practices as the small colleges in NEPA and it should employ them in the future regarding maintenance and construction projects. $300 million or more in assets is an awful lot of real property to neglect and ultimately waste.

Whereas WBASB thinks construction planning and control and preventive maintenance are fine when relegated and deferred to the back burner as *afterthoughts*," organizations that are proper caretakers of their hundreds of millions of dollars' worth of real property assets see facilities management as a vital and even strategic part of their organizations. Without the buildings on campus, how can there be an educational institution? There cannot.

The WBASB and its superintendent have chosen not to use generally accepted facilities management and preventive maintenance procedures. And so, the result is that the long-term health of their facilities has not been assured. That is why at WBASD, buildings like

Mackin School in its day, and now Meyers, Coughlin, & GAR, are always facing a handy emergency that must be solved or all will be lost.

So, here we are in late 2019, after a number of false starts and blocked decisions about what the board can and should do regarding its ever-changing plans to eliminate Meyers, Coughlin, and GAR. This board wants all Wilkes-Barre students to take the bus every day of every school year to their Consolidated Mine Shaft High. What a shame.

And so, since the sane citizens of Wilkes-Barre Area are not suicidal and do not wish to bring on taxpayer bankruptcies by overtaxing themselves or others in the area, many have joined the Save Our Schools Group. This organization is determined to do what is right for the community, regardless of the tyranny, malfeasance, and incompetence of the tyrants serving as members of the board of directors.

The idea of abandoning the notion of neighborhood schools for the *one big school fits all idea* has never made the taxpayers, parents or students happy or better off wherever it has been implemented and it is not about to work here. Moreover, from their lousy track record when trusted with major property assets, this board and its Superintendent put forth clear proof they cannot handle such a big decision. It is a bungle boondoggle as proposed.

Please consider that they have been serving as the caretakers who permitted all of these schools to be neglected and fall into a state of disrepair. Why would anybody with a choice if this consolidated coal-ash toxic-fill monstrosity is forced upon us all, vote to retain this bunch of irresponsible, careless derelicts, whose actions mimic those of imbeciles. Would we not expect that they would take a 40-year school as the Plains school is expected to be, and have it torn down in 25 years. It is their MO.

Just look at the history of the Wilkes-Barre Area School Board and you will believe they are the worst custodians of taxpayer property there could ever be. The secret folks is to vote them out of office. That is what this book is all about. The people do not need a School board made of tyrants who find no problem with figuratively spitting in the public taxpayer's faces.

The only candidates to consider in the November General Election are as follows:

(WBASD Candidates Endorsed by Save our Schools)

- Terry Schiowitz
- Robin Shudak
- Debra Formola
- Beth Anne Owens-Harris
- Jody Busch

This is the final list of candidates sponsored by Save Our Schools. Running five candidates from SOS gives the people the opportunity to command the control of the WBASD by a 6-3 margin. That is why it is important to forget your friends in this election. Elect the candidates that will help education results rebound. The same candidates will assure that the elderly will not have to sell their homes to live.

Please read Chapter 4 which describes the difference between the incumbents and what the citizens will find by entrusting our schools to these five fine people, who are endorsed by the Save Our Schools Group. Thank you very much.

Chapter 4 Wilkes-Barre Area School Board New Candidates for the People!

Please don't forget that first and foremost nearly all evidence says don't consolidate schools because it harms academics, student sense of well-being, student participation, and that it increases costs. Having said that, the site is receiving such attention because outside of perhaps Chernobyl, it would be difficult to find a worse spot to build a school.

The only candidates to consider in the November General Election are as follows:

(WBASD Candidates Endorsed by Save our Schools)

- Debra Formola (write DEBRA FORMOLA)
- Jody Busch (write Jody Busch)
- Terry Schiowitz (on ballot)
- Robin Shudak (on Ballot)
- Beth Anne Owens-Harris (on ballot)

Debra Formola   Jody Busch   Terry Schiowitz   Robin Shudak   Beth Anne Owens-Harris

Low turnout May 18 2019

Wilkes-Barre elections are known for low turnout. Thus, those with name recognition win even though they are the politicians and the perpetrators in many cases. My congratulations to the SOS primary election winners as well as to the two, Bob Holden and Debra Orlando Formola who put in a valiant effort for a cause well worth it. Thank you. For the fall election Bob Holden cannot run but has passed his write-in candidacy to Jody Busch. Both Bob Holden, DOD Vice President and a very active member of SOS, and our new write-in candidate Jody Busch will work together to assure that the board is represented by only those who want the best for the students, the teachers, the staff, and the taxpayers. That means of course the current board must go.

I would like to see as much chatter about this election as possible. Talk to your friends about Debra Formola and Jody Busch as their write-in campaigns for the board are extremely important for us all.

If you are for saving Wilkes-Barre from bankruptcy and you are for saving our schools, please help the cause. It is a good time to write your first letter to the editor or call in to talk shows, write to the TV stations and send your cards and letters to the current board to tell them how you feel. Nobody would complain if they called off the Big Toxic School even before the election. Would that be nice.

The objective of SOS and the objective of the concerned citizens of Wilkes-Barre area is to have five new elected board members. Especially big thank you's to those supporting our cause not on the ballot in November (Busch & Formola) for permitting their names to be cast as write-ins. We can never give up.

The board is already improved with three candidates on the ballot. We need as much free publicity as possible to make the names of the SOS write-in candidates well known so that when you take your card with Debra Formola and Jody Busch into the machine with you, will already know their names and you can write them in lickety split without a stumble. Thank you.

There are so few voters who show up to the polls that with the group write-in campaign being launched, with discussions at eateries and taverns and the letters to the editors and call-ins, it is possible that the few additional voters necessary to bring in the whole SOS slate of five candidates could be found. Thank you again.

Those who voted against the SOS slate will be back so if we can keep the votes we have and attract a small percentage more, we can win with the four that ran in the primary plus Jody Busch Not just three. Again, please do not give up. We need four but we want all five so that all board decisions in the future support all of Wilkes-Barre area. Please remain active.

The candidates have all done a wonderful job in getting us this far. We can do it if we do not give up. Thank you again to the candidates for your great efforts and thank you to the residents of Wilkes-Barre area for coming out to vote in November and bringing home a big **"W"** for our Wyoming Valley. It's time for the people to run the school board again.

I have been a regular member of SOS from the beginning. We have a similar purpose in our desire to rid the board of bullies and corruption. The SOS people I have met are wonderful community-minded people just like you and I. They are not relatives of past great school board members and they have no name recognition just like you and I have no name recognition but we care nonetheless.

I had no name recognition and I got trounced when I ran for mayor of Wilkes-Barre in 2015. I am hoping that my experience in running for Congress and in running for Mayor will help me in this book present the reasons why we need a big change and help all the people believe that we can do it. We need to vote for the school board and the candidates need to be those supported by SOS:

Debra Formola | Jody Busch | Terry Schiowitz | Robin Shudak | Beth Anne Owens-Harris

 We do not want politicians to fill these offices as in the past. We want regular people like you and like me. To help the people in 2018, when Melissa Etzle Patla made it to the board on behalf of SOS, I wrote a small essay that was not published by either paper. Note the date and how close it was to Christmas and I hoped but did not expect the school board to give us all a big Christmas present. Here is my essay:

School Board is Incompetent
Brian Kelly
December 6, 2018

It is clear the school board is incompetent. If you've looked, you know it. I've looked and I know it. They are full of greed, self-importance, and other inadequacies. WB Area would be better without them. They can give us all a big Christmas present by doing the right thing for their community, by stepping down from the board so that this district can start fresh and undo the mess they have created.

Thankfully Kim Borland is on the case. He is one of the best lawyers in the country. Many thank you's to the SOS folks who continue to fight for the communities in the WBASD.

Few people have such tenacity. The people of WB Area did not expect to get a dishonest school board and surely have the right to fight back. Those who wrote in negative comments about this group after Attorney Borland's recent article ought to get a life. In particular the trouble-making disrespectful Irish guy who has no connection to WB Area ought to go back to his own school district where he belongs. If he had another good thought, it would be lonesome.

BTW, just one board member stepped down, Dino Galella, and was replaced by the board with Mark Atherton who has decided to go against the people on the Big Toxic School issue. Technically James Geiger also stepped down as he had also voted with the majority and so we are happy to see him go.

A fact: corrupt school board members destroy our children...

The facts in this coming August 9, 2018 article were written by a disgusted blogger about their school board and it was downloaded from the ubiquitous blogosphere where many such ideas are available for the reading. Whether Wilkes-Barre Area's School Board is corrupt may be a matter of opinion and may be a matter of fact.

In examining the competency of the board to manage over $300 million dollars-worth of real estate assets, we have presented innumerable facts showing that the tyrant members of the school board, by choice, or by corruption have not done the will of the people and their poor decisions have been very costly to the taxpayers.

From the first page of this book, the facts have been laid out. One may conclude this is corruption or incompetence but for sure something is way out of line in the board decisions that have been made. The long-standing practice of cronyism and nepotism in the district adds to the concern that we may have corruption at work here as much as any other factor. The board simply cannot be that stupid.

While functioning officials have some culpability, the top Wilkes-Barre Area board members can be deemed as the real criminals if the newly initiated audit bears fruit as expected. Their corruption and bickering with the public, kills children's futures. But, despite their transgressions, far too many of the public think that the board will not be punished in any way. Too bad that until now (and things are expected to change after the audit and the new election) the people have been correct. The board thinks they already got away with it. They are wrong. Wilkes-Barre Are voters have a long memory and in this book we give you their names. This SOS group is filled with vigor and vim and a major dislike for dishonesty.

There is a deep fear among regular people who see politics for what it is that the board will be rewarded by being reelected to create more damage to this community. Only the voting public—"We the People"—can put an end to the board's misdeeds by firing each and every one of them. It is up to all of us to vote against the tyrannical incumbents in the Wilke-Barre School board. While we are at it, we should ask the incumbents not running to step down immediately for the sake of the people.

Can it be that plenty of corrupt people are in power in this district, but the only ones who get punished are those that want to do the work of the public. If not, why is there only one school board member, Melissa Etzle Patla, who favors neighborhood schools? She is to be commended as she remains steadfast despite pressure to turn on the people who support her.

As in so many districts, the problem starts with school boards. Even if they are not corrupt to start with, school board members are tempted continually and they are often ignorant of legal matters when they begin their first term. Consequently, they rely on unethical lawyers—even those employed directly by the district. If a corrupt lawyer says it is OK, then it must be. Not so!

I had a lengthy email discussion with Rev Shawn Walker who has relatives working for the school district and who has a big stake in the election game. They say he wanted the vice chair job on the board. As a Reverend I expected better but got the same ole politics as from my eyes, Walker turned on the people when the vice presidency was dangled before him. Those who told me may be wrong and I may be wrong but I don't think so. So, I recommend we vote him out of office before all others because he knows what he is doing and he benefits from his decisions.

After a few years of going along with unethical lawyers, school board members become compromised legally and morally, and they decide to cover up their wrongdoings. As noted, even Reverend Shawn Walker, who for years was the most refreshing member of the board, has been in the company of the wrong people for too long and I regret from my perspective, he has fallen.

He started off being for the people and neighborhood schools but all of a sudden, he is voting with the big-shot incumbents on the board for the big monolith planned for Plains Township—The Big Toxic School. It makes me sad to say that. Then again his relatives would not be safe if others got on the board. Humph!

Let's face it. There is nobody better for covering up the wrongdoing of school officials and board members than the lawyers who instructed them to commit such transgressions in the first place. Sometimes the board members get so bold, they try to convince the public that the board is not raising taxes enough.

For example, feeling good about his popularity, incumbent candidate board member Shawn Walker argued in a recent meeting the district should have raised taxes even more—by another percent to get a bonus of about $500,000 annually taken directly from the people's shallow pocketbooks.

You see Walker knew the district decided to raise taxes by just 2.2 percent instead of the 3.2 percent allowed by law and which Walker preferred. Walker noted the district did substantial layoffs a few years ago, and that when the three high schools are consolidated, he claims there will be even more opportunity. Opportunity for what Shawn— for getting more taxes from the people and perhaps more layoffs?

Those of us who have lived in the area for years are well aware that *nepotism, cronyism,* and of course *tax increases* are a major cause of concern on many local school boards, the three have been especially prevalent in the tainted Wilkes-Barre Area.

We all know that in the last ten years, and actually much longer, this board has seen three of its members convicted of federal corruption charges. This was not suspicion as these big shots are doing time now if they have not been released. Who's next? If they were not criminals then what were they? How many on the board voted to boot them before the feds made it a Dunn deal? Don't be a dummy folks. Do not vote for an incumbent school board member— especially this time when the health of the kids is at stake.

Yes, Nepotism and people with the same last name or the same church or social affiliation has plagued the district for decades and continues to be a problem as just last year two board members openly lobbied to have their wives promoted. The board members think we forget. We can no longer afford to forget. We are being cheated. I

t's coming out of the poor people's pocketbooks and shallow wallets. Why are people with long family ties to officials the only people who can get a job, even a simple job in this area? Who in your family has ever worked for local government?

This school district is for gouging residents until they have to sell or lose their properties—especially seniors. If that is not the case, why do taxes go up every year when wages in NEPA are not going up at all? Though the state allows school districts to slightly raise property taxes every year, it does *not* have to do so. Yet this greedy board has hiked them—for the past 13 years. Property owners have seen an increase of 4.5 percent from the district in the last three years alone. Who does that help. It surely does not help John Q. Public. Ask the incumbents how many of their wives or husbands have lucrative teaching jobs in the district. How many of your relatives are driving an old truck or cleaning floors because no teaching jobs are available to them?

The Save our Schools group was formed to help residents achieve the best possible education in schools for the least amount of taxpayer dollars. This group's charter is to stop all the wasteful nepotism and cronyism and people not showing up for work but getting huge salaries. Overall, in this chapter, you learn the major differences between the incompetent incumbent tyrants who control the board today and how things can and should be with an effective board of your fellow citizens who care about the students and their educational opportunities. The citizens have a lot to gain by entrusting our schools to the five people noted above who are sworn to the people and they are endorsed by the Save Our Schools Group. Thank you again.

Across the country in school district after school district schmooze artists are conning their way onto school boards and then doing as they please. So how does this happen? And more importantly, what does it say about the state of school board governance in the United States? Humph!

"Our national and of course local conversation on education should include more discussion of effective school system leadership, and not just of increasing test scores and global competitiveness."

Having said that about the US, the fact that WBASD, our district is at the bottom on test scores in the state offers no consolation. We lose academically as well as financially. Yet the fat cat officials we hire and pay never have a meatless Sunday.

American taxpayers are very generous to school systems and the boards that dole out the money. We entrust more than $550 billion in spending to public education every year. And while national education reform dominates media coverage, local school boards wield the most significant influence over student performance. Our board has watched the quality of education in our area slide more and more each year. Soon it will be better to not have a HS degree than to possess one. What a travesty?

Board members who do their jobs diligently are tasked with solving such large-scale problems as achievement gaps, budget shortfalls, and aging facilities. However, the discrepancy between effective and ineffective school system governance is clear among the more than 14,000 public school districts nationwide. Would it not be nice if Wilkes-Barre Area School District were at the top instead of the bottom of the pile.

November's election gives the people the opportunity to speak with a big broom that we can use to sweep those who misused our trust— right out the door.

Ineffective governance is often the byproduct of what has been called "school board dysfunction," the situation in which board members lacking in organization, leadership, and an understanding of their role diminish a board's capacity for good decision making and strong educational leadership. Quite frankly, they consistently make bone-headed decisions. Mine Shaft High, the Big Toxic School is at the top of the bad-guy list.

The inherent difference between managing a campaign for the school board and actually leading a school system is one of the key drivers of this dysfunction.

Board members spend considerable time campaigning for their posts. Being elected is more important than serving the people once elected. In a large district, this can mean fundraising for thousands of dollars, speaking to tens of thousands of constituents, completing dozens of interviews, and networking with countless other politicians.

Campaigning, at its heart, is an entrepreneurial experience. The difference is, instead of pitching a product, candidates are selling their ideas, and often more importantly, marketing themselves. A politician seeking office must inspire his or her staff to work insane hours for a shockingly low amount of money on a project with a high potential for failure. The problem lies when a board member moves from tinkering in the garage to elected office.

While candidates are kings and queens of their own campaigns, they do not hold that level of power in a legislative board position. There is room for a board member to work on policy, establish direction, and ensure continuous improvement, but in reality, he or she is merely one of many in the decision-making process. The public cannot expect that a duly elected board for example, will elect a capable chair person. If the person is a doofus, but related to a friend, they have a great chance of being the chair.

This is the inception of dysfunction. This is the moment in which things go awry. This is why public schools such as ours or for example purposes, the Franklin Township public schools in New Jersey hired four superintendents in the span of one year. We do not have that same problem here as the superintendent salary is a hugely handsome amount. But, are we getting our money's worth?

Bickering and backstabbing and a power struggles between board members have reportedly consumed the Seattle school board. Are they representative of America? This is why a board member is said to have used personal attacks as leverage to attempt to change a vote on the Richmond, Va., school board. Most of all, this is why a successful superintendent with a national reputation for positive change and vision was made unwelcome to continue his work by board members in Montgomery County, Md. Some of the board members that fired him had only a few weeks of experience. Power drunk!

Students suffer big time when politics becomes a priority. School boards become the target of voters not because of poor platforms, insufficient creativity, or lack of effort, but because of naiveté and unprofessional conduct and yes, an awareness of their power and all the contracts to be let.

Elected school board directors and the big shots they create such as Financial Managers or neophyte superintendents begin to read their own press clippings and become untouchable by mere mortals—even in their constituency. Our national conversation on education should include more discussion of effective school system leadership, and not just of increasing test scores and global competitiveness.

These studies do not even get into a board abdicating its fiduciary responsibility as WBASB has in permitting real estate assets to be so neglected they become almost unusable. This problem is so egregious, it seems it is the home brew of NEPA politics. Nobody would pay face value for any of the buildings in WBASD if available for sale. They are a travesty because nobody cared for them.

Voters must consider past behavior in addition to statistics when choosing their local school boards. Sometimes the only way to fix a toxic relationship is to end it. A dysfunctional board can mean years of stalled progress on improving schools. Allowing the campaign mentality to tarnish relationships at a cost to students, teachers, and parents is never good governance. This is the fault of our school boards. Save Our Schools offers a solution to WBA. Fire the board and start anew. Such opportunities do not come often. We can't cry and gain sympathy later when we can change direction right now.

We are in the process of presenting to the public the November 5, 2019 escape from tyranny that we are recommending. Please ignore the pleas of incumbents who for too many years have neglected their sworn duty to fulfill the wishes of the people. They have chosen not to preserve the school property of the taxpayers.

To accomplish this mission and become a politics-free board again, I am asking you to cast a vote for these Wilkes-Barre Area School Board (WBASD) candidates— Beth Anne Owens-Harris , Terry Schiowitz, Robin Shudak, Jody Busch (write-in), , and Debra Formola (write-in). They are running at the people's request. Together, all five being on a new school board will form a large enough voice for the people to survive and reverse the WB Area School Board's betrayal of the citizenry. Finally, the people will prevail in this sham that has gone on far too long.

Let's examine the SOS candidates briefly

Jody Busch

Jody Busch 69, is currently the Business Manager of Advanced Hearing Solutions 209 Old River Road Wilkes-Barre Pa where clients are welcome to call for an appointment. Jody is the Father of three, all graduates of Meyer's high school, and a grandfather of four. Jody has been an Educator, a Musician, and an Engineer. He is well remembered by his students and fellow teachers for his days as a teacher at Meyers High School. Most people in the Wyoming Valley know Jody from the band he formed and led for years playing at weddings and other great venues.--The New York Times Band. He was also a founding member of the successful local band, Side Street. His HQ for years has been the famous McCrindle Bldg Studios in Laurel Run PA. Jody spent a lot of his work life as a musician and teacher.

He also studied Special Education at King's College and he enjoyed his high school days at G.A.R Memorial Junior/Senior High School where he was a 1968 graduate. Jody is ready to serve Wilkes-Barre Area as an advocate for the people.

He is an active member of the Save Our Schools Committee and is running as a write-in candidate in November to become a member of the board of directors for the Wilkes-Barre Areas School District . He strongly favors neighborhood schools and is against the Big Toxic school. Please type in **J-O-D-Y B-U-S-C-H** when you engage the County Voting Machines. If this is your first time writing in, it should be fun.

Debra Formola

Debra Orlando Formola, 55, is a dedicated member of the Save Our Schools Group. Her mission in this major endeavor is to help the people in Wilkes-Barre Area take back their school board and to help enact policies that will assure that the people will continue to be able to afford their homes. She is a major advocate of neighborhood schools v the huge consolidated super school approach. She is a registered nurse and always ready to help.

Debra is an active member of the Save Our Schools Committee and is also running as a write-in candidate in November to become a member of the board of directors for the Wilkes-Barre Areas School District . She strongly favors neighborhood schools and like all the SOS candidates is against the Big Toxic school. Please type in **D-E-B-R-A F-O-R-M-O-L-A** when you engage the County Voting Machines. If this is your first time writing in, it should be fun. In fact, it should be even more fun after typing in Jody Busch's name.

Beth Anne Owens-Harris, 34, works as a psychologist for the Carbondale Area School District and has worked as a public-school psychologist for the last 10 years. With her vast experience in school activities, she is a key player in the Save Our Schools Group.

Beth Anne Owens-Harris

Beth Anne has a bachelor's degree in elementary education and special education, a master's degree in child psychology and a post-graduate degree as an education specialist in school psychology.

A life resident of Wilkes-Barre and a Meyers graduate, she is married and has three daughters, ages 10, 7 and 3. Her school-age daughters attend Wilkes-Barre Area schools. She is as capable as anybody can be and she works hard for saving our schools.

Beth Anne is on the ballot.

Robin Shudak

Robin Shudak, 44, is a 1993 graduate of Meyers High School and received a bachelor's degree in environmental and public policy in 1997. She is a graduate of Texas A&M University. She received a master's degree in 2000 at Penn State in social psychology & climate science. She knows what she is talking about.

Robin also interned at the Pennsylvania Department of Environmental Protection's Mine Subsidence Insurance Program and learned how to evaluate and educate those living in subsidence-prone areas. She knows that Mine Shaft High is not good for people because all people breath air. Toxic air creates cancer even in kids.

She has worked as a small business owner and managed projects and accounts for CatzEye Studio, a multi-media production company that made videos, graphics and scripts for various clients. She loves the SOS mission and is ready to serve WBA for the benefit of the citizens.

Robin is on the ballot

Terry Schiowitz, 64, has lived most of her life in Wilkes-Barre and is a 1972 Meyers graduate. She is retired and worked as a registered nurse and certified registered nurse anesthetist.

Terry Schiowitz

She is a 1975 graduate of Mercy Hospital School of Nursing and a 1980 graduate of General Hospital School of Anesthesia. She has 38 years of clinical and didactic anesthesia experience. You can bet she is on our side in this big fight against tyranny in our school board.

Her husband, Dr. Mark Schiowitz, served on the school board in 2011 after an appointment to fill a vacant seat. He is very active in SOS matters. They have three adult boys.

Jody Busch and Debra Formola, two great people who, like you, want to reinvest in neighborhood schools, not a huge consolidate high school built on toxic mine ash, have engaged their candidacies and have promised to serve the people 100% of the time if and when they are elected to the board . Won't that be refreshing.

There is only one gotcha and we have a way around that. Neither Busch, nor Formola will be shown on the November ballot as neither won a party nomination. The people of the area did not pay attention as much as needed to assure the incumbent tyrants would not be on the November ballot. That is another purpose of this book—to alert the public that these two individuals can still be given your vote. This is a must to free the board of the tranny it now displays every day.

For your information, Busch and Formola do not have to be on the ballot to win a board seat. Pennsylvania law offers the opportunity for a write-in for any candidate. Save our Schools recommends you exercise this privilege and learn how to cast your write in vote for two candidates who back your wishes.

Simply write in the name of each of these two candidates instead of selecting an incumbent. Jody Busch and Debra Formola are the names you write in. It will be the same as if you picked them from the ballot. Instead you type in their names. This is very important. We will show more information in this book about how to use the write-in capabilities of our voting machines.

The collective promise of all five candidates, Busch and Formola as write-ins, plus Owens-Harris, Schiowitz, and Shudak--the three SOS candidates on the ballot, will save the WB Area taxpayers hundreds of millions of dollars in wasteful spending. Plus they will enable the elderly and the un-rich from having to sell their properties and move out of the area just to afford life. This new board will shut down the monster boondoggle school—the **Big Toxic School** that is planned by the corrupt board full of tyrants to be built over an unhealthy toxic mine waste dump in Plains, PA after all three Wilkes-Barre high schools are destroyed.

As you know, for years now, the current board has taken action against the best interests of the people of Northeastern PA, whose children / students are in attendance. This may be our last chance to end this abomination before it is too late.

Candidates Squared Off in a Forum on July 10, 2019.
By Mark Guydish, Times Leader

[Our candidates from SOS stood their ground and did well against entrenched politicians who are the WBASD incumbents.]

Eight of the nine candidates for Wilkes-Barre Area School Board showed up at a forum Friday night. Incumbent John Quinn said he couldn't attend for medical reasons. - Mark Guydish | Times Leader.

It helps to know that Mark Guydish is often the reporter the Times Leader sends out to do a hit piece on those who oppose the Wilkes-Barre Area School Board. Yes, it is a shame but it is what it is. Various members of SOS have responded to Guydish's articles in the past and some have been published in the paper.

WILKES-BARRE — The prelude may have had some serious friction — enough to force a last-minute change of venue — but the two-hour forum for Wilkes-Barre Area School Board candidates was civil from start to finish.

Incumbent Shawn Walker called for unity in his opening comments, primary challenger Bob Holden headed straight into the audience to talk, and challenger Robin Shudak said her research of paperwork filed with the state showed the new high school is already over budget and that the pad for the building has been relocated several times.

But there was no shouting or name calling.

And at the end, the five challengers — who generally have been running independently — handed out papers with a new mnemonic to show they are all on the same page: "WHOOS" Short for Weigh in for Holden, (Debra) Orlando Formola, (Beth Ann) Owens-Harris, Shudak and (Therese) Schiowitz. Since the forum, Bob Holden has had to drop out of the race as a write-in and he has been replaced on the SOS slate by Jody Busch, another good guy.

The five hope to unseat four incumbents: Walker, Mark Atherton, James Susek and John Quinn. Quinn did not attend the forum, citing health concerns from recent surgery.

If they succeed, the challengers are vowing to try to alter the current work on consolidation of the three high schools into a new building in Plains Township. It's time for a moratorium on any more building while the people figure this one out.

The format called for brief introductions in which Walker said that if there are sometimes heated exchanges between the consolidation pro and con sides, the differences arise "because we are so passionate about our concerns."

Atherton cited his years as a coach in saying he feels he can have a positive impact if elected to a full four-year term. He was appointed to finish the term of Dino Galella, who moved out of the district.

Schiowitz first joked about her decades teaching anesthesia by telling the crowd of about 60 at St. Stephens Church to "nudge the person next to you, I know how to put people to sleep," then spoke of a deteriorating tax base, low test scores and voter apathy. "This can't go on," she said.

Several of the political newcomers conceded some difficulty in public speaking. Formola paused briefly in her opening remark and apologized, then got personal, recalling a bout with a serious illness that, she said, she got through because of the friends she met at GAR Memorial High School. She also repeated her concerns about cost of the new school and safety of the property, which was a former mining site where coal ash was dumped.

But it was primary candidate Holden who became most animated as he spoke of his two daughters in the district, then opted to step away from the podium and closer to the audience. "We had two children who had to come to our house," he recalled from his coaching days, saying the children had a bullet shot through their home's window.

"They stayed at our house for two, three days not because we're good people but because we didn't know what to do."

"This is why I'm running,"Holden added. "This is their future. I want to be an example for them." I regret to say Bob Holden had to step down after doing a great job in the primary. Jody Bush, a very competent replacement is now in his slot as one of the two write-in candidates along with Debra Formola.

The candidates were each given two minutes to answer a single question, then had the same time to address one of the nine questions of their own choosing. Mostly they covered familiar ground, with the challengers disputing the costs of renovating the existing schools and the price of transporting all students to one new school.

Walker addressed the former by noting the new school will add $3.5 million to the annual debt service but should save as much in operating costs.

[BTW, Large school project typically result in higher expenditures regardless of Rev. Walker's opinion.]

Atherton conceded transportation costs will rise but will be manageable. He also vowed there would be an activity bus for all students who want to participate in after school events. "We would never let a child stay at the school waiting for a ride."

[With neighborhood schools, the chance of somebody waiting for a bus does not have to be factored in.]

Owens-Harris, a former school psychologist in the WBA district, said the savings may cover the increase in debt service, but noted that doesn't account for other cost increases. She noted special education costs have more than doubled in nine years, and said she knows ways to reduce those costs.

[This board will never ask anybody for advice.]

Shudak noted she has been reviewing documents related to the school site preparation, made the claim of cost overruns, and promised she will do the research necessary to "make decisions with the facts in front of us, all of them." Shudak also said she believes students at Coughlin High School, now divided into two buildings, need to have a new school, and that building a smaller school in Plains Township might make sense, but not building the larger one.

[Anybody who looks at it honestly, cannot in good conscience be in favor of Mine Shaft High, the Big Toxic School. The best solution of course is to rehabilitate over a long period the oldest school building in the state, the former Wilkes-Barre High / Coughlin High School. Two to five artisans can be assigned full time until it is usable.]

Susek addressed concerns the board could work together if new, anti-consolidation members win seats. Noting he was first elected in 2011, he talked of often-heated executive sessions behind closed doors that lead to action at meetings with everyone accepting the outcome. "People aren't mad at each other at the end. Win, lose or draw at the end you move on," he said. "It's that simple, that easy, but it isn't always" — he paused briefly — "quiet."

[The SOS candidates are not interested in going along with the existing board just to get along. This monstrosity must be stopped dead in its tracks—A moratorium first]

Schiowitz cited studies she said show smaller schools are better for students. "The existing board says we can't afford three secondary schools, and I say we can't afford not to have three secondary schools."

[Me too!]

For the last half-hour of the forum, candidates mingled with the audience.

Do not vote for school board incumbents, period. Please!

In the primary election for the Wilkes-Barre Area School Board, the incumbents did not receive a resounding endorsement from the people for their plan to build a new high school in Plains Twp. on top of toxic mine waste. The Save Our Schools Group sees this as a major weakness despite School Board President Joe Caffrey's insistence that the incumbents have the election sewn up. They do not have anything sewn up because the people have yet to speak!

Neither Caffrey nor the pundits who second guess the power of the people of Wilkes-Barre Area, know about the SOS plan revealed in this book and elsewhere for the two members of the group who are not endorsed by the incumbents and who did not win a party's nomination in May. As the people will see, the plan is to conduct a very active write-in campaign to assure these two candidates will join the majority voting against the consolidation right after the November 5 General Election.

The current board thinks they have it made but their power over the people is slipping and it will end on November 5—election day. There were four incumbents on the primary ballot. Current board member James Geiger is leaving the board at the expiration of his term in December. Some may gain confidence from this and say they are dropping like flies or the people are getting rid of them. But so far, it is not quite enough. We need a few more positive steps in the general election in November.

All incumbents have consistently voted against the people. Geiger left on his own, and only one, Dr. James Susek, failed to win a Democratic or Republican nomination and so he did not advance to the November general election. SOS is pleased that this one board member will not be back to fight against the people. In the general election, it is a must to defeat all incumbents except for one who is not running–Melissa Etzle Patla, as her term continues for two more years.

Only one of the nine current school board members has aligned with the SOS group by opposing the high school project. To form a new majority, four new members from SOS are needed. With the people's help, all five candidates from SOS, shown above can be elected and this will provide a 6-3 majority in favor of the people against the tyrannical anti-Wilkes-Barre Area School Board that consistently votes against the people.

Members of Save Our Schools, a group opposed to the plan to build what just a short time ago was estimated to be a $121 million high school in Plains Twp., aggressively campaigned against the incumbents. Last October 30, 2018, the board upped the ante again saying that the new maximum cost for the project is $137.3 million. With all costs considered, there are current estimates over 40 years for the cost to exceed a $Half Billion. Wyoming Valley is not Las Vegas and no bet will bring billionaires here to bail out our communities.

Beth Anne Owens-Harris, one of the five challengers from Save our Schools surprised the incumbents by receiving the most votes in both the Democratic and Republican elections.

However, school board President Joe Caffrey said the primary results show voter approval of the current board, predicting the three incumbents to win primary nominations Tuesday — Mark Atherton, the Rev. Shawn Walker and John Quinn. Caffrey says they will be tough to defeat in the general election.

SOS agrees they will be tough but we are ready this time for a big win both for the three ballot slots and the two write-ins. The people in Wilkes-Barre Area are energized and we are sick of people like Joe Caffrey and the rest of the tyrants on the board pushing us around.

According to unofficial results, the Democratic primary winners are **Owens-Harris**, 2,570 votes; Atherton, 2,229; Walker, 2,178; Quinn, 2,020; and **Terry Schiowitz**, 2,000.

The unofficial Republican winners are: **Owens-Harris**, 916; Atherton, 828; **Schiowitz,** 805; **Robin Shudak**, 798; and Quinn, 797.

SOS asks voters to redirect their votes for Atherton, Walker and Quinn to SOS as it would be like voting against what is best for Wilkes-Barre Area. The SOS candidates on the ballot are Beth Anne Owens-Harris (D&R), Terry Schiowitz (D&R), and Robin Shudak (R). Remember in the General Election, all voters can vote for any candidate whether on the D or R side. Don't forget the two write-in candidates to give the people's position a great victory—**Jody Busch and Debra Formola.**

Caffrey said many votes were based on the individual candidate and not based on opposition to incumbents. SOS begs to differ with Caffre's take on that point. Incumbents are a known entity and in the fall, that advantage will be minimized as the increase in publicity for the SOS candidates will make them all known entities.

Of the five, please remember, Jody Busch and Debra Formola are not on the ballot and must be written down. Here is a picture again of the five Save Our Schools candidates.

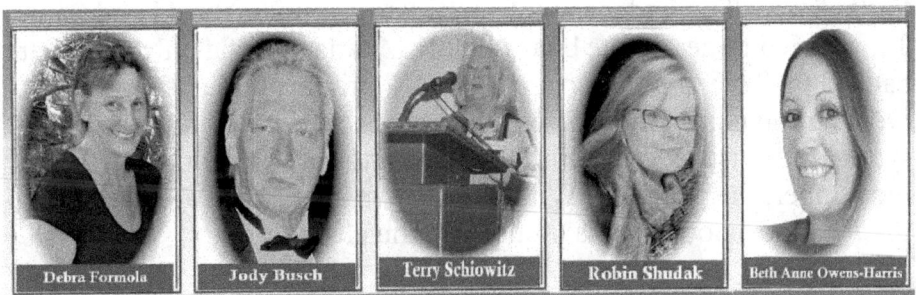

Debra Formola | Jody Busch | Terry Schiowitz | Robin Shudak | Beth Anne Owens-Harris

Owens-Harris said she is a little surprised but pleased by her first-place finishes. The Wilkes-Barre resident works as a psychologist for the Carbondale Area School District and worked for Wilkes-Barre Area for nine years.

"Being active in the community, being involved and showing up to events," Owens-Harris said, trying to explain her success in the election. "I have experience working hand and hand with families. Being a psychologist allowed me to build relationships with families. People might trust me, having worked with me and knowing I am very students focused. I also have a track records of really believing in the city and remaining positive on what our city could be."

The high school consolidation project was "the hot topic," but voters looked at other issues, [such as the negligent school maintenance] she added.

"I hope to be a collaborator," she said, noting she has "good relationships" with Wilkes-Barre Area officials and prefers "neighborhood schools."

Eight of the nine primary candidates cross-filed and were on both the Republican and Democratic ballots. Walker only filed as Democratic candidate.

Five candidates in the general election will win four-year terms on the board.

In the 2017 general election, the four winners were: Caffrey, 3,959 votes; Denise Thomas, 3,841; Ned Evans, 3,722; and Melissa Etzle Patla, 3,553. Two independent candidates, John Suchoski and Sam Troy, failed to get on the board in 2017. Patla was the only candidate backed by Save Our Schools in the 2017 primary and she won a Democratic nomination. She is returning to the board for the next school year and together with the five victories SOS anticipates in November, the people of Wilkes-Barre Area will have a 6-3 lead on the neighborhood schools' issue after the election

Chapter Summation by Richard A Holodick from March 15, 2019 Includes underfunding by state

Though this short essay by Dr. Richard Holodick was written before the primary election, it is the perfect summation for what is at stake in this election. Your vote matters. Save Our Schools and return to the neighborhood school philosophy. Here is Dr. Holodick's essay:

"It doesn't take a CPA to see a major problem in this school district. Setting the stage, our school district is underfunded by the state. We have a low tax base. The average salary is under $40,000, and the students are at a 76% poverty level. We have three historic high schools. One, Coughlin is the oldest in the state at about 110 years, built in 1909.

Both of these schools were neglected by this board so bad that one was closed, another they say needed $51 million in repairs, and the other scheduled for demolition at a cost of $13 million. Six other district school buildings are old and none meet state standards, except the recently renovated Mackin which was closed down as an elementary school ten years ago.

The property tax has been increased the max allowed by law for the last three years, and it appears this will be an annual event for many years.

[While elderly are vacating the Area so they can afford life.]

The need to raise taxes is not related to the renovations or new construction. Replacing common sense in using existing facilities, the board has a pie in the sky plan to build a large box consolidated high school on top of a coal mine and coal ash dumping ground. All costs considered, construction, site purchase, interest and bussing over the 40 years will reach a HALF BILLION DOLLARS. To take care of a third of the students, what about the other two thirds? To solve a three-school problem, what about the other six school buildings?

Additional summation comments from Dr. Holodick Essay of May 18, 2018

It is vital to 7000 students, the taxpayers and senior citizens to "hold elected officials accountable." The belief of Save Our (neighborhood)

Schools Board is that the education of all students is vital to our community. Neighborhood schools are vital to our city; the quality of education and financial stability of the district. safe/quality facilities and the aforementioned notions are fundamental to our citizens.

We need to hold elected officials accountable for a deplorable student state wide ranking; six million spent with nothing physical to show for it, and a potential deficit of $29 million dollars, without required construction; the destruction of historic high schools due to neglect; the need to raise taxes to the max allowed by law just to cover errors and omissions.

Yes the district has been underfunded by the state, all the more reason to handle the funds you do have vigilantly. This city is on the re-bound with center city, the colleges and universities, riverfront, and sports/entertainment. Desperately needed is the restoration of our neighborhoods. The Wilkes University study pointing to the growing neighborhood blight and number of family residents' homes for sale are vivid examples that the neighborhoods are heading in a reverse direction. We truly believe that the restoration of the neighborhood schools will be the needed beginning of bringing the neighborhoods back to what they once were. What is your opinion?

Chapter 5 The Plan: ~~Three High Schools to be Consolidated in Wilkes-Barre~~

Please don't forget that first and foremost nearly all evidence says don't consolidate schools because it harms academics, student sense of well-being, student participation, and that it increases costs. Having said that, the site is receiving such attention because outside of perhaps Chernobyl, it would be difficult to find a worse spot to build a school.

"Three-In-One" is not a good oil for Wilkes-Barre Area

Coughlin HS   **GAR HS**   **Meyers HS**

The board plan is for all three Wilkes-Barre high schools, Coughlin, GAR, and Meyers are to be consolidated into one.

The people of Wilkes-Barre, Pa and immediate surrounds never asked their school board to destroy their high schools and they never asked for their lives and the lives of their children to be turned upside down. Nonetheless for politics or for greed or for a combination of both, or perhaps leadership incompetence, life may never be the same in the small communities comprising what they call Wilkes-Barre Area.

Nonetheless, the Wilkes-Barre Area School Board, the top politicians in Luzerne County PA, whose honesty is clearly in question, are in charge of the plight of schools in this section of Northeastern PA. They made their decision and nobody with a functioning brain would approve of what they have decided.

Let's explore the competence notion and let the politics and greed sit for now. We will get back to that in this book.

Dr. Richard Holodick, a strong supporter of the people and of the neighborhood schools' notion has served as the President of the Save Our Schools Group for many years. He is a major reason why this group has become so active recently. Through his work, hopefully this year, we will arrest power back from the tyrants on the WBASB. I have the pleasure of reading his work and communicating with him regularly about the sad state of affairs in which this school board and its administration have placed the citizens of the WBA.

Here are some powerful words from Dr. Holodick:

Good morning Brian. ...Another angle I am working on two issues that have brought this board or will bring this board to their knees [which is where they belong]. The first is this quarter to half billion-dollar project [The consolidated, unaffordable Taj Mahal super school in Plains TWP]. Can you believe that there is no curriculum/facility master plan? I provided an example of an RFP [high quality] done by the Harrisburg Community College. It was ignored by the board—no consideration.

The second concern is of course nepotism and cronyism, [rampant in the school district for years]. This is capped off by hiring and promoting the seriously inexperienced. Consider the academics, finances, and facilities in dire straits with three historic facilities in jeopardy. The two top positions vacant, superintendent and business manager. The board's solution was to hire Brian Costello, who has a grand total of 4 years as an assistant principal;. The business manager was promoted from within though he has never held the position. Both of these new hires could feasibly be a big part of the problem.

With no architect or engineer in-house to provide guidance to the new superintendent or the board, major issues were discovered that were overwhelming; yet, they needed to be dealt with by neophyte political appointees.

With historic high schools in the balance they hire four architect firms with zero, yes zero large school restoration experience; and sparse large high school construction experience. Even at the board level, with all the district's problems they needed leadership at the top. They elected Denise Thomas as the board president. Her background is as a former district attendance clerk.

It would be humorous if the job were not so serious. To solve the myriad of problems and to "lock-in" the notion that the Plains albatross is a real happening. they opt to consolidate all sports without any construction for a new school. Then, they post the head football coach position where once there were three head coaches.

------ end of Dr. Holodick's remarks

The all-powerful Wilkes-Barre Area School Board, exercised its solitary power by choosing to force all Wilkes-Barre Area high school students to go to school under one roof. Of course this cannot happen until their Taj Mahal boondoggle consolidated high school is built over a toxic mine waste site. So the board voted and it is not about to be readily overturned though the citizens of the area are not happy. Life for Wilkes-Barre students and parents may never be the same again. Taxes are expected to blow through the roof as more and more parents leave town for relief.

The Save Our Schools Group was formed to stop this insanity and that is why it is so important for the public to vote for the slate of candidates including two-write-in candidates, Debra Formola and Jody Busch that have been brought forth by the group.

After a large number of misfires on where to locate the new consolidated high school, which nobody seems to want in the first place, the Wilkes-Barre Area School Board voted 6-3 to add GAR High School into its consolidation plan. Citizens continue to challenge the board for many reasons including the desire to have schools without any worry of breathing in toxic waste fumes from coal ash and other carcinogens under the new high school.

Additionally, the citizens clearly prefer neighborhood schools rather than a huge consolidated blown-up high school serving "everybody" in the Area. The board says they have the new solution by making GAR a middle school under a recent iteration of their overall "plan," expected to be completed in 2022. But, the Citizens want three neighborhood High Schools and there is no reconciliation in sight.

Among the misfires, at one time the board had a plan to merge Coughlin and Meyers high schools at a site in Wilkes-Barre but with objections, they changed these plans to the current site in Plains Twp, while in this iteration, GAR would remain a high school. The best laid plans of mice and men gang aft agley.

With its major inexperience in the top management ranks, the WB Area Board seems to not know what the right thing is to do but it seems that when the citizens offer their thoughts, they are always quickly rejected. The inexperienced officials in the District are know-it-alls, and they have apparently adopted the catch phrase "What Me Worry?" as they never seem to worry about being incompetent. After all, they expect the taxpayer to always bail them out.

"What Me Worry," as many know is the catch phrase attributed to Alfred E Newman, the mascot / symbol for Mad Magazine. It symbolizes the irreverent and often caustic humor of the publication. Our own Alfred E Neuman serves as the superintendent and has become the district's chief fireman. As the board creates neglect fires all over the area, our own Alfred E Neuman believes he can put them all out without needing any help.

The board's action

The August 8, 2018 rendition of the Wilke-Barre Area School Board's "final decision" on consolidation came about on a 6-3 vote . This vote added GAR High School into its consolidation plan, which is still being challenged by citizens who prefer neighborhood schools. GAR will become a middle school under the plan, expected to be completed in 2022.

"It's a wonderful night in the Wilkes-Barre Area School District," board member Ned Evans said prior to voting yes. When Ned is up for reelection the citizens have to remember the glee he showed in taking an action against the wishes of the people.

Other board members voting yes were Joe Caffrey, Denise Thomas, James Susek, John Quinn and the Rev. Shawn Walker. They all must be fired the first chance we get.

Some board members who voted "no" couched their vote for apparent political reasons by explaining that they didn't have enough time to review the idea.

Walker had made the motion near the conclusion of the meeting and some board members appeared to be caught off guard. So, the No vote from Dino Galella may have been taken back after he gets his Dutch Uncle talk. It did not happen because Atherton was appointed to the board when Galella left town. James Geiger did not run for reelection and is off the board in 2019 and Melissa Patla is against the consolidation.

"I didn't know we were voting on it [Tuesday night]. I think we as a board should have talked about it more," Galella said. Humma Humma Humma! Galella resigned from the board after this when he moved out of the area.

Parents, teachers, and students did not react well and have protested the consolidation of the three Wilkes-Barre area schools into one. In one particular protest, they marched from Meyers High School all the way to the school district's administration building. Protesters had strong words for the board but typically, this board operates under a rule by tyranny and they pay little attention to the concerns and the needs of the people,.

The people are clearly against the consolidation of GAR, Coughlin, and Meyers High Schools into one brand new high school being built in Plains Township. Most cannot believe that the board is serious about actually going through with such a poor idea. They are surprised that with so much negative pressure, the board members have not relented. The SOS group has a solution to avoid this big mistake. Fire all board members when they come up for reelection. It is the only way.

"I was honestly shocked because I've lived in Wilkes-Barre my entire life and I've always expected to go to Meyers," Meyers Freshman Sam Grimm said.

School officials said the average class size in the new high school would be about 24 students, but protesters still have their doubts. "The neighborhood schools are definitely a better choice, a better option," Meyers High School teacher Amy Basham said.

Costello said he hopes the new high school brings in a new sense of community, but protesters don't think that's going to happen.

"What community? Number one, the school is in Plains it's not even in Wilkes-Barre," Tracy Hughes, a parent of a Meyers High School student, said.

Even though the school board is moving forward with its plans to build the new high school, protesters said they'll keep voicing their opinions.

"To those people who say that the deal is already done - this is a democracy. No deal is ever actually done. The will of the people should prevail," Protest organizer Lois Grimm said.

Several other comments levied by citizens over the decision to consolidate and build the boondoggle school over a tox mine dump:

1. No tax base any longer in Wilkes Barre= no money for the school districts. It's a matter of financial survival. Don't these people realize you can't get blood from a stone? Caused by the cost of teacher pensions, which need to be re-structured.

2. I am for the standing up against those making wrong selfish decisions! Power to the Parents!.

Chapter 6 A Look at the WBA Schools' Issue

Please don't forget that first and foremost nearly all evidence says don't consolidate schools because it harms academics, student sense of well-being, student participation, and that it increases costs. Having said that, the site is receiving such attention because outside of perhaps Chernobyl, it would be difficult to find a worse spot to build a school.

Atty. Kim Borland addresses the audience at a recent Wilkes-Barre Area School Board meeting. -

Spread out in the chapters of this book are the many issues that have been documented about the Wilkes-Barre Area School Board's intransigence in the matter of ripping down all the high schools in Wilkes-Barre to build a monster school—now in Plains. It was not always to be in Plains. It is tough to find a complete time line on the Board's decisions but it would not be fun to read anyway. We begin this chapter on the issue with what was going on in 2016 when Meyers High School was the issue.

This article was published October 3, 2016 by the Times Leader. It was written by Bill O'Boyle - boboyle@timesleader.com

Save Our Schools waiting on Wilkes-Barre Area board to decide on Meyers study

WILKES-BARRE — The Save Our Schools Committee is awaiting a response from the Wilkes-Barre Area School District regarding a proposal prepared by a construction company that would provide an independent assessment on the feasibility of repairing Meyers High School.

According to Kim Borland, an attorney and member of SOS, the group sent a proposal from Bancroft Construction Company to the district on Sept. 9, but there has been no response from the administration or school board.

"We are disappointed that, after 14 months, the school district has refused to have an independent study done of Meyers," Borland said Monday. "So SOS went out and found a firm with similar experience. We feel it would be best to get an independent assessment of Meyers to see if it can be fixed at a reasonable cost."

Wilkes-Barre Area Solicitor Raymond Wendolowski said the school board hasn't met since it received the Bancroft proposal. The board is scheduled to meet at 5:30 p.m. Oct. 17 [2016] in the cafeteria of the Solomon/Plains Complex, 43 Abbot St., Plains Township.

"The board will consider (the proposal) at that meeting," Wendolowski said.

Wendolowski said the October meeting will be the first time the board can review the proposal and discuss it before making a decision.

Borland said one of the issues that SOS has had with the district is it does not have confidence in the information the district has relied upon in making its decision to consolidate Meyers and Coughlin.

"Because of the enormous investment and impact it would have over the next 30 years, we asked that they get an independent review of what would be required to keep Meyers open," Borland said. "That's why SOS feels an independent study should be done."

Borland said SOS decided to seek a company to perform an independent study "because the school district couldn't agree to do it." Borland said SOS found "numerous inconsistencies" with the district's approach to the matter of consolidation.

"We wanted someone else to take a look at this and tell us what they think," Borland said. "A lot of the district's plan is based on Meyers not being usable."

The school district wants to build a new high school where Coughlin stands on North Washington Street that would consolidate grades 9 through 12 from Meyers and Coughlin.

Bancroft proposal

In a letter dated Sept. 9 sent to Brian Costello, superintendent, and Joseph Caffrey, school board president, Bancroft Construction detailed what it would do to assess Meyers and what the assessment would cost — $100,000.

"Our objective is to provide an opinion as to what repairs and renovations are reasonably necessary to make E.L. Meyers High School fit and suitable for use as a secondary school for the foreseeable future and at what projected cost such repairs and renovations can be made," the letter states.

Bancroft would review the assessment documentation already created, visually assess the building itself, review current recommendations and associated back-up data and evaluate costs associated with these recommendations.

"Since the option for new construction is already provided in the 2014 report, we will limit the scope of this study to renovation/rehabilitation of the existing building, taking into consideration its historical significance in the community," the proposal states.

Bancroft has assembled a team to do the feasibility study:
• ABHA Architects would provide full design services, ranging from master planning, site studies, space needs programming and feasibility studies through architectural and interior design,

preparation of bidding and construction documents and construction contract administration.

• Bancroft Construction Company is a full-service construction management, general contracting, design-build and program management firm serving the Mid-Atlantic United States, including Delaware, Pennsylvania, Maryland, and New Jersey.

• DEDC, established in 1965, is a privately owned, full service multi-disciplined engineering and design firm offering in-house expertise in mechanical HVAC, electrical, plumbing, process/chemical, structural and instrumentation/control engineering and design services.

The Bancroft proposal would be an analysis of the Meyers building based on survey information and data provided by the district and will need to include:

- A demographic review of district needs with enrollment projections
- An educational program review with facilities analyses of all buildings
- Building capacity calculations
- Summary of educational deficiencies
- Structural analysis dated December 2014
- Masonry façade analysis dated December 2014 and attached to the structural report
- Floor plans and elevations

Bancroft said its representatives would travel to Wilkes-Barre three times while developing the report — first to tour the site, with two subsequent trips to meet with representatives of the district/school board to review recommendations.

Mark Schiowitz SOS re Abandoned WBASD board Plan and now

Admin · July 21. 2019 at 11:10 AM

Photo of Dr. Mark Schiowitz when serving temporarily on WBASD School Board

The SOS leadership and the most active discussants in this group have read a lot of the literature about consolidation, school size, operational costs, the longevity of buildings, educational models, middle schools, even the opinions of Plancon. We have forged an alternate plan based on data.

More recently, surprised by 2 completely different school siting plans, much attention turned to the sites: One plan which was not very good, had multiple parts and was expensive, was not supported by the taskforces the district assembled. The plan was promoted without a thought to zoning consent. Exit $5 million. SOS specifically warned the superintendent & board that we would oppose them at zoning, yet they persisted with site prep which didn't even include appropriate clean up and that potentially could have harmed CHS students in the annex.

When that plan was abandoned, it was clear, the leadership was intent on punishing city residents when they extremely quickly and petulantly announced they were moving the site to Plains. They promptly picked the site with the fewest advantages by their own evaluations. Then they bought it for 4 x its value, claiming a bargain because the mining company, with its checkered past, wanted double that amount.

When the land's full mining history and its use as an unlined coal ash landfill became known, the educational issues went to the rear a bit: This is a soft, air-polluted contaminated site which still has not been checked for several very significant toxins. The remediation plan is second-rate when you cull the literature. Cap in place is not even being permitted in some locations and 21 states would discourage or forbid the use of this site.

A link to EPA's outline of school siting (and other literature) is under files on this group [Save Our Schools Web Site]. Because this land gets reclaimed and looks better, does not mean a school should be placed there. I'm a physician. I know the potential of these toxins to harm. Again, check the coal ash section [of the website]. Look at info from Earth Justice, Environmental Integrity Project or the Sothern Environmental Law Center. The site has escaped the EPA, to date, because they are the only federal agency with a coal ash rule and it was established after the last shipment was dumped in Plains and because they don't regulate mining sites. OSM does and they have opined that the management and timing of this sale is most unusual.

So, this fight, this group, is truly about education and health first. SOS leadership gains nothing via our alternate plan. The district's plan is simply not supported by available research, at all. My frustration is why don't reasonable, good people read what we have found (and anything else?) I do not see how caring and good people can support the district's position.

Information about Dr. Mark Schiowit:

Not only is Dr. Schiowitz a leader in the Save our Schools movement, he is still active as a volunteered for over 10 years in the Meyers sports program. He is also on the side line a s a volunteer coach. Ironically, though available, this school board is too self-centered to recognize that they have had a surgeon on the side line as well. Dr. Schiowitz served on the board as a replacement for several years and performed outstanding work. Nonetheless, he was rejected by President Caffery and this board for Dino Galella's board seat when he stepped down. They also kept Dr. Schiowitz from the external task force committee, though he is clearly an expert in school matters. Why you may ask; Mr. Caffrey's exact words were "he has a plan." Dr. Mark Schiowitz sure does have a plan and it is a workable plan that would not bankrupt the communities in the Wilkes-Barre Area. You can tell who Mark is by reading the essay above and many other essays and opinions that we have captured in this book. Thank you Dr. Schiowiz for all you do.

From: **Richard A Holodick** July 23, 2019

Tribute to Mark & Terry Schiowitz

Not just a thank you but also a tribute to one of our school district's and community's most dedicated leaders/activists. Two individuals that are accomplished alumni of WBASD. Fifty years in this business I have worked with the best educational scholars; the most creative problem solvers; and dedicated community leaders; Mark & Terry Schiowitz are high on that list. Dr. Mark Schiowitz is a graduate of Coughlin High School; a surgeon at the General Hospital. Terry also is a Meyers grad, and is a retired medical professional, and candidate for the WBA school board.

<<< They have three sons Josh, a grad of Elmer L. Meyers High School. A chip off the old block, Josh is now involved in assisting SOS, most pointedly getting Mom elected to the board.

Meeting an immediate need Dr. Mark volunteered to fill a vacant board seat after the resignation of Theresa McGuire. He has for many years volunteered in the MHS football program, providing not just as a volunteer coach but a medical professional on the sideline.

His wife Terry was one of the organizers of Save Our Schools, Inc. As expected Terry, captured the most votes in both parties. I would attest; a complete professional couple dedicated to the children of the WBASD; not to mention the poverty-ridden residents.

Dr. Mark without question has been the leader extraordinaire in educational research and the creator of an educationally sound, cost-effective alternative plan that maintains the acclaimed neighborhood school concept; based 100% on his and SOS research.

[Along with Dr. Holodick, my hat is off to the great work done by Dr. Holodick, Dr. Mark Schiowitz, and Terry Schiowitz, soon to be Board member. Thank you all very much.]

Walls begin to rise for new W-B Area high school

WBASD Construction and Facilities Manager Brian Costello, who also doubles as the Wilkes-Barre Area School District Superintendent, stands near what will be the base of an elevator shaft on one end of the "Main Street" hallway bisecting the new consolidated high school under construction in Plains Township. Footers and foundation can be seen in the background. You can see the mine waste in every part of this picture.

On the next page begins some additional information from July 22, 2019

Note: Brian Costello, in the pic on the prior page, is the front man on the construction project because the Board has failed to hire a competent maintenance staff and no architect or engineer are on the team so Costello does this work while grades and test scores are falling throughout the school district. You can't be the construction guy and superintendent of schools anywhere else but in Wilkes-Barre Area. Nobody even Superman could do both jobs.

Information is from a Mark Guydish newspaper article in Tomes Leader.

PLAINS TWP. — Foundations have been poured, walls are rising around door frames, and the stage is literally set for the stage, at the site of Wilkes-Barre Area School District's new consolidated high school.

"I'm walking down Main Street," Superintendent Brian Costello said as he trod a black, flat bit of ground. And while his optimistic vision of the school has previously been purely in his head, this time footers of concrete outline the main hallway — "Main Street" — of the future building.

On one side Costello pointed to a corner of the concrete foundation and noted that will be the planned ticket stand for the public coming to attend an event. On the other side, the outline of the stage front and beginnings of the orchestra pit are clear.

Nearby, steel door frames stand with walls of concrete masonry units (old-timers would call them "cinder blocks") already about halfway up the frames. A large hole has been excavated for the natatorium. The land where the four classroom "pods" will jut like fingers from the main building is under preparation or already with foundation underway. The base of an elevator shaft has been excavated, framed with wood and latticed with reinforcement bar, awaiting the pouring of concrete.

[Look at the black ugly mine waste in the pictures being buried under the "new school." Should the Board and Costello be risking the student's health building on top of this toxic site?]

As construction manager Michael Krzywicki [Apollo Group Inc., the district's building project manager – not a WBA employee] drove his pickup truck around the site for a tour before stopping to walk "Main Street," Costello kept track of where they were, regularly pointing to a rendering of the finished building on his phone screen, showing what part of the building will be where the truck was. "We're in the cafeteria." "We're driving through the gym."

[One might suggest Krzywicki should be a WB employee and Costello should be pretending he is the superintendent of schools.]

Krzywicki repeated his expectation that at least two of the four classroom wings should be ready for interior work — walls and roof complete — before winter weather sets in, allowing construction inside to continue once the weather blocks outside work.

[WB residents hope there is not too much building over the next few months as the SOS group is running five candidates for the new School Board which begins its term in December. The objective is to stop the project in its tracks. Then, Costello will have to go back to his real job of School District Superintendent.]

The wall sections that were already visible Monday were not part of those wings. They were athletic rooms. But Krzywicki said the contractors are doing whatever they can in one part of the site where foundations have been poured while waiting for foundation work to be completed elsewhere.

In fact, he said, he likely would have been unable to get so close to the construction site if it hadn't been raining on and off Monday morning. More than a dozen heavy construction vehicles sat idle around the area, and he said on a clearer day most, if not all, would be in motion.

Costello clearly prefers to focus on what he sees as a big plus for school district students. He points to where the STEM (Science Technology, Engineering and Math) rooms will be, then to what he estimates will be the front of the new auditorium. He envisions a state-of-the-art facility that, at an estimated $121 million, he insists is still coming in under budget despite some additions since the basic contracts were awarded. "I think our kids deserve this," he said of a school that will house students from three existing buildings, each either past or near 100 years old.

Krzywicki is less sanguine when it comes to responding to critics. The plan for this school on this site has been pilloried repeatedly by those — including candidates in November's school board race — who contend it is unsafe due to dumping of coal ash and elevated levels of cadmium and arsenic in some soil samples. They also accuse the district of spending too much on the project.

Much of the criticism, Krzywicki noted, comes on the Facebook page for Save Our Schools, formed after consolidation plans were initially announced with the goal of retaining the current system of three smaller high schools.

[Krzywicki, of Apollo Group a favored contractor, not of Wilkes-Barre, knows where his bread is buttered so he supports Brian Costello and the Board, his benefactors]

At the end of Monday's tour as the rain picked up for a while, Krzywicki sat in his truck and rebutted some of the criticism.

I wonder if he got paid for his PR work or was it gratis.]
…
[There are more examples in the Guydish article]
[BTW, Krzywicki is not a doctor and he has disdain for those wanting students to breathe clean air. Dr. Mark Schiowitz is a Medical Doctor. He is with the Save Our Schools Committee and he knows the school to be built is not safe. How many patients does Krzywicki see in a day?]

[Nonetheless] Krzywicki chafes most at the recurring claims the site is a health risk. In the past, he has stressed that no coal ash has been unearthed in any excavation where the building will sit, and that the only place it was encountered was digging an entrance road to grade. While considerably more excavation has been done since he first made the claim, he repeated it Monday.

[What do we expect this biased contractor to say – that it is all bad and should be shut down so he loses his big contract?]

The debate is sure to continue, but as the tour showed, it has not stalled construction. **[That is a shame.]**

Pictures Work proceeds among foundation footers with reinforced bar jutting up to support concrete masonry unit walls — like those partially completed in the background — at the construction site of WB Area's consolidated high school. Bill Tarutis | For Times Leader

The front of the auditorium stage is outlined as workers continue construction of Wilkes-Barre Area's new consolidate high school. Bill Tarutis | For Times Leader

The base of an elevator shaft awaits concrete pouring on the construction site of Wilkes-Barre Area's consolidated school. (Mine Shaft High) Bill Tarutis | For Times Leader

Contractors work on part of the foundation for the new Wilkes-Barre Area consolidated high school Monday foundation Bill Tarutis | For Times Leader

Construction continues on the swimming pool, front, in the athletic wing of the new Wilkes-Barre Area High School in Plains Township . Bill Tarutis | For Times Leader

Workers have begun building concrete masonry unit walls at the site of the Wilkes-Barre Area consolidated high school. Foundation work is well underway at the construction site of Wilkes-Barre Area's consolidated high school. . Bill Tarutis | For Times Leader

-----

So folks, as of today, July 23, 2019, as we get ready to release this book, I was really taken back by the above June 22, 2019 Times Leader article by Mark Guydish (mguydish@timesleader.com). Most of it is shown above. One would think the bevy of negatives about SOS were dictated by Brian Costello himself. All the quotes in this piece by favored construction team Apollo Group Inc's manager Michael Krzywicki appear to be part of a well-orchestrated joint hit piece intended to dupe the people of Wilkes-Barre Area into loving Mine Shaft High That is my opinion. I found it shocking that the Times leader would be part of a story that stabs Wilkes-Barre residents in the back.

First of all if my supposition is true, even after I did not repeat a number of the unverified quotes from this derogation, then the Times Leader colluded with the Board and Costello and Apollo Group Inc. in this published Times Leader ax job. Regardless of your opinion of Mine Shaft High, nobody can contest the lousy effect that ripping down three refurbish-able high schools in Wilkes-Barre will have by leaving the city without even one high school. This is not good for Wilkes-Barre students or resident taxpayers. Since the Times Leader is located in Wilkes-Barre City, why would they not take a position in favor of the citizens of Wilkes-Barre, their customers, and not the powerful members of the School Board and a favored contractor, Apollo Group. Think about it. The paper could have taken the side of the people. When Wilkes-Barre is no more, what happens to the Times Leader?

Joan Finn:
Both papers only print "fluff". Where is the investigative reporting?

Richard A Holodick:

[This is Dr. Holidick's response to the hit piece article by the Times Leader's Mark Guydisht. Can we get access to the school board's payroll to see if Guydish's name is on a pay stub someplace?]

I share with you my response to the Times Leader front page Mark Guydish story.

(Holodick's response)

Krzywicki is less sanguine (confident? Upbeat? Optimistic?) when it comes to responding to critics. The plan for this school on this site has been pilloried (defiantly denounced) repeatedly by those (would "those" be Brokavitch or the Louisville University study where 300 children have been studied ?)— including candidates in November's school board race — who contend it is unsafe due to dumping of coal ash and elevated levels of cadmium and arsenic in some soil samples. (It is not the candidates who are making these hazard claims of cadmium and arsenic in some soil samples' its actual case samples including the State Correctional Institution at Fayetteville where 13 inmates have cancer from being near a contaminated site.) They also accuse the district of spending too much on the project. (Michael K, a quarter of a billion dollars in a district with a 76% poverty rate to solve the district inflicted problems of 2400 students, out of 7000 just does not make me sanguine regarding the rationale thinking of the board or their construction manager.)

Much of the criticism, Krzywicki noted, comes on the Facebook page for Save Our Schools, formed after consolidation plans were initially announced with the goal of retaining the current system of three smaller high schools. (SOS supports the neighborhood schools as supported by the board that claim they "consolidate to save money." The PFM and the board's own half million-dollar study state closing the neighborhood schools as a "Disadvantage." Lets see. $4.9 million purchase price, $9.5, million site work, $4.9 million Washington Street, $1.3 million Kistler expansion, nearly $22 million to date; have we started to save the taxpayers money yet?)

One SOS post, he noted, said the pool for the school was costing $17 million. He said it had been budgeted at just under $5 million and so far totaled $3.7 million. Even if it is expanded from six to eight lanes, he estimated, it would cost at most about $4.1 million.

(we repeat poverty; the miss info, if in fact it is miss-info came from an unexplained $17 million payment on the list of board approved payments. WOW $4.1, $4.2, $4.9 seems to be a favorite in the losses category for this dysfunctional board. There is no question that $4.1 million for a pool is irresponsible spending in a district that already has a swimming pool they are obligated to maintain.)

Krzywicki chafes (annoys?) most at the recurring claims the site is a health risk, (because it is Mike). In the past, he has stressed that no coal ash has been unearthed in any excavation where the building will sit, and that the only place it was encountered was digging an entrance road to grade. While considerably more excavation has been done since he first made the claim, he repeated it Monday. (He is "chaffed at health concerns? Seriously? I find that most irresponsible and a need for the chafed to do a little research. His response scares the hell out of me.) And he rejected claims by SOS critics who have said developers would not be able to build residential homes on the site because of the materials in the soil. "DEP, the state Department of Environmental Protection Is holding the district to residential standards," Krzywicki said, meaning clean fill caps of a specific required depth. "A developer would have to do the same thing if he were building a home." (Hum caution meaning there is concern?)

Richard A Holodick: More TL:

Much of the criticism, Krzywicki noted, comes on the Facebook page for Save Our Schools, formed after consolidation plans were initially announced with the goal of retaining the current system of three smaller high schools. (SOS supports the neighborhood schools as supported by the board that claims they "consolidate to save money."

The PFM and the board's own half-million-dollar study state closing the neighborhood schools as a "Disadvantage." Let's see. $4.9 million purchase price, $9.5, million site work, $4.9 million loss on Washington Street, $1.3 million Kistler expansion, nearly $22 million to date; have we started to save the taxpayers money yet?)

Marilyn Jones

Ignorant no good paper too don't forget that we were going to use that building too!!! money in their pockets too 😠 😠 😠 Bull 💩💩💩 SO MANY UGLY PEOPLE IN THE WILKES-BARRE SCHOOL BOARD 💩💩💩 HEADS!!!!

Mark Schiowitz, SOS Committee
Admin · Captured 2 hrs. after posting 7/23/2019

I've sent a longer letter but suggest something like this for the DOE. The terms moratorium or temporary halt can be used. Of course add any details about consolidation, busing, neighborhood schools, parental access, site purchase, effects on neighborhoods, planning, etc. that you like:

Dear Secretary Rivera:
Please request the Wilkes-Barre Area School District bring to a halt any construction on their tainted consolidated high school site. A Departmental Hearing is pending and multiple candidates opposed to this project are on the school board ballot for the fall. Thank you. See contacts under files on this group page. Other contacts are found there too, like Atty general, AG, etc.

Duncan Yoyo

Holding the world by a string

When I was a kid, there were cheap YoYos and there were Duncan YoYos. Duncan was the Cadillac. It is the same today. Donald Duncan, is the man that brought YoYos into prominence starting in the 1930's. These days Duncan-brand YoYos are still extremely popular—with a history like they have, why wouldn't they be?

Citizens of Wilkes-Barre Area have had enough of being treated as YoYos. They've had their fill of being played with like a cheap YoYo. The people want one thing on the school issue—relief from the board's tyranny. The board pretends to listen but they always snap the YoYo back gaining control back with their YoYo finger.

They forget that their job is to serve the people, which is the idea of democracy in the United States. Just because they were elected to serve in office does not mean that the school district is their private erector set and they can do whatever they want. The people are sick and tired of being toyed with.

Politicians at all levels of government like to say that it is against their makeup to ever let a good emergency go to waste. When I was the computer consultant for example in the late 1990's for Wilkes-Barre City, I outlined a plan for the City to prepare for and survive all of the potential hazards of the Year 2000 aka Y2K. With the two-digit date changing from 19 to 20 and the year 2000 closing in, the City was still not motivated to fix its software so it would run in 2000. At the time, I did not understand their logic for testing fate.

Computer programs across the world needed to be examined and changed to perform properly. Wilke-Barre City officials at the time said "No" to spending a dime on preventing an emergency. In fact, one astute official told me that "the public won't pay for planning but the public will always pay for an emergency."

And, so, for politics, they were ready to deal with an emergency, because they knew it would be funded. It is the same game that the school board has played for years and years. Here we are with another emergency. This time, a HALF-BILLION DOLLAR high school to be built on toxic waste.

Without such a neglect strategy, why else would all of the schools in the district be in such a state of disrepair. The three high schools are already at doom's door thanks to the board choosing never to apply an ounce of prevention but instead seeking major funding for the cure for neglect and disrepair. The people must deny them their boondoggle funding and fire them all.

Don't forget that five candidates for the people opposed to the current board's poor decisions are running in the November General Election.

The definition of *an ounce of prevention is worth a pound of cure* fits perfectly here as the dilapidated state of the high schools is in need of a major cure. It would have been much better and easier for the board to stop the problems from maintenance neglect from happening than to stop or correct them now that the results are coming in quickly. It has started. It is intentional . It is the game the board plays to get the funding for new buildings.

And, so the board is not ashamed of the job it did as caretakers of Meyers and Coughlin in particular. They came up with one stop-gap plan after another. One of their plans suggested that parts of Meyers High School could actually be saved while the rest of it would be demolished. Who would you pick, the superintendent or the business manager to decide which parts can be saved and which parts must go. After all, the board is so inept there is nobody with construction or building expertise on staff to help make the determination. That too is a shame. There is not an architect or an engineer to be found.

Along the way to today, the school board actually voted in one of its Monday meetings in favor of a plan that would eventually demolish most of Meyers while keeping the magnificent auditorium and the only football field for four schools. Meanwhile Meyers graduates from many different years are talking together more and more about their school and in almost all cases, they still think that all three major sections of Wilkes-Barre need their own neighborhood school as do many of the smaller communities in WBA.

What about auditoriums and gymnasiums

Let me take a small diversion to bring up the notion brought up when the board considered keeping a piece of Meyers High School. How many auditoriums does a school need. The sane answer is one. But, how many are needed when you put three or four schools in one? Well, one that is three times bigger. That's a lot of space.

Actually, Meyers, GAR and Coughlin have beautiful auditoriums and nobody would consider sending GAR students to Plains or Meyers or Coughlin for programs needing an auditorium. An auditorium is needed for plays, concerts, daily assemblies, honor roll assemblies, pep rallies etc.

A gymnasium is also a great item to have. One per school. At one time, Meyers had two gymnasiums and tore the wall down between the girls and boys and made a bigger gym. GAR and Coughlin have their own gyms and rightfully so. They serve a lot of students.

Coughlin had one of the largest gymnasiums where District 2 wrestling etc. and larger events were often held. Gymnasiums are used also for gym class for all the sections of all the grades several times a week. Plus, there are indoor intramural sports such as basketball that use the gym.

What about swimming pools? Somehow our parents were able to afford to build two pools into the Meyers complex in 1930. One was for girls and one was for boys. With the damage sustained from the 1972 flood, the two pools ,which were at the very bottom level of the school at the football field level were both filled-in and never used again for swimming. Too bad. Somehow the board could not afford to fix the pools but could build a huge pool in the Kistler complex.

My point is not to bring back these swimming pools but just to note times are different. Right now Meyers uses Kistler Elementary School (across Hanover Street from Meyers Stadium] for its pool needs and there are no more swim classes for students like I had during the day at Meyers—back when male bathing suits were made of the same material as the emperor's new clothes. Our more recent school boards seem ready at all times to reduce the opportunities for students rather than fix existing facilities to increase the opportunities.

When Meyers seniors graduated in their school auditorium in June, 2019, they may not have realized they could be one of the last classes to go to school there. With this YoYo school board, what is today is not always tomorrow.

Quite frankly, it is not just Meyers students and parents who have been jerked around by the board. One day GAR is going to be ripped down, then it's back as a high school and then it is to be a middle school. Humph! That is especially poor management.

Coughlin students had the most treasure to lose. The board did such a poor job of maintaining the part of that school that was once Wilkes-Barre High, they actually were forced to close it before there was a solution to the board's so-called high school dilemma. I drove past the fenced in historically significant Coughlin High school the other day to get a look at it.

To the naked eye, it is a filthy mess but the grandeur of the historical building still comes through even though no time has been spent by anybody trying to make it look even just a bit more presentable. Coughlin needs to be preserved in my opinion as a City and school district historical treasure even if it is never reactivated into being a fully functional high school.

Coughlin with board applied fencing and scaffolding as beautification artifacts or what???

What would I do with Coughlin? I would hire two to five artisans with skills in multiple building areas. Perhaps some craftsmen would even volunteer. They would go to work every day in the old Coughlin building—the oldest school building in Pennsylvania. I would give them a budget and no time limit. The budget would permit them to bring in special contractors as needed for special parts of the restoration. Every day they would move forward until one day, full restoration would be in sight.

All the time the work was progressing, Coughlin students would know it is still their school and they would know that one day it would again be magnificent. We, the people of Wilkes-Barre Area must save it from the only master craftsman which the WBASB is willing to hire -- *The Axe Man*.

When Terrance Williams, a Wilkes-Barre resident was interviewed by WNEP TV for one of their shows, his comment was perfect:

"It's historical and really should be preserved."

In their Rube Goldberg half-way approach, the board produced an artist's birds-eye rendering showing how the Meyers' auditorium would look. Part of the school building on Carey Avenue would be demolished. Part of it would be transformed into a performing arts center. The football field would also be renovated by fixing the school side bleachers. And, then the board could work on the Brooklyn Bridge—that's a joke folks. Sometimes it seems that simple things in WBASD are as difficult to get as getting a good price for the Brooklyn Bridge.

Having an auditorium at Meyers would not mean one would not be needed at The Big Toxic School. What would the board do after that? Would they bring in busses from Plains when there was to be a major chapel / assembly program? Another bone-headed idea by the board! Not the first and surely not the last until we can fire them all.

Though nobody wants a historical building in any neighborhood to be ripped down, one Meyers graduate offered that "The building isn't nearly as important as the idea of a neighborhood high school in the City of Wilkes-Barre. I think the neighborhood high school is the anchor."

These preliminary plans still have a long way to go, but if the plans and funding are all approved, demolition on Meyers High School could start as early as 2022. The school board must be replaced so this demolition never sees the light of day.

The Wilkes-Barre Memorial stadium had a different look before and after it reopened in 2017.

Concrete Bleachers hugged Meyers High in the stadium's Glory Days. They are now gone.

Note that in the pic above, there is real grass. The above pic is from a long-time ago. Artificial turf makes the stadium better looking but the grass days were very nice.

The picture on the following page shows the artificial turf. It is **COURTESY OF WILKES-BARRE SCHOOL DISTRICT. Fans packed both sides of the stadium stands for a 1995 PIAA playoff game between Berwick and Manheim Central. The school side stands no longer exist. Next pic is the current look with no bleachers hugging.**

Meyers with bleachers hugging school and artificial turf

Meyers Bleachers Gone

When Wilkes-Barre Memorial Stadium reopened, it was half-sized after nearly a month of repairs. It was a typical restoration by the board. There was less stadium left after the stadium was fixed. If we gave the board another month, perhaps the stadium would have been reduced by another 25% to ¼ size? Who knows? Do any of us feel we can trust the current school board to make decisions that are in the best interests of the people in the Wilkes-Barre Area? They must be replaced.

The Johnny come lately *"What me Worry!"* school board led by what appears to be a trusty team of Alfred E. Neumans, showed how astute it can be in *taking care* of $300 million dollars' worth of real-estate facilities. They reopened Meyers Stadium on a Thursday night in week three of the 2017 football season.

It was a game between Nanticoke and GAR. It was the first game of the year at the 87-year-old stadium. Only during the 1936 flood and the 1972 flood had the stadium ever been closed. This time, it was under the control of the Costello School Board and it was preventable since it was closed from neglect and disrepair. The current board's rules are not based on the norms.

Rather than a planned preventive maintenance gradual repair, the board had to use one of its patented big-bang approaches to maintenance. It involved some destruction, which is immediately noticeable to anybody who has ever visited the historical stadium for a Friday Night or a Thanksgiving Day football game. Those bleachers visible in the first and second pictures on prior pages are gone and so the home fans now sit on the visitors' side.

Yes, they are gone. See in the bottom picture on the prior page. The bleachers on the school side, which were built of concrete are no longer there. Why? I wonder if a few building tradesmen experts on staff could have saved this historic part of the stadium. Was all the concrete bad after 87 years? The only bleachers they left were the wooden "away" side bleachers.

Now both teams playing each other get to know each other better as they share the "away side." In this particular reconstruction, crews had to race to fix the tunnel to the locker rooms and they closed off the old elevated walkway. The board's experts, though they have nobody on staff with any building expertise, claimed that both elements were starting to crumble due to years of wear and tear. Amazing isn't it that they just noticed it?

Concrete does not crumble in one day after 87 years unless there is 100% neglect. Check out the Roman Coliseum. It is still there. Years and years of neglect, running the stadium with no maintenance on the thin edge of safety, bad things could certainly happen. Surprise, the WBASB could not open its only stadium in time for the 2017 football season because nobody had checked to see if it was OK for football or taking a shower or anything.

The stadium as we previously noted is critical to Wilkes-Barre Area football. There is no other stadium for the City's high schools and for Bishop Hoban. Four separate high schools play their home games at Wilkes-Barre Memorial Stadium. Consequently, all home games for the first two weeks of the season had to be moved to other stadiums. The board and the top officials of WBASD are simply incompetent. But, for the time being, until we fire them, they are ours to live with. We elected them. The other venues collected all the booster proceeds.

Adding to the repair woes were the unhappy football team supporters who depend on the stadium for booster revenues. The concession stands produce no income when there are no games. The stands at games serve as fundraisers for the teams, the boosters, and the bands. For those not on the board, this is all important.

"We were concerned about what we were going to do. Like I said, this is a big fundraiser for us. We were really concerned with what the future would hold for us as far as the rest of the season," said Ellis Hall.

This great stadium first opened in 1930, and it has hosted some big games over the years. It was attached to Meyers high school until just recently, when the board ripped those bleachers down. Whatever the future holds, fans of the Wilkes-Barre schools say there's no place like home.

Despite creating the recent maintenance debacle, Wilkes-Barre school officials claim they want to keep Memorial Stadium and fix it up, even after Meyers high school is torn down.

Knowing that keeping the stadium was in their future plans, one would ask why the board would permit the stadium to begin to crumble with no short-term maintenance plan?

It makes you wonder about the board, does it not? If we cannot trust them with small stuff like half a football stadium to maintain, how can we ever consider giving them a half billion dollars over forty years to build and operate a Taj Mahal school they chose to build on top of a coal ash toxic heap? What do you think the board will do when the first kid gets sick from toxic ash in his throat? What then for the board after the Taj Mahal is built. Will the board sue Plains TWP? Who knows. They are tough to figure out.

Chapter 7 The Best Thinking on Consolidation.

Please don't forget that first and foremost nearly all evidence says don't consolidate schools because it harms academics, student sense of well-being, student participation, and that it increases costs. Having said that, the site is receiving such attention because outside of perhaps Chernobyl, it would be difficult to find a worse spot to build a school.

Sometimes you eat the bear and sometimes the bear eats you. My friends often throw that line at me when things don't go as planned. In other words, we all have to manage our expectations. Sometimes managing expectations is beyond the pale such as when trying to deal with an incalcitrant board of directors who have sworn allegiance to the people but in their actions show they were only kidding.

Instead, they choose to flip the people one of their small wrist center appendages at the end of either arm. Wilkes-Barre Area residents have unfortunately become accustomed to that particular finger.

At some time in early 2019, Richard A. Holodick, the patriarch and lead man of the Save Wilkes-Barre Schools movement did announce that he was stepping down as president of Save Our Schools, the group formed to oppose the consolidation of high schools in the Wilkes-Barre Area School District. The board was especially happy he was leaving because Dr. Holodick knew their ways better than anybody else and he fought so that the people, not the board had their way.

Holodick had gotten sick of battling a board that did not care with a WBA population that thought things would go right without their involvement. He was not kidding but as luck would have it for we the members of this group, there was nobody available to accept his resignation. So folks, much to the board's chagrin, he is still on duty.

Dr. Holodick is still on duty smiling as he had the board really going. He is doing his finest work at this time. He is making other analyses again available to help the cause of Save Our Schools. Dr. Holodick will be listed in each neighborhood high school resulting from his work as the man who awakened all the people to do the right thing for the community. If you are not awake yet, please splash water on your face and join the fray, we are fighting the board together. Dr. Holodick is our leader.

Holodick, 81, is a great leader but much to my personal chagrin, he is not immortal. When he decided to cool it, he cited health issues and frustration as reasons to resign his position. How would you like to have to work with a tyrannical school board that does not care that it took an oath to serve its constituency in the Wilkes-Barre Area. Dr. Richard Holodick is by far one of the best if not the best; and he was ready to go but he never left. Sometimes God intervenes directly as needed.

Holodick is a 1956 graduate of Meyers High School, who retired after a lengthy career as an educator in 2001. He lives in Wilkes-Barre, which is more than some Wilkes-Barre officials can say. .

"I am concluding my efforts (resigning) because this board is now willing to gamble with the health and safety of 3,000 students and the employees who will be on a contaminated site isolated from all neighborhoods; and I have failed to prevent it from happening! Be assured SOS will continue to rectify this deplorable plan," Holodick wrote in a letter about his decision.

A brief note about Dr. Richard Holodick

There is a lot I can say about what a great man and a great Educator Dr. Richard Holodic is but you will see that in the material he has written to help the Save Our Schools cause- Neighborhood schools, no big toxic school, and the elimination of a school board that does not represent the people. Dr. Holodick has received many plaudits during his career as an educator and I would like to show you one below of which he is especially proud. Here it is

Thomas Payzant, former Assistant U.S. Secretary of Education, served as the superintendent of the Oklahoma City School District. Following a national search, he recommended Dr. Richard A. Holodick to work as his assistant in the K-12 city school district. Dr. Holodick's unique assignment was to create a new school district, researching program offerings, recruiting, interviewing and recommending for hire all employees from the administration, teachers, maintenance and custodial staff, and to develop all policies and procedures necessary for the district.

In short, his mission was to create a long-range plan for the development and implementation of all aspects of the new district.

He was responsible for working with the State Department of Education, community, an architect and to plan a new vocational-technical center in an amusement park that the center city had built-in 1928. Thirty years have passed and the Metro Tech School has become a state model if not national. Thirty years later we can attest to the fact that **we have followed the master plan developed by Dr. Holodick and the many community leaders and advisory groups he recruited and coordinated.**

The Save Our Schools committee is very fortunate to have a true professional such as Dr. Holodick on this very important team.

The deplorable Wilkes-Barre Area School Board began excavating the land to build a new consolidated high school in Plains Twp. this spring. The new high school would theoretically allow the consolidation of all three district high schools — Meyers, GAR and Coughlin — sometime during the 2021-22 school year, and the sports teams at the three high schools are being merged this fall. The board is making it hard to undo their actions but a bad idea is a bad idea and we won't stop until this idea is reversed.

Members of Save Our Schools have criticized the construction project for many good reasons over time but recently it is because of previous mining activity at the Plains Twp. site. It is not safe for students, teachers and other workers to breather there.

School officials have said the site will be safe because of environmental safety measures that will prevent exposure to potentially harmful soil. Yet, no executive on the board is willing to accept liability for the first sick child or worse than that, an epidemic or God forbid, a death.

"The district has gone through this with DEP (the state Department of Environmental Protection)," school board President Joe Caffrey said. "I have had conversations with Dr. (Superintendent Brian) Costello and the solicitor (Raymond Wendolowski) that this project will be monitored every step of the way regarding the soil." Joe, how will we know for sure, when nobody gets sick after the first month?

Then what? Remember folks, this is the same board that promised to be vigilant caretakers of District assets such as the very dilapidated school buildings in question. They did not do their jobs. Why should we believe that our kids will not develop respiratory issues or die young from issues and illnesses first encountered in the school the board says is safe. SOS members have challenged the board to move their Administrative Offices to the site.

The district recently upped its dollar bogey to borrow up to $137.3 million to fund the construction of the new high school between Maffett and North Main streets in Plains Twp. The district bought the 78-acre site from Pagnotti Enterprises for $4.2 million. Who else wanted the site? Nobody! Are we sure 10% of that sum would not have been enough? Cronyism and Nepotism have always been the two big words that matter at WBA. Three past board members did time for corruption. Even though School Director is an unpaid position, those on the inside somehow seem to get a lot of perquisites from positions that have no salaries.

Save Our Schools has backed a plan to build a new Coughlin building in Plains Twp. and renovate existing GAR and Meyers facilities. Despite that, Brian Kelly offers another thought that is OK'd by Dr. Holodick.

Kelly (your author writes the following paragraph:)

What would I do with Coughlin? Let me repeat this for effect. I would hire two to four artisans with skills in multiple building trade areas. They would go to work every day in the old Coughlin building--the oldest school building in Pennsylvania. I would give them a budget and no time limit. The budget would permit them to bring in special contractors as needed for special parts of the restoration. . Every day, they would move forward until one day, full restoration would be in sight. Coughlin Students would know it is their school and they would know that one day it would again be magnificent. We must save Coughlin High from the only master craftsman which the WBASB is willing to deploy -- the Axe Man.

"I depart disheartened and disappointed at the apathy of the residents and city council that have said nothing to speak of. The state refuses to even answer their own formal complaint process," Holodick said.

"What is pathetic is the board has concluded all this public apathy, and the state's avoidance, to be approval of their dysfunction."

[It is not approval, folks!]

The initial plan in 2015 was to merge Coughlin and Meyers at a new high school built at the current Coughlin site in downtown Wilkes-Barre. After the city zoning board rejected that plan, the board chose the Pagnotti site in 2017. The board added GAR to the consolidation plan last August. [It has always been a moving target which has confused many residents.]

"I cautioned them, providing an example that the zoning approval request could fail; they ignored the caution. Had they listened they would have saved the district taxpayers $4.9 million dollars," Holodick said.

[It's like money provided by the taxpayers does not matter to this board.]

School officials have said the high school consolidation will save more than $2 million a year by eliminating more than 20 teaching jobs, and they argued building a new consolidated high school is less costly than renovating current facilities.

[Show me the money!]

-- end of Dr. Holodick's letter

And, so, here we are in Wilkes-Barre Area in a state of dysfunction in which neither the board nor its acolytes and disciples can show why their plan has any merit at all. They do not have to. They were elected and reelected. Folks, that is our fault because we did not pay enough attention to what the mice were doing.

Additionally, the board cannot prove to the residents that the children in the high school will not suffer from cancer as a result of the known carcinogens in the mine dust that is prevalent in the building tract. Should that not be enough cause for us all to vote them out of office?

Perhaps the builders of the school like the 911 first responders should get their own special insurance so that latent issues with toxic refuse does not begin to cause the demise of workers, teachers, students and others who frequent this site. If the chance of a toxigenic disease were 25%, would it be negligible enough for parents to be pleased to send their children to this unsafe school. Why take the chance?

Four years ago believing that the school board was made up of intelligent people who wanted what was best for the people, Dr. Richard Holodick wrote the following position paper hoping to get the board to think of the consequences about what it was doing.

I present to you this alarming position paper by the esteemed Dr. Richard Holodick, who is one of a very few in the WBA who actually know what the board's double-talk is all about. After you read it, ask yourself if this school board deserves your trust. I already know my response if that were ever a question on a ballot.

After this chapter with the position paper, there are two additional chapters which make the case against building new buildings v renovating the better built buildings that are more than sixty years old. The first is from the PA Dept of Education and the second is a federal perspective about whether to build new or renovate. You will find that no matter where you look, the WBASD has made all the wrong turns.

The Dr. Holodick paper begins in the next chapter. There has been some editing license taken on the paper in the next chapter, which originally was written for an 8.5 X 11 presentation but in this book because of the smaller page size has been reduced to 6 X 9.

Chapter 8 Position Paper to School Board

Please don't forget that first and foremost nearly all evidence says don't consolidate schools because it harms academics, student sense of well-being, student participation, and that it increases costs. Having said that, the site is receiving such attention because outside of perhaps Chernobyl, it would be difficult to find a worse spot to build a school.

A Position Paper

TO: The Wilkes-Barre Area School Board

BY: Richard A. Holodick, Ph.D.

WBA's PLAN: Invest $150 million to consolidate ~~two~~ three schools to meet the facility needs of 2000 students omitting 5000 students and five schools. Not a dime for student achievement needs. While destroying the much acclaimed neighborhood schools and communities. I had the opportunity to save the taxpayers nearly five million dollars and failed! This paper has the potential of saving one hundred million dollars and improve academics.

RE: Restore or Rebuild

DATE: August 2, 2018

Richard A. Holodick, Ph.D.

Eleven years in the private sector, construction electrician IBEW local #163. Degrees from Temple, Penn State, and Colorado State universities. The Ph.D. earned through a U.S. Department of Education Scholarship. Completed professional goals to work at the secondary, community college, and university levels. Assistant superintendent in Oklahoma City SD, 5000 employees, 40,000 students; Director of Planning, City Colleges of Chicago, one of the largest community college systems in the US; the Pennsylvania State University, main campus. Twenty years part time consulting for an international master curriculum/facility firm, Grand Rapids Mi.

INTRODUCTION

At the outset, this board and previous boards were in agreement that the neighborhood schools' concept was the best for our children in this district. The board and community took pride in their Crusaders, Grenadiers, and Mohawks. The district has a relatively low tax base; it is seriously underfunded by the state; coupled with aging neglected facilities.

A study completed through the state conducted by a respected accounting firm determined that the WBA school district could not continue (afford) to operate the present schools; of course not—they have been neglected and are far from energy efficient, and are seriously over staffed. And if major changes were not made the district in a few short years would face a $70 million-dollar deficit.

[The WBASB as always showed remarkable restraint in ignoring the recommendation. Not one notion was changed from learning how things could be improved.]

The district's board contracted with two architect firms and two engineering firms to do a district wide facility study. Considering the three neglected historic high schools, and the other six school facilities the estimate to make all facilities meet state standards had a price tag of a quarter of a billion dollars; yes BILLION not million!

The historic 114 years old high school, the state's oldest, was so neglected that the board closed the school entirely.

[The board, faced with a facilities issue and having never hired anybody ever in the district with architectural or engineering facilities expertise were forced to accept the words of crony architectural and engineering firms, who also had affiliated restoration and construction firms and thus had a fiduciary stake in which decision the board would make. Why would the people expect a decision favoring the people?]

The estimate of $113 million dollars to renovate historic Meyers High School, brought the board to conclude that this facility like Coughlin should be demolished at a cost of $13 million dollars with a five-year date established. Four years have lapsed, (as of 8/2/18) eight million taxpayer's dollars spent without a purchased site or a brick laid, but we do have two renderings.

Restore/rebuild?

There is the historic factor, the pride factor, but most important is at this point and time the economic factor. The misunderstood conclusion derived by the board from the "architect/engineering" firms and the PFM accounting study was to consolidate the three high schools.

In the educational public-school system there are two main stay organizations, the **Pa. Department of Education** and the **Pa. School Boards Association**; in the private sector you have the **American Institute of Architects**, and the **Historical Society**. All four of these organizations have co- published in support of restoration over new construction. The research predicts a forever shelf life of schools over 50 years old that are restored.

[Our schools fit their definition of lasting forever What does this mean to John Q. Public. It means that only a board of directors attached to some organization not part of the citizenry would ever approve something that would eliminate the probability of restoring well-built facilities to the point of becoming never dead buildings . Instead our board has a preferred modus operandi of

deciding to declare buildings dead while they still have substantial useful life. How can a school board with no building expertise at all in-house make any decision that is in the best interests of the people they represent?]

Statement of the Problem

Millions were spent "evaluating sites. Six evaluated sites would have negated a state reimbursement of $12 million dollars; why spend $100,000 to evaluate those sites? At the very beginning someone should have said we need a long-range curriculum/facility master plan, that would have cost at least a million; but would have saved $7 million taxpayers' dollars and without question there would have been a ribbon cutting ceremony for the Coughlin students by now. But there isn't as the Crusaders have been split in half with half in a renovated elementary school the other half warehoused in an annex.

The board needed a building site so they returned to the facility feasibility study and selected the site with the most listed dis-advantages—the Pagnotti site.

There are several verified reasons that consolidation does not save money. For example the Pagnotti site as described in the study is isolated from all neighborhoods. This will eventually require 2400 students to be bussed twice a day to and from the site. Need we add the cost to demolish Meyers? $13 million!

[In all of this it was difficult to tell whether the board cared one iota that their premise might be 100% off the mark.]

Solution to the Problem

In a school district facing a $70 million dollar deficit [or substantially more] in a City approaching distressed status, where the average income is under $40,000 a year, all existing resources must be used, all possible avenues to save tax dollars must be considered. And by all means meticulous planning and impact considerations on all board actions are mandated.

Then all internal and external professionals must be held to the strictest standards and held accountable. Last but not least, due to the depth of the problems, student achievement, finances, and aged facilities experienced personnel and professional services must be sought out and employed/contracted.

The Schiowitz Plan favored by Dr. Holodick

Through extensive research by SOS, headed by Dr. Mark Schiowitz, a one-time respected member of the WBASD board, an alternate plan is in place that is educationally sound, affordable, maintains the neighborhood schools, and follows the published recommendation to restore rather than build new by, **The Pa. Department of Education**, **The Pa. School Boards Association**, **The Historical Society**, and **The Architects Association**. And, it has the potential of saving one hundred million dollars over the long haul.

Due to years in the construction industry, consulting for an international facility planning firm, and the visit to P.S. DuPont middle school in DE, without reservation I can tell you Elmer L. Meyers High School can be restored for half [or less] than the projected $113 million estimate and have a forever shelf life. The same holds true for GAR High School.

Bottom line, we renovate the two historic high schools, and build a new high school for the Coughlin students. [An alternative would be for two to five local artisans to be hired to be working on Coughlin today. They would finish eventually in an affordable fashion and the dollars would be better spent that that about which the board dallies.]

The projected three-facility cost of $150 million that can be phased to be made affordable for the taxpayers [is a better notion.] The plan is to consolidate; both the PFM and the feasibility studies disagree; the plan to convert the GAR high school to a middle school is listed as a disadvantage four times, in the feasibility study, and rejected in the PFM study as they recommend K-8 schools.

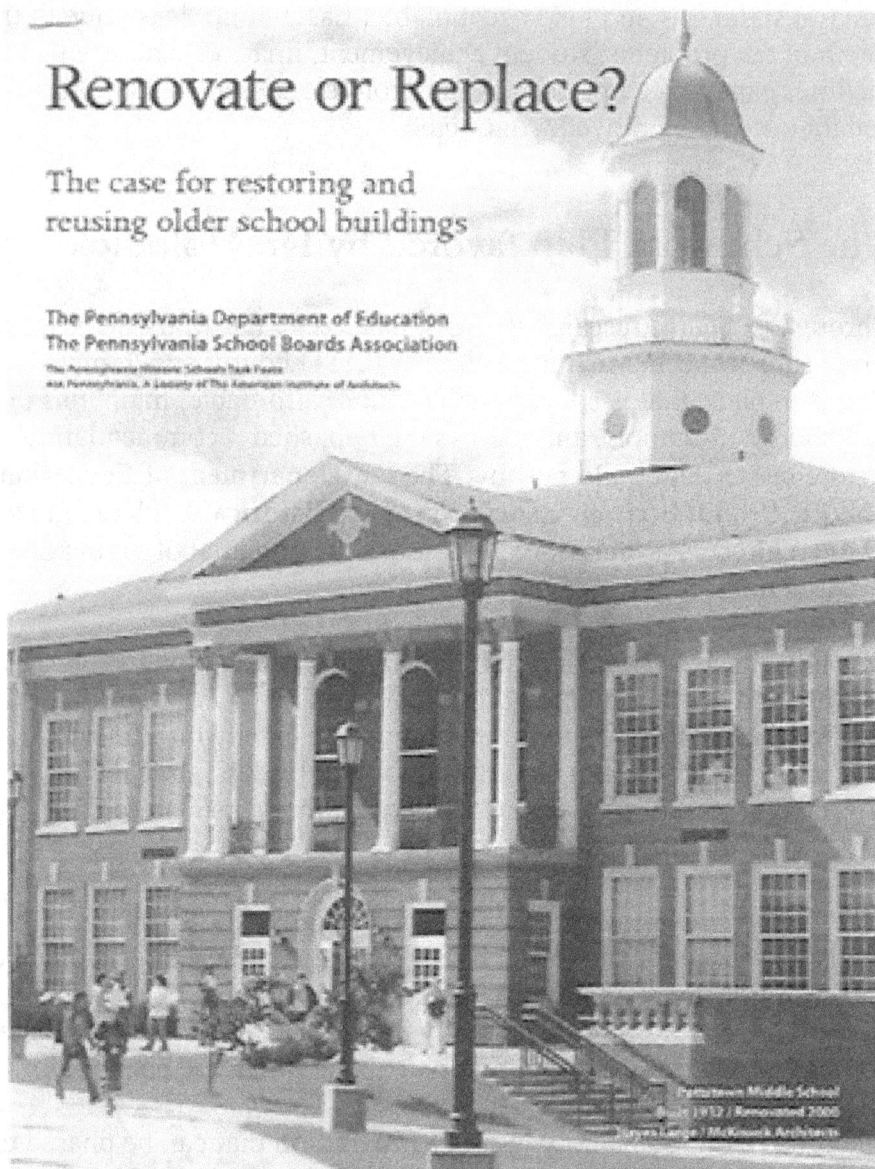

Renovate or Replace?

The case for restoring and
reusing older school buildings

The Pennsylvania Department of Education
The Pennsylvania School Boards Association

The Pennsylvania Historic Schools Task Force
AIA Pennsylvania, A Society of The American Institute of Architects

Pottstown Middle School
Built 1932 / Renovated 2000
Bryce Lange / McKissick Architects

The Department of Education, the School Boards Association,
the Architects Association, the Historical Society &
BUSINESS & INDUSTRY RECOGNIZE THE VALUE OF
RESTORATION.
Why doesn't the WBA school board?

Does the WBASD subscribe to professional ideas of what their actions should be?

"Renovate or Replace." Publication Statements

"Many Older Schools Can Be Renovated to 21st Century Standards"

"Renovating Older Schools Can Help Conserve Resources, Revitalize Older Communities"

Small Schools Can Make Ideal Neighborhood Schools

Neighborhood Schools Can Help Keep Older Communities Vibrant

Too Much Busing
Pennsylvania spends more
than $1 billion each year
busing children to school.
Altogether, school buses
travel more than 381 million
miles annually in the
commonwealth.

Listed on next page are some successes – Check them out

Manheim School District Goes Green with Historic Schools

Mount Lebanon Achieves Academic Excellence, Retains Character with Neighborhood Schools.

Hazleton Area School District Saves Its Castle from the Wrecking Ball

North Penn School Board Preserves Much-Loved Neighborhood School,

Lifespan: A well-constructed building can last indefinitely with periodic renovations.

[Why folks can one of the success stories above be us? Answer: The board does not want success. It wants to spend taxpayer dollars.]

A review of more than 100 studies on school size in 2001 by researcher Kathleen Cotton showed:

- Students in small schools have better attitudes towards school and higher attendance rates.
- They do better in standardized tests.
- Students in small schools are more likely to participate in extra curricula activities.
- There are fewer discipline problems.
- The level of parental participation is higher.
- Teachers feel more satisfaction in small schools
- Moreover, it's not clear that large schools really are less expensive to operate

The following are pictures of a number of WBA schools sold and renovated/restored for business and industry use. The point is that WBASB could not make them work as schools but other outside firms could productively use WBASD buildings to make them successful. Some of the schools are simply presented here for a perspective.

WBA DOBSON SCHOOL

WBA MAFFET STREET SCHOOL

WBA Meade Street School
The district's oldest school

The Lackawanna College

The former Scranton School District's High School was considered not useable as a school, the college thought otherwise. This facility has a forever shelf life as compared to new construction that must be replaced every 40 years.

[What is the cost value of a forever shelf life? Confidence and a resolute school board dedicated to the people. How do we get it. Fire everybody but Melissa Etzle on the current school board. How? Vote!].

A MUST–READ PAGE

P.S. DuPont Middle School, Brandywine School
District DE
Restored by the award winning Bancroft Firm

P.S. DuPont Middle School, DE The school is similar in size and age
of Meyers High School

Owner: Brandywine School District Method: Construction
Management Architect: ABHA Wilmington, DE The largest school
renovation in Delaware state history – Bancroft completed the P.S.
DuPont project on-schedule and within budget.

The scope of work included the replacement of MEP systems,
exterior repairs and upgrades, security upgrades, renovation and
restoration of the main lobby, classrooms, administration area,
library, cafeteria and auditorium as well as a separate 13,000 SF
natatorium. Bancroft was successful in retaining and restoring 90% of
the original wood trim, plaster ceilings, and terrazzo and oak floors.

[Those who think they can't are always right!]

The WBA's "TEAMS" estimate to renovate Meyers was $113 M. The estimate included $25 M for not needed seismic bracing for earth quakes; reducing the cost to $88 M. According to Superintendent Costello, the entire building would include "gutting the facility." Unnecessary!

At the $88 M figure, using the estimated cost per square foot the estimate is $338 dollars a square foot. We believe this is high; problem two every square foot in the facility need not be renovated. Problem # 4, the TEAM has stated prior to all estimates that the renovations will meet "all state standards."

The state that encourages restoration will allow for variances when a district is restoring historic facilities. We believe $50 M is more realistic. Try this comparison: A new replacement high school for Coughlin cost $50 M. In forty years the new school will need to be replaced. The renovation of Meyers, with regular maintenance, will have a **forever** shelf life.

So, in forty years Meyers is still standing; Coughlin must be demolished and replaced; what is the dollar value of that fact? Couple that with the most important fact of what "Restore or Replace," prescribes as benefits of the small neighborhood schools for students and their families and the 100 M dollar question surfaces:

The Rendering Factory

Kistler Old River Road

Coughlin + Meyers Replacement Washington Street

The Pagnotti site Maffet Street Plains

Chapter 9 What Does the PA Dept of Education Think?

Please don't forget that first and foremost nearly all evidence says don't consolidate schools because it harms academics, student sense of well-being, student participation, and that it increases costs. Having said that, the site is receiving such attention because outside of perhaps Chernobyl, it would be difficult to find a worse spot to build a school.

Harrisburg's 1924 high school was undergoing a $55 million makeover, including renovations and an addition that doubled the size of the facility. Students moved into the newly completed addition in September 2006. Wilkes-Barre Area can do the same.

Wilkes-Barre Area School District is ignoring the Guidelines for Renovate / Replace projects put together by The Pennsylvania Department of Education The Pennsylvania School Boards

Association, The Pennsylvania Historic Schools Task Force AIA Pennsylvania—A Society of The American Institute of Architects.

The olden days of poor education was when schools consolidated. It is no longer the right thing to do to create a big bang construction project for a forty-year school. Forty years is so close in, why not include the wrecking ball and the rebuilding cost to stretch the useful life to eighty years. Facts show that older schools built before 1950 can actually be renovated and gain a lifetime status as a forever school with normal maintenance. How is it that Independence Hall has never been ripped down. Maybe somebody cared and wanted to save taxpayer dollars.

These agencies make the case why it is a better deal to restore and reuse older school buildings rather than rip them down. Renovate is the better option especially when historical buildings are part of the mix. Try to find anything built as well as Wilkes-Barre High (Coughlin) or Meyers High. GAR is none too shabby of a school either. There is so much already in place as assets for WB Area. To tear it all down; is not the recommended approach. To build a new 40-year school on top of a toxic mine field is not a project many smart leaders would attempt to undertake. Why is our board so hell bent on bucking what is best for Wilkes-Barre and surrounds? What's in it for them?

Older school buildings are significant community assets that should not be discarded without careful evaluation. The educational, health, and community benefits of older schools may be compelling. Older schools located in established neighborhoods offer easy accessibility for students to walk or bike to school, rather than having them be driven by their parents or bused to a school far away. There are no bullies on the bus when there is no bus.

A school's presence often stabilizes and sustains established neighborhoods by facilitating community involvement and providing a center for community activity. Open up the gyms on the weekends for the community and watch the community love their schools. Experience has shown that it's generally less expensive to alter and rehabilitate an existing well-built school rather than build a new Plasticville model.

What part of that statement may I ask, did our Wilkes-Barre School Board leaders not hear. They certainly did not get it. Their regard for such malfeasance and disregard for the public of course says they must be to be voted out of office. The tyranny is palpable. The board is working against the citizens. I wish they were not but it is conclusive.

Of course, many older schools are in poor condition and don't meet current educational needs. That is not the case with Coughlin, GAR or Meyers. The challenge, which apparently was too much for the board, is to determine whether these schools can be rehabilitated efficiently and cost effectively to meet 21st century educational standards. Tough to do so with no trustworthy inhouse architects or engineers.

The historical cost borne by the people because of this incompetent WBA School Board is incalculable. The old Coughlin High Building is the oldest school building in Pennsylvania and the Coughlin High School operating in multiple buildings to day still prints the nation's oldest school newspaper but it is awaiting its fate as Coughlin High School faces demise. Somebody should save this building and this newspaper. There is too much wrecking ball destruction in Wilkes-Barre and now this great school newspaper tradition is going to die along with the high school. Why>

At the beginning of this year (2019) Mark Guydish wrote a piece in the Times Leader noting the demise of the Coughlin School Paper. Would it not have been nice if he said that the Times Leader would keep the paper going but that was not his news this day in January.

"Truth is, the editors have spent more time this year on old news than new. Only one issue of the Coughlin Journal has been printed, and another remains in limbo as they scurry to save more than a century of newspapers."

"I started packing them in October," said sophomore Kallie O'Donnell, standing in a room in the Coughlin High School annex with what few Journals remained in a building now half-closed. "It was so sad."

Newspaper adviser Heather Johnson recalls walking into the sorting room one day and asking, "Why does it look like a funeral in here?"

"The old Journal office is vacant and off-limits. Most of the newspapers have been moved to another building. Demolition of the Coughlin High School building could begin this summer, and no one knows if the publication recognized as the nation's oldest, continuously-published school newspaper will vanish with it. Yet, if it "looks like a funeral," that's not because the paper faces an uncertain future. It's because the paper holds such a sweeping past."

That is the sordid legacy of the Wilkes-Barre Area School Board.

WB Area School District hires cronies and minimizes the skill-level to its own detriment. The patronage system overrides what is best for the preponderance of the people. Why is there no expertise available within the WBASD to make such an assessment? Because WBASD hires custodial personnel and pays them maintenance personnel wages. Their skills do not measure up so clean buildings fall apart.

As noted, the people closest to being experts are located in the custodial staff but they are far from the level of skilled craftsmen needed and not close to being architects or engineers. How can an inexperience Super know what/ who, he or she needs as the top facilities manager in the district? He/she cannot but don't you be the one to speak up or your kid may not ever get a teaching job in WBASD. That's how it is. A number of good people were ready to run for the board to Save Our Schools but they feared retribution on their children in sports, or other areas in control of district personnel.

Many historic school buildings were constructed with materials and workmanship that we cannot duplicate today. Just 100 miles south of us, we find The Harrisburg School District, for example. They are in the process of renovating and adding to their 1924 high school.

Our own GAR High School was originally built in 1925. The original Harrisburg structure boasted an elegant exterior graced with limestone columns and carvings, complemented within by spacious hallways and airy classrooms. GAR measures up.

Many older schools can be renovated to 21st century standards

Creative design means that the architect preserves the building's unique character, while transforming it into a state-of-the-art facility with a modern library, science labs, classrooms, and special purpose rooms equipped with nearly 400 computers.

In the brochure put together to show what can be done, Harrisburg School District brags about their PlanCon process for school boards and communities by spelling out what is required (and what is not required) for PDE reimbursement approval.

State officials hope school boards consider a wide range of factors when exploring the need for new or upgraded facilities. In many cases, our best schools may be the ones we already have.

Facts above provided by Dr. Gerald Zahorchak PA Secretary of Education

School board malfeasance

There *Oughta Be a Law!* against the type of decisions, actions, and inactions taken and not taken by the Wilkes-Barre School Board leading up to this dilemma that by plan will be capped off with a cost prohibitive albatross school building built over a toxic mine shaft. It is a comedy of errors that is surely malfeasance in office and sometimes that is a felony.

Most of us know that malfeasance is the doing of an act, which a person ought not to do at all. To legal theorists, negligence can arguably be divided into misfeasance and, in limited cases, nonfeasance whereas malfeasance is an intentional tort. In either case the WBASB is guilty on all counts or so it surely seems. The Trump Campaign, like it or not would say to those like our school board, "Lock Them UP!" Amen! Say no more.

By the way "There Oughta Be a Law!" was an old cartoon strip that many of you may remember. It was a single-panel newspaper comic strip, created by Harry Shorten and Al Fagaly, which was syndicated for four decades from the mid-1940s to the mid-1980s. The gags illustrated minor absurdities, frustrations, hypocrisies, ironies and misfortunes of everyday life, displayed in a single-panel or two-panel format. Does that sound like the problems we face here from a recalcitrant tyrannical Wilkes-Barre Area School Board. It sure does. The cartoon below is not about school boards but it is about human nature, which board members use more than care for the public

WB Area SD waits for an emergency to do due diligence

It would clearly be a better situation for all if the board treated the public with respect and acted like the big boy in the room at all times. The differences between the public and the board should be able to be discussed without the board getting all huffy and using their bully power to make decisions they know will not sit well with most of the silent majority in the Wilkes-Barre Area.

If there is a public relations person working for the WBASD, they are not doing their job well because the board should not be fighting with the public, period. There oughta be a law that says the board must do the people's bidding and not the reverse. Or they lose their offices.

If we were to draw a cartoon, such as the one above, we would depict the board with a huge fist coming after a skinny stick figure representing the 100-pound weakling general public. This approach cannot work well for the board in the long-haul as more sooner than later, the public will want a board that does their job well and treats the public with respect. Perhaps it is too late to change this board's modus operandi at this point but it is not too late to fire them.

Summary

ON RENOVATION

From The Council of Educational Facility Planners International: Keeping schools in older neighborhoods is inherently better for the environment because it takes advantage of existing infrastructure and public transportation.

"Compact building design preserves land. Rehabilitating older buildings reduces the need to manufacture new steel and other building materials. Historic school buildings can usually be renovated to state-of-the-art educational standards at less cost than new construction."

Renovate or Replace:
The chronological age of a school is no indicator of its construction quality. Most schools built between 1900 and 1940, for example, are masonry bearing structures that rely on massive walls to provide structural stability. Many were overdesigned in load-bearing capacity by today's structural standards. Most of these older schools are easier and less costly to renovate than schools built in the postwar suburban era, when cheap materials and inferior construction techniques became common.

From Renovate or Replace (The Pa. Department of Education and Pa. School Boards Association)

"Small schools with many grade levels make ideal neighborhood schools. Families know their children will attend a nearby school for many years. The school lends a sense of permanence to the neighborhood and helps keep it healthy. But above all, it can be a superior place to learn.

Renovate or Replace—another look

"Older school buildings are significant community assets that should not be discarded without careful evaluation. The educational, health, and community benefits of older schools may be compelling. Older schools located in established neighborhoods offer easy accessibility for students to walk or bike to school, rather than having them be driven by their parents or bused to a school far away. A school's presence often stabilizes and sustains established neighborhoods by facilitating community involvement and providing a center for community activity. Experience has shown that it's generally less expensive to alter and rehabilitate an existing school rather than build a new one."

To make this less-costly approach even more attractive to school districts, the Public School Code was amended in 2005 to provide additional state funding for renovation projects. And if a renovation project conforms to the "green" building standards certified by the U.S. Green Building Council or the Green Building Initiative, the reimbursement is even higher
"

Chapter 10 What Does the National Center (NCES) Think?

Please don't forget that first and foremost nearly all evidence says don't consolidate schools because it harms academics, student sense of well-being, student participation, and that it increases costs. Having said that, the site is receiving such attention because outside of perhaps Chernobyl, it would be difficult to find a worse spot to build a school.

National Forum on Education Statistics

Sponsored by the
National Center for Education Statistics
U.S. Department of Education
as a component of the
National Cooperative Education Statistics System

Major national think tank

Just like the PA Dept of Education in Chapter 9, the **National Center for Education Statistics** has a lot to say about how public schools in the US should maintain their precious school facilities. In fact, the Center has produced a great book titled, *The Planning Guide for Maintaining School Facilities.* (https://nces.ed.gov/pubs2003/maintenance/).

In Chapter 5 of their guide, they hit on the topic of most importance for the Wilkes-Barre Area School Board: Maintaining School Facilities and Grounds

What do you suppose the Center's goals are for this project. They are obvious. There are so many districts in the USA that build way too many new buildings unnecessarily. And so the goals for this publication and the Center's work in this regard is as follows:

1. To remind readers that an ounce of prevention is worth a pound of cure.
2. To convey strategies for planning and implementing "best practices" for maintaining

The Center staff wrote an executive summary for this book that can serve as the first training manual for a new Superintendent of Schools and for a new school board member.

Pennsylvania Law says that every two years, portions of school boards must be replaced. On the odd years, five board members either run again or they are replaced by new members. In the even years, four board members get the same opportunity. If incumbents choose not to run, they would not be on the board the following year, beginning in December.

Their work really nets out the issues well. As you read it helps to recall that the WBASD's issues have arisen because of neglect. The board failed to hire the proper people and then they failed to build a maintenance plan to assure all buildings would at least reach their useful life. The issues are simple but they cannot be ignored as has been done in WBA by the Wilkes-Barre Area School Board. The people's solution is to simply choose other members of the community to be on the board. .

As America's school buildings age, we face the growing challenge of maintaining the nation's education facilities at a level that enables our teachers to meet the needs of 21st century learners. Facilities issues arise at all educational levels, from prekindergarten through postsecondary, and at all sites, from classrooms to administrative offices. Challenges arise in new and old facilities alike, although the types of concerns may differ.

Because routine and unexpected maintenance demands are bound to arise, *every* education organization must proactively develop and implement a plan for dealing with these inevitabilities. A *sound facilities maintenance plan* helps to ensure that school facilities are, and will be, cared for appropriately. WBASD through its board has never chosen to implement such a worthwhile plan.

Negligent facilities maintenance planning such as that practiced in WBA, can result in real problems. Large capital investments can be squandered when buildings and equipment deteriorate or warranties are invalidated. Failure to maintain school facilities adequately also discourages future investment in the public education system.

However, school facilities maintenance is concerned about more than just resource management. It is about providing a clean and safe environment for children. It is also about creating a physical setting that is appropriate and adequate for learning. A classroom with broken windows and cold drafts does not foster effective learning. But neither does an apparently state-of-the-art school that is plagued with uncontrollable swings in indoor temperatures or drifts of toxic gasses through the AC ducts or the open windows if they are openable.

The Planning Guide we reference in this chapter is designed for staff at the local school district level, where most facility maintenance is planned, managed, and carried out. This audience includes school business officials, school board members, superintendents, principals, facilities maintenance planners, maintenance staff, and custodial staff. The document is also relevant to the school facilities interests of state education agency staff, community groups, vendors, and regulatory agencies.

The Planning Guide has been developed to help readers better understand why and how to develop, implement, and evaluate a facilities maintenance plan. It focuses on:

- ✓ school facility maintenance as a vital task in the responsible management of an education organization
- ✓ the needs of an education audience
- ✓ strategies and procedures for planning, implementing, and evaluating effective maintenance programs
- ✓ a process to be followed, rather than a canned set of "one size fits all" solutions

✓ recommendations based on "best practices," rather than mandates

The document offers recommendations on the following important issues, which serve as chapter headings:

✓ Introduction to School Facilities Maintenance Planning
✓ Planning for School Facilities Maintenance
✓ Facilities Audits (Knowing What You Have)
✓ Providing a Safe Environment for Learning
✓ Maintaining School Facilities and Grounds
✓ Effectively Managing Staff and Contractors
✓ Evaluating Facilities Maintenance Efforts

The Planning Guide for Maintaining School Facilities is the product of the National Cooperative Education Statistics System and the collaboration of the National Forum on Education Statistics (http://nces.ed.gov/forum) and the Association of School Business Officials International (ASBO(r)) (http://www.asbointl.org).

Would it not be a great circumstance if an architect or engineer employed by WBASD had the opportunity to know this information and be in a position to advise a good manager such as a superintendent about how to deal with any facilities issue. Hiring contractors with other goals is not the best use of District funds. Unfortunately with so many real assets involved, WBASD thinks it needs neither an architect or an engineer. That is why it makes so many mistakes.

The project was sponsored by the National Center for Education Statistics (NCES)(http://nces.ed.gov), U.S. Department of Education. Roger Young (ryoung@haverhill-ma.com), Haverhill (MA) Public Schools, chaired the Forum's School Facility Maintenance Task Force, which was charged with developing the document. Lee Hoffman managed the project for the National Center for Education Statistics.

The full document is available electronically at no cost via the World Wide Web at http://nces.ed.gov/forum/publications.asp. One free copy of the Planning Guide for Maintaining School Facilities can be ordered from the U.S. Department of Education's ED PUBS Online Ordering System at http://www.EDpubs.gov/ or 877-4-ED-PUBS.

Multiple copies can be ordered for a fee at the U.S. Government Online Bookstore at http://bookstore.gpo.gov/ or 888-293-6498. For more information about this Planning Guide or other free resources from the National Forum on Education Statistics and the National Center for Education Statistics, visit http://nces.ed.gov/.

For a starter, I would ask all readers of this book, to call the superintendent's office and ask if you can review their copy of this great book about how to avoid needing consolidated high school.

Don't be surprised if they do not have a copy as this board and the officials they hire claim to know everything without having to do any research. Their shoddy work product is a testament to the neglect such an attitude will foster. With so many people such as this organization as well as their own organizations telling them what they do wrong, why would they buck the trend; go own way?

The Center staff offers the following as a final summary for their excellent work:

Experience at the Local, State, and National Levels Suggests That Effective School Facility Maintenance Planning Can:

contribute to an organization's instructional effectiveness and financial well-being improve the cleanliness, orderliness, and safety of an organization's facilities reduce the operational costs and life-cycle cost of a building help staff identify facilities priorities proactively rather than reactively extend the useful life of buildings increase energy efficiency and thereby help the environment

One would think that with all the knowledge necessary to manage over $300 million in real estate assets and to manage the rejuvenation and/or rebuilding of parts of the WBASD campus, every official in the district would have a pocket copy of this guide to refer to at all times and all places. Then, just possibly, nobody would be planning to build a new school on top of a toxic mine shaft.

What do you think?

Chapter 11 The History of Meyers, Coughlin & GAR Should Be Preserved

Please don't forget that first and foremost nearly all evidence says don't consolidate schools because it harms academics, student sense of well-being, student participation, and that it increases costs. Having said that, the site is receiving such attention because outside of perhaps Chernobyl, it would be difficult to find a worse spot to build a school.

Who wants to kill schools?

THIS IS A ETTER TO EDITOR THAT WAS PUBLISHED: JUNE 13, 2015. RESIDENTS HAD BEEN ASKING THE BOARD TO SUPPORT NEIGHBORHOOD SCHOOLS FOR A LOT LONGER THAN THIS. COUGHLIN & GAR ARE VERY IMPORTANT TO WILKES-BARRE

FRONT OF MEYERS HIGHS SCHOOL IN BETTER DAYS EVEN HERE, THERE IS A CONSTRUCTION FENCE???

Editor:

This letter is addressed to the Wilkes-Barre Area School Board concerning the closure of the high schools—Coughlin and Meyers. School board members, I know your minds are already made up about building a new high school and Meyers will most likely be torn down. Please take a good look at Meyers before you tear it down. The beautiful marble staircase and the stained-glass windows in the auditorium. They cannot be destroyed with the school.

Meyers' auditorium: Steeped in history, tradition and genuine Mohawk pride

They are history and should be preserved somehow. To just let them be destroyed with the rest of the building is a sin. It would be nice if they could somehow be incorporated into the new school for everyone to enjoy. If that isn't possible, put them somewhere where they can be enjoyed as a part of history.

[Of course there really is no need at all for the new monster school nicknamed Mine Shaft High]

Do not forget about them [craftsman items]. Please take a walk through and look at the beauty in Meyers and you'll see why it can't be destroyed with the building. I am deeply saddened that the school board members of the last 20 or 30 years have let these buildings get in such condition. When you own property, you take care of the upkeep of that property. These buildings should never have gotten this bad. Keep the marble staircase, brass railings and the stained glass windows.

Ruth Hagenbaugh, Class of 1972, Wilkes-Barre Meyers

Bottom of marble Staircase in Front Entrance – From Class of 1965 Yearbook

I (your author) am one of the males in this picture. All the men have wide shoulders so I cannot use that as a distinguishing mark. But, how about that, your author is a Mohawk and is in this picture. Don't look at any of the ladies to find me as I am one of the gentlemen. ;

There is a lot of Wilkes-Barre history in the Meyers, Gar, and Coughlin schools and they should be preserved somehow. To just let them be ripped down is a sin. Saving parts like the staircase and the auditorium might be smart but it won't make opponents happy.

None of them—Coughlin, Gar, or should be torn down because they are a part of a lot of Wilkes-Barre history that should be preserved. Both should be made forever schools and Mine Shaft High, the little bit that is built can be torn down right now, with no tears from anybody.

School board leaders possess no building or trade school experience whatsoever and they choose not to pay a full-time architect or engineer to study structural matters somehow get to say that the big moose high school would be a huge improvement over the district's current high schools. I say they do not know what they are talking about. They have no skills in building maintenance or construction. Why should anybody ever listen to these clowns?

All Wilkes-Barre high schools are from 70 to 110 years old. The district has sold schools in the past, which are being used for residents and businesses even though the board had previously given up on renovations looking for more taxpayer money.

What does this board really know about buildings after the poor job it has done in maintaining over $300 million worth of building properties. To dupe the people into giving them millions of dollars now for new construction is foolhardy.

If you simply look at the outside of the buildings in recent years, it's not difficult to see why Wilkes-Barre area school leaders are ready to build a big Taj mahal school (Mine Shaft High.). At Meyers High School on Carey Avenue for example, for the longest time, the building had a net strapped under part of its front façade. Now there is an ugly dark blue particle board façade with PVC pipe dangling out of it. This is your first look at Meyers because that must be what the board wants you to see. They'll do anything to make everybody who sees their handiwork say Meyers is bad! bad! bad! But it is not bad at all. The board is bad! bad! bad! And how! Meyers needs a little love and attention from a caring school board but it gets none.

At Coughlin High School on North Washington Street, for years, students had to walk under scaffolding before the board decided to shut down the oldest high school in Pennsylvania. It's like Ben Franklin Jr. Jr. Jr. Jr. Jr. saying the US should shut down Independence Hall. Humph! But, of course, Ben would never do that.

A third high school—GAR—is over 90 years old. The board thinks that is bad also. Look at GAR now. It is in great shape, for a building built in 1925. The Bog Toxic School desired to be built by the board in Plains is estimated to last forty years. Why replace a ninety-year old school with a school that will need to be replaced in 40 years? Logic dictates that you simply fix what you have and Coughlin, GAR, and Meyers will last forever. Maybe that is too long for this board of directors.

Residents know why things look so bad:

"They deteriorate. They don't keep them up," said Wilkes-Barre resident Rich Burrier.

Chapter 12   Surprise!!! Nobody Responsible for WBASD Dilapidation

Please don't forget that first and foremost nearly all evidence says don't consolidate schools because it harms academics, student sense of well-being, student participation, and that it increases costs. Having said that, the site is receiving such attention because outside of perhaps Chernobyl, it would be difficult to find a worse spot to build a school.

And nobody is responsible for the state of disrepair at Coughlin, Meyers, Mackin, etc."?"

High School Stadium in Wilkes-Barre Closed for Repairs

Written by Brian Kelly
Published: 19 June 2015
Hits: 21637
Press Release:
June 18, 2015

This article, which I wrote, was submitted and posted four years ago. It was originally released as a press release to all the local papers and media outlets throughout the Northeast. The date shown is only important so that the reader knows that the issues we speak about in this book have been lobbied against by many constituents in the Wilkes-Barre Area. The article is printed as it was written four years ago so if there are some time anomalies and/or anachronisms, it is because that was then and this is now. [Items in brackets are recent additions]

The Wilkes-Barre Area School Board, after going through the motions, pretending it was not a Dunn Deal, on Wednesday, June 10, 2015, finally announced their plans to build a brand spanking new high school [Not Mine Shaft High]. They not only made a poor decision, they made it worse by picking the smallest spot available where Coughlin now stands.

At just about two and a half acres, the Coughlin site is too small even for Al Boscov to build another fine department store. Yet, the magicians on the board think they know something about building a mega-school that is not obvious to the rest of mankind. Too bad they know nothing about how to maintain a school building or the new mega school would not even be a consideration.

Ask yourself, which of the students from GAR and Meyers will be able to walk to school and make it on-time? Ask yourself how do the students from Parsons and Miners Mills and Plains and Laurel Run get to Coughlin today? We know that most students from Meyers and GAR walk to school today. Is it fair to ask if anybody on the School Board plans to take a stake in a School Bus company?

The board has just made a decision about which, nothing seems right and nothing seems OK. The idea stinks; the site stinks; and the board thinks we are all dumb by throwing this bogus deal at us and hoping we let it stick. More and more residents have recently awakened to the reality of a poor educational system, morning traffic jams, and massive property tax increases in their future. Finally the people are beginning to look at the problem seriously. They are concluding that more than likely, it is the board itself that stinks.

Cheers to Parent Lois Grimm who at the big decision meeting asked for a show of hands to see who opposed the board's determination to build a new school. The GAR auditorium was packed for the meeting with those who came to oppose the measure. The crowd quickly raised their hands high. Supporters of the board plan must have taken the night off. Still the board chose not to understand the overwhelmingly negative message from the people. Without formally saying it, the board declared: "What is best for the students does not count and of course the people of Wilkes-Barre, aka the voters, do not count."

Gabby Richards, a 2011 Meyers graduate let the board have it both barrels: "By making a decision of this magnitude without consulting the public, the community in which this decision affects, you are not honoring the trust that we put in you to respect this community."

If you are looking for a testimonial to the current high school configuration producing fine educational outcomes, look no further than Gabby Richards. Will future students do as well as Gabby in a mega-school environment in which they are small dots in a great abyss?

Current Meyers student Josh Schiowitz (son of Dr. Mark Schiowitz & Terry Schiowitz, who is a candidate for the School Board) showed he too is no slouch in the learning department thanks to his Meyers Education. He offered the board his opinion and requested they not lower any standards for the students: "I don't want to see a combined school because how detrimental to education that is. All three city schools have the perfect number of students as far as enrollment; as far as educational opportunities; as far as academic achievement; and as far as extracurricular participation." Sometimes the teachers need to listen to the students.

School Superintendent Dr. Bernard Prevuznak meekly offered his assessment of why the board had to take action immediately: "Both James M. Coughlin and E. L. Meyers High Schools were showing signs of years of deterioration and neglect."

[Who was in charge of maintaining the schools? – The same board that now wants to build a new school.]

Dr. Jeffrey Namey, led the District for sixteen years then retired in 2012. Dr. Prevuznak took over from him in 2012. Prior to this, Prevuznak was Deputy Superintendent for 11 years before becoming Superintendent. The deterioration occurred on Namey's and Prevuznak's watch.

[And of course the board members at the time – three board members went to jail during this period as I recall].

Prevuznak is the leader of a system that provides education to students, and that is surely a big job. He is not the guy to come to about soil composition or the structural integrity of school buildings. There is no such person [architect or engineer] on the WBASD staff of over 500 employees.

Though the Superintendent does not have an executive advisor on staff with any of the required technical talents to manage building assets properly, he is still tasked with the job. As we have seen with the demise of many District structures in recent times, paying contractors for ad hoc projects does not produce effective long-term building maintenance plans.

[and it is very costly.].

Dr. Prevuznak is known in the district as a fine man, and a real gentleman. I think they are right. He is all that and more. Teachers and staff really like him. However, he is not an architect or an engineer. He is not an operations manager. He is not a facilities manager. Dr. Bernard Prevuznak is none of these and so he is not even able to properly assess technical proposals from outside contractors. He also is not Superman.

Compounding the Superintendent's shortfall in personal technical abilities, he has nobody with such talent at the ready by his side. In other words, no employee in the district carries a title such as Executive Director, Facilities Management and Services. Thus, nobody is specifically responsible for the dilapidation and disrepair which has occurred in the school buildings.

[Let me repeat that four years later—Nobody is responsible for the dilapidation and disrepair that has occurred in the school buildings— yes nobody! Well, why did we hire these guys then?]

Otherwise, as we know, he or she would have been at the decision meetings to provide the explanation for the problems. All fingers would be pointing their way. Their head would have been on the block so the leaders could save face.

Yes, hard as it may be to believe, even now, with a $100 million deal on the table, there still is not one single person employed by the District with the proper qualifications to advise the Superintendent on facilities' matters. If taxpayers let this new building scam go through, who will be the person to assure the new structure is being built properly?

[Nobody again!]

There is not one person whose mission it is to assure that the hundreds of millions of dollars' worth of school district real property are well maintained and properly managed. Likewise, there would be nobody qualified to advise the Superintendent and the board that new construction is being done correctly. Who will help assure that we do not create a big $100 million mistake?

[Nobody! That's Who]

It is no wonder the school district properties are mismanaged and neglected. It is no wonder they deteriorated without any attention. We can count on more of the same for all WBASD schools and other structures that ultimately are owned by the public.

Knowing what they now know, it would be malfeasance for the Leadership (Board and Superintendent) to neglect their responsibility to hire the proper facilities leadership and the necessary qualified staff to avoid or at least minimize such huge complications in future years.

[Yet in the four years since this article, no such people were hired.]

To summarize this point, the Wilkes-Barre Area School District has a Superintendent, whose major mission is Education, not facilities management, and so the facilities have not been managed at all. In many ways, neither Dr. Prevuznak nor Dr. Namey could have prevented the deterioration and neglect, because they do not have the skill set required to manage buildings.

However both agreed to take care of the District's assets when they took the jobs. They were in charge when buildings started to fall apart. Even then, neither hired the right people to address the problems to protect the several hundred million dollars in building assets owned by the people. Their failure to hire who they needed makes them culpable for all of the neglect.

What I see in the brief statement by the second highest ranking school district executive for eleven years, who has been the highest-ranking executive for the last three years is a suggestion that the two nasty culprits that created this problem were deterioration and neglect, and not mismanagement.

Dr. Prevuznak was only partly correct. Deterioration happens only when neglect is permitted by management. During this period, only the Superintendent and board leaders were empowered to change the status quo. Instead of doing nothing, they could have insisted that publicly-owned property be sustained and not neglected.

With over $300 million in building assets under their control, they should have insisted on continual status reports and a proper maintenance schedule. The cost for this and for people on staff who can fix things when they break should have been worked into each budget. In this way, deterioration would not have occurred.

There could have been a big payback if Dr. Prevuznak, Dr. Namey, and the school board paid attention to all parts of their jobs rather than permitting and in fact overseeing neglect. That payback would be huge to the tune of $100 million. Yes, with due diligence on the part of School District Leadership, $100 million would not be due from District taxpayers who are now bracing for a huge tax increase.

[Somebody has to pay for the board's dereliction—John Q. Public!]

One thing we all know is that nothing is free and when somebody gives an estimate of "exactly" $100 million without showing a blueprint, we also know that the cost to taxpayers will be substantially more.

[In 2019, four years later than this press release, the 40-year cost of Mine Shaft High is estimated at almost a HALF BILLION DOLLARS.]

Stay tuned as www.savewbschools.com becomes a focal point for this major issue for residents within the Wilkes-Barre Area School District.

We must remain vigilant and committed to solve this problem.

Just like Coughlin, GAR & Meyers, where nobody is responsible for the neglect and subsequent dilapidation, nobody will be responsible for the upkeep of Mine Shaft High. The inadequate staffing begs the public to know the board will do no better with $100 million in funding than they have in the past.]

This is a follow-up article

LETTER TO THE EDITOR / PUBLISHED: DECEMBER 9, 2015

Editor:

With over $300 million in building assets to protect, where is the qualified Wilkes-Barre Area School District facilities director? There was a recent attempt by a well-meaning former school board member to make some order out of the chaos the Wilkes-Barre Area School Board has created. His suggestion was to build a smaller school and replace Coughlin High School with a new school in the vicinity of the Solomon complex. I commend him. His idea is better than the board's. However, I do not agree that we need a new school at all.

Our school board controls over $300 million in property assets and yet it uses a rag-tag maintenance force of political appointees to keep the properties in repair. I have written a number of articles, some published by The Citizens' Voice and on www.savewbschools.com that talk about a real solution that will last a long, long time.

There should be no new school construction or it too will fail, decay and crumble like so many of the buildings in the district.

A trip to the Wilkes-Barre School Area District's main webpage shows the importance that the "Building and Grounds Department" for $300 million in assets has in the scheme of things. There is not a mention of a building plan or maintenance plan or a maintenance team or a maintenance/facilities leader on the site.

And, so when buildings self-destruct because there is no plan to keep them in good shape, should the taxpayers be surprised? Where is the leadership in the district for facilities planning, engineering, construction and maintenance? Are we now expected to turn over the new $100 million school to a building and grounds unit that has proven that it cannot do the job?

Brian Kelly
Wilkes-Barre

Chapter 13 History of Board's Recent Poor Decisions

Please don't forget that first and foremost nearly all evidence says don't consolidate schools because it harms academics, student sense of well-being, student participation, and that it increases costs. Having said that, the site is receiving such attention because outside of perhaps Chernobyl, it would be difficult to find a worse spot to build a school.

MARK MORAN / THE CITIZENS' VOICE Students leave Coughlin High School in Wilkes-Barre in December, 2015. Where students would attend the next school next was undecided. Look at the front of this school. And our board is not ashamed.

Three and a half years ago in February 2016, the Wilkes-Barre Area School Board still had not finished its decision process. Things began to appear to move very quickly back then as the board would make or almost make decisions, then make other decisions and then undo the decisions and then some of the decisions were stopped by factors such as zoning orders, etc. Without a program, like you would get in a football game, it continues to be difficult to follow board actions. But, nobody was selling programs then and they still aren't. Few really knew at this time what was happening and what was going to happen.

The May before in 2015, the board had voted for a controversial plan to demolish Coughlin High School in downtown Wilkes-Barre and merge Coughlin and Meyers high schools into a new high school built on the Coughlin site. The vote came in the face of massive opposition from the Meyers community in South Wilkes-Barre. The South Wilkes-Barre Area would become a ghost-town without Meyers. Coughlin was a step child that had always been mistreated by the board.

Rendering--Board Decided to Build on Coughlin Site. N. Washington St. July 2016

In July 2016, the school board decided to build a four-story structure for 1,800 students that extended along North Washington Street from Union Street to Butler Lane in downtown Wilkes-Barre. The cost of the new high school was projected at $82 million. The latest design also incorporated use of the nearby Times Leader newspaper building. The notion wound up being rejected by zoning so the renderings such as the one above are all that are left of this now defunct notion.

The school board had voted in June 2015 to build a consolidated high school on the 3.7-acre Coughlin site in downtown Wilkes-Barre. Since then, dozens of critics attended school board meetings to question the building plan.

As I see the history over time, more and more people began to question the board's decisions on school consolidation and destroying Wilkes-Barre high schools.

In January, 2016, the district closed Coughlin's main building and moved the 11th and 12th grades into the Coughlin Annex and they moved ninth and 10th grades into the renovated Mackin school in the city's East End. Coughlin students were feeling like the wooden sphere on the bottom of a cheap yoyo string.

Using the Times Leader building was not part of the original plan until February 2016. The newspaper building became part of the plan so that the district could relocate 500 Coughlin students in 11th and 12th grades at the start of the 2017-18 school year, district solicitor Raymond Wendolowski said.

The plan became the following—when renovations to the Times Leader building were done, the district would rip down Coughlin's main building [the oldest school building in PA] and the Annex to the left along North Washington Street. The demolition was to last three or four months and the board felt it could take place when students were no longer in school such as in the summer of 2017, according to officials.

A firm known as Panzitta Enterprises, had a key role in the plan at the time. Based on the Panzitta proposal, the district expected to become owner of the Times Leader parking lot along Butler Lane. That additional land would permit the district's design team to increase the size of the new school's cafeteria, gym and auditorium.

The District was engaged in a lot of planning at the time that would go no place. In fact for a while, they planned a $15 million enlargement to Kistler School. It seemed to many like a folly orchestrated by buffoons.

The city zoning board met in July on the day many of these plans were announced but it was not for judging compliance of these new plans. They were to review the district plan to expand Kistler Elementary School in South Wilkes-Barre. The district's $15 million plan this time was for an addition at the Kistler School to provide space for seventh and eighth grades.

This, along with the new humunga high school on North Washington Streets would allow Meyers to close. The Save Our Schools Group as well as Wilkes-Barre Neighborhoods were not on board with the board's plans but the board did not care. Meyers is a stone's throw from Kistler on Old River Road and when all the plans crashed, Meyers survived and still (2019) is used for grades 7-12. Back then it was scheduled to be demolished. Meyers seems to have gained nine or more lives after the board declared the school "unsafe at any speed."

No kidding as hard as it is to believe, on May 30, 2014, it could not have been planned better. It "just happened." First, after years of board neglect, it was Coughlin High in Wilkes-Barre. Then in mid-2014, the board and the superintendent announced that there were structural concerns with a second of three high schools in the city. If the board had a secret plot to build a new high school, things could not have gone any better for them.

They say in Wilkes-Barre that only when they build something does the school board get paid for their work otherwise by law, their jobs are unpaid. Who knows? As predicted some parents were very worried about safety and the district's image. Others were already saying that taxes would be going up. It could not have been going better if the board had planned it. An unplanned emergency often makes the people part with their tax dollar increases more readily. How convenient in 2014 for another problem with a school to emerge "all of a sudden."

To make it more ominous, the board made sure that the orange fences went up outside Meyers High School as the school year was coming to an end. "Don't worry folks, it is just a safety precaution about a crumbling facade." Even summer school was canceled because Meyers was now so bad! bad! bad and it was getting "worser.

It might not even last another day after 84 years. Humph. Yet, mysteriously as the board's new construction folly played out 'til now in 2019, Meyers became necessary in the board plot to build a new high school. All of a sudden Meyers had to live another day or the boards plans would not work. Mysteriously nobody talks about its structural defects anymore. Here we are in 2019--five years later and Meyers still has at least four lives left. Like a cat, Meyers is surviving. All the board had to say was nothing much and the problem went away. Perhaps it will even outlast mine Shaft High. Then what?

Kistler supposedly was expected to join Solomon Plains Elementary/Junior High School as a district facility for grades K-8. The new N. Washington St. high school was to be for grades 9-12. GAR at the time was to remain a facility for grades 7-12. Since the board makes plans like some people eat breakfast—every day, nobody really knew what would happen next?

Wilkes-Barre Area School District solicitor Raymond Wendolowski gives handouts to members of the Wilkes-Barre Zoning Board Architect Kyle Kinsman of WKL Architecture spoke during a hearing about the new Wilkes-Barre Area high school on Wednesday, Dec. 7, 2016.Christopher Dolan / Staff Photographer

The best laid plans of mice and men gang aft aglay. That's how it was going for the WBASD board. The Wilkes-Barre Zoning Hearing Board was another bad day for the board and Brian Costello, the disappointed super.

The Zoning Board apparently had little love for the Wilkes-Barre Area School District. They voted 2-1 on Wednesday Dec 7 2016 to reject the application by the school district to build a new consolidated high school on the Coughlin High School property on North Washington Street. Many in Wilkes-Barre were very pleased with the decision.

The Save Our Schools Committee had cautioned the board that they would not win zoning board approval because the site was too small, but the board wasted millions of taxpayer dollars anyway and got no results from their effort.

School Superintendent Brian Costello reacted as expected by preparing to punish Wilkes-Barre for denying the district their building rights in downtown Wilkes-Barre.

"It is unfortunate that the zoning commission did not want the school within the city," superintendent Brian Costello said, adding the district will now look to building the new high school "outside the city." There are other places and other options but the fiery Costello was obviously "ticked." He no longer liked the city of Wilkes-Barre PA.

As discussed previously, the school district had hoped and had spent a lot of money planning to demolish Coughlin's vacant main building and the adjacent annex, which is still used for students. As noted, the plan was to build a new 350,000-square-foot public school building to be used for Coughlin and Meyers. The plan stunk and the Zoning Board saw it for what it was. It was a stinky plan put forth by what some would call stinky people.

Costello and the board hoped that the new high school would allow Coughlin and Meyers high schools to merge in 2020, to accommodate 1,800 students who the board had previously placed in its WBASD netherworld.

The Zoning Board did approve the conversion of the Times Leader newspaper building on North Main Street into a school building, but to no avail. Panzitta Enterprises had proposed buying the old newspaper building from Civitas Media and then leasing space inside to the school district as a tenant.

However, that was just a part of the bigger plan. The district's interest in the Times Leader option was based on the construction of the new consolidated school on the nearby Coughlin lot. The board and the superintendent were quite upset and said they would meet and review all future options. A downtown school with or without the Times Leader building appeared to not be in the board's future.

The board was denied needed zoning approval for a special exception to enlarge the floor area on the Coughlin property. Zoning board member Vaughn Koter voted against the Coughlin-site plan and for the Times Leader proposal. Carl Naessig voted against both, and Edward DeMichele voted for both.

John Bergold, who recused himself from voting on both plans, made a comment after Koter seconded Naessig's motion to reject the new school plan and according to onlookers, he appeared stunned. Zoning Board Solicitor Charles McCormick told Bergold to be quiet because he had recused himself. We'll never know what that was about.

Attorney Walter Grabowski testified at Wednesday's hearing and made his case against the new consolidated high school on the Coughlin property. "They are trying to fit a size 12 foot into size eight shoe," Grabowski said during a long meeting of the city zoning hearing board. The Board was ready for anything to get itself a new school and destroy the Meyers and Coughlin buildings.

<<SOS's Holodick meets Dept Of Education.

The size of the Coughlin lot is 3.7 acres, but that acreage amount is only 5 percent of the size that the state Department of Education recommends for a school with more than 1,500 students, attorney Joseph Borland said. Borland is a member of the

Save Our Schools Group, which opposes the district's current school construction plans.

The WBASD board always believed it could dupe all Wilkes-Barre residents all of the time. They sure have yet to stop trying.

Coughlin supporters object

There were all kinds of permutations to the board's plans. One brought about massive opposition from the Coughlin community — which stretches from the north and east ends of the city to Laurel Run, Laflin and Bear Creek, Plains and Buck townships. They did not like a plan for a split schedule for Coughlin students. The board most often chooses not to listen to the cries of its constituents and the cries of those who cared about Coughlin at the time were not noticed and obviously not addressed.

Annex is on the left

The split schedule supposedly was a solution to one of the iterations of the board's plans which created a scenario of not having enough classrooms for Coughlin students after the current school year. Why?

Well, because of the planned demolition of Coughlin's historic building and annex on North Washington Street in downtown Wilkes-Barre. The Zoning Board hearing made them all feel better. Now there was more time to think.

As discussed, the ninth and 10th grades moved in January 2016 into the renovated Mackin school in the city's East End. At the time, as noted, the district planned to build a new high school on the 3.7-acre Coughlin site. When it was to be finished in four or five years, it would allow the merger of Coughlin and Meyers high school.

At the same time, the school district closed the historic main Coughlin Building and moved the 11th and 12th grades into the Annex and as noted, moved the ninth and 10th grades into the former Mackin Elementary School. See the fence and scaffolding in front of Old Wilkes-Barre High?

Split schedule unpopular

Under a split schedule to have been implemented this year by the board, all Coughlin students would have gone to Mackin with the 11th and 12th grades there from 7 a.m. to 12:30 p.m. and the ninth and 10th grades there from 12:30 to 6 p.m. How would anybody live with that?

Other options included buying modular classrooms for extra space, keeping the annex open and buying or leasing the Times Leader building, which is next to the 3.7-acre Coughlin site. When the Zoning Board rendered its verdict, the board eventually decided to go with Mine Shaft High in Plains Twp. instead of the Coughlin site.

It is easy to conclude the truth that the benefit of the students was always last on the board's priority list.

Building a new $75 million high school [note the number keeps changing] was expected before the rejection to take four or five years, and during that time, Meyers would remain open, and the district would continue to use Mackin for Coughlin students. Meyers kept having its ultimate execution stayed.

The consolidation was not expected to impact GAR Junior/Senior High School, which (as of 3.5 years ago) was to continue as a facility with grades 7-12 in the Heights section of the City. That too is changing daily. To get the picture today, you have to visit the Plains site where all current action is taking place—Mine Shaft High.

Modulars

Not wanting to have students with no desks and no roofs, the board voted the prior November to authorize a purchase of up $2.25 million modular classrooms, also known as trailers. But the district never finalized the purchase, and by December, officials seemed to prefer the split-schedule option.

In November, officials said the modular classrooms would be installed at either The Bog fields in the city's Miners Mills neighborhood or Guthrie Field behind Flood Elementary School in the city's North End section. The modular buildings would accommodate up to 500 students and include an all-purpose room for eating and a fitness room for physical education, Superintendent Bernard Prevuznak said. And, of course there would be busses galore to accommodate all the variations in student schedules.

From Preservation Pennsylvania

Despite Wilkes-Barre Area's lackadaisical opinion of its great historic high schools, more and more attention is being given at the state level and the National level for saving buildings simply because of their historical significance.

For example a group called PlanCon, in their Part A: Project Description states that "School districts should take all reasonable efforts to preserve and protect school buildings that are on or eligible for local or national historic registers.

However, because renovations or alterations to an existing building are usually less expensive than new construction, the proportion of reimbursement is usually greater for work on existing buildings than for new buildings. Wilkes-Barre Area leaders reject new ideas and consequently make many big mistakes,

ON NATIONAL REGISTER

A statewide survey of historic schools is underway, as well as a history of the development of public schooling in Pennsylvania from the colonial period through the mid-20th century. This study will help facilitate the nomination of historic school buildings to the National Register of Historic Places.

We invite you to visit this site at: http://www.phmc.state.pa.us/bhp/schools.asp. Currently, Pennsylvania has about 350 schools or former schools listed in the National Register, but there are hundreds of historic schools that have never been surveyed. Wilkes-Barre should have focused on this fact to save these magnificent structures.

ON CONSOLIDATION

NATIONAL REGISTER OF HISTORIC BUILDINGS - If any buildings, structures, site conditions or site features on this site are more than 50 years old, the school district should contact the Bureau for Historic Preservation in the Pennsylvania Historical and Museum Commission at (717) 783-8946 to determine their historical significance.

School districts should take all reasonable efforts to preserve and protect school buildings that are on or eligible for local or national historic registers. If for safety, educational, economic, or other reasons, it is not feasible to renovate an existing school building, school districts are encouraged to develop an adaptive reuse plan for the building that incorporates a historic easement or covenant to avoid the building's abandonment or demolition.

from Howley, et al and the National Education Policy Center (http://nepc.colorado.edu/publication/consolidation-schools-districts)

What happened next?

PLAINS TOWNSHIP, LUZERNE COUNTY (WBRE/WYOU)

In 2017, the Wilkes-Barre Area School Board was plotting again to build its new big consolidated toxic high school. In May, The Wilkes-Barre Area School District offered its new plan for its high schools.

At a Wednesday night school board meeting, the board members voted 7 to 2 in favor of pursuing an 80-acre Pagnotti Enterprises site in Plains Township for a new consolidated high school. Apparently as Wilkes-Barre Zoning had rejected the Coughlin Site, the board pulled a power play on the City and began negotiating with the Plains Twp. Commissioners who were very pleased to be the benefactors of a brand new monster high school. It was like Christmas in May in Plains. They were getting rid of a big ugly culm bank and more money would be rolling into the township while Willes-Barre Officials simply let it happen.

Two years prior, the school board had approved a plan to consolidate Meyers and Coughlin high schools. They had not given up on that idea. You recall in this chapter we discussed how the new facility back then was going to be built on the Coughlin site, but the board got rid of that plan after the city zoning board rejected it.

Three other sites were under consideration—1. A site off State Route 115 in Plains Township, 2. A Geisinger Health System site in Plains Township, and 3. A Pagnotti Enterprise site in Wilkes-Barre Township. Notice that after having upset the superintendent with a zoning rejection, Wilkes-Barre City, the town that was to lose its three high schools was out of consideration.

The positive word of all the glad handers at the time was that there were just some simple tests that needed to be done before the plan could move forward, so the other three options were still on the table in May 2017.

Back then, the school board had an architect looking at the pros and cons of each site. As noted, all the potential sites are four to five miles away from Public Square in Wilkes-Barre. It's still within the district, but outside Wilkes-Barre City limits. That angered many people who live in the city. And it should, yet somehow Wilkes-Barre politicians (Mayor & Council) remained silent on their opinion of losing three high schools.

May 3, 2017 Plains Maffet Street site is picked

The only folks who are very disturbed at the new Plains site where the consolidated school is to be built seem to be from Wilkes-Barre as one might expect. The Save Our Schools Group expressed deep concern over the site selection in Plains.

Regardless, the board ignored them and it took another step in deciding where a new high school would be built—a site in Plains Township not far from the Solomon-Plains Education Complex. Perhaps Plains Twp. will change its name with all the schools it will have to "School Township." Seems like a good fit.

Before the board voted, they got out their token ears and heard a lot of opposition to the project from taxpayers and parents.

"I am totally and vehemently opposed to this new school construction plan. I'm opposed to the consolidation plan and I'm opposed to it on practical and moral grounds," said Wilkes-Barre resident Sam Troy.

There was no mincing of words as residents addressed the Wilkes-Barre Area School Board as they opposed both the building of a new school and where the board is looking to put it.

"I don't think you guys should vote, but if you do vote, I'd just like full explanations on why you guys think that whatever site that you're voting for is the best site," said John Sochoslsi of Wilkes-Barre.

As discussed previously in this chapter, the school district is planning to close two of Wilke-Barre City's high schools, Coughlin and Meyers. They plan to consolidate students at one brand new school.

This board meeting was at Solomon-Plains Education Complex. At the meeting, the board selected one of four locations on where that school should go and voted to move forward with a site located between the Cross Valley, Maffett and Main Streets near the Solomon-Plains Complex in Plains Township.

The other three options are noted just above in this chapter. Ironically, the board showed it was not prepared for objections when members admitted not seeing all the sites. They were asked to table the vote. They rarely do what the public asks.

"It's beyond mind-boggling to me that we could possibly have a vote when the entirety of the board hasn't toured the entirety of the sites," said Atty Joe Borland of Wilkes-Barre.

The board says a new school is the only option financially. Others with better information believe the board is either lying or they have their facts wrong.

"How we can continue to do what we're doing, because we've been doing it, and look where we're at with our facilities and look what we face in our deficit," said board member Joe Caffrey.

Although the board picked the location near Solomon-Plains, they said it does not mean the three other options are off the table. Well, then what does it mean? Theoretically, the board could default back to the other options if problems arise with the first site picked. That gives one a comfortable feeling

Groundbreaking eventually came on April 12 2019. I was there

The board pushed for a groundbreaking

Anybody who was anybody in politics in NEPA was at the groundbreaking. It was a big day for the Plains Commissioners who were thanked profusely by WBASD superintendent Brian Costello. Perhaps the district will be renamed as the Plains Area School District. Why not? Plains is now the centerpiece location for public schools in the area.

Yes, there were some protestors who came to see Brian Costello fawn over the Plains Commissioners in the groundbreaking ceremony for Mine Shaft High

The protestors rightly are concerned that the land the school is being built on could be harmful to students' health. Not just students' health but also teachers and workers and neighbors. Many of us do not believe the land is safe for students because it used to be a mine and it was never properly reclaimed. Carcinogens have not been removed from the soil.

"It's very concerning," said parent Lois Grimm. "You wouldn't even be able to build a house on this property because of the levels that they found in the soil but we're putting a school on it. I mean, that right there should give the school board members pause."

We spoke with a representative from the DEP who says the land is safe to build on. What choice did he have when all the politicos from Pashinsky to Yudichak were there to cheer on the board and say to H___ with the people.

"I think the school district has identified the site. They've studied it. They know what contamination is here and they have appropriate measures to deal with it to make it safe for reuse for a school," said DEP official Michael Bedrin.

Michael, which school district person was the lead decision maker on the safety of the site? Where did they get their degree in Environmental Schience?

In addition to the health concerns the protesters have, they're also upset about losing their neighborhood schools. I was surprised that nobody from Wilkes-Barre City Hall was there to express concern.

"For me to drive up here took 15 minutes. I can't imagine on a school bus and having to start at 8:10 in the morning and how to get to practices," said Grimm.

The new high school is expected to open in 2021. The Save Our Schools Committee put together its own slate of candidates to replace the incumbent members of the WBASB who are running for reelection. THE SOS members believe they have the people's support and the candidates are as follows

List of all Save Our School candidates.

- Debra Formola (write-in Debra Formola)
- Jody Busch (write-in JODY BUSCH)
- Beth Anne Owens-Harris (on ballot)
- Terry Schiowitz (on ballot)
- Robin Shudak (on ballot)

Chapter 14 What is the SOS Plan for WBASD?

Please don't forget that first and foremost nearly all evidence says don't consolidate schools because it harms academics, student sense of well-being, student participation, and that it increases costs. Having said that, the site is receiving such attention because outside of perhaps Chernobyl, it would be difficult to find a worse spot to build a school.

The first part of any plan for WBASD is for the taxpayers to remove the four incumbents running in the November 5 election and replace them with the five candidates supported by the Save Our Schools Committee (SOS).

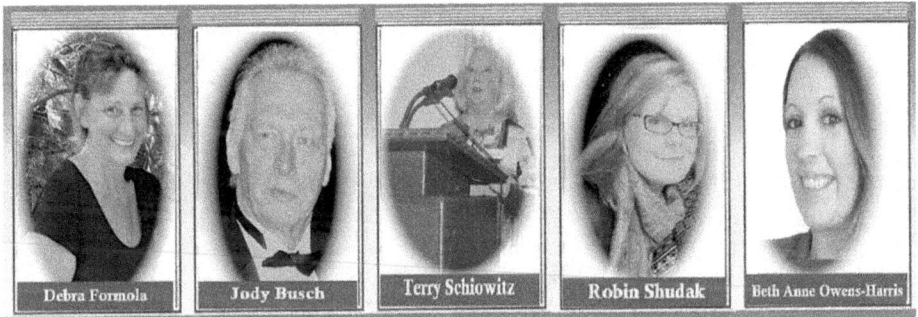

Debra Formola | Jody Busch | Terry Schiowitz | Robin Shudak | Beth Anne Owens-Harris

Five supported candidates—SOS endorsed

The SOS Plan Dr. Mark Schiowitz

Please note that all plans from the board and SOS are subject to reevaluation even though construction has commenced at Plains site.

Mark Schiowitz post on SOS
Admin · December 5, 2016
For those unfamiliar, here is the SOS Facility Plan:

1. Educational model thru district: Grade K-6 elementary schools, Grade 7-12 High schools. No middle schools, no transition year.

2. Sell downtown CHS property,

3. Build a much less expensive grade 7-12 CHS @ or near Plains/Solomon

4. Restore Meyers,

5. Upgrade GAR.

6. Mackin reverts to elementary use. (No Kistler expansion, no demolition, no Heights expansion, no Times Leader lease, No MHS/CHS consolidation, no 2nd stadium, alumni +/- corporations restore Memorial Stadium without tax money)

This plan conserves property values in residential neighborhoods, gives smaller schools, limits busing, is educationally superior, increases participation in school, helps with elementary overcrowding and saves millions. Please share extensively.

I really thought everyone on this site (Save Our Schools) was aware of this alternative.

Other SOS members or I would be happy to present this plan to interested groups.

I think the snapshot above nets it out for all who did not know.

There are few notions the board has put forth that pass the smell test for sanity. This does.

It requires a new board to pull it off.

Here again so we do not forget is the new board for your consideration:

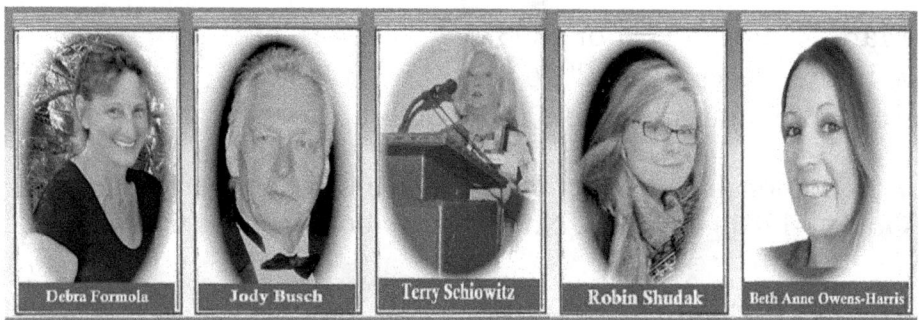

Debra Formola | Jody Busch | Terry Schiowitz | Robin Shudak | Beth Anne Owens-Harris

Each of these fine people are giving up a lot for a job that pays $0.00. Please let them help us all.

Chapter 15 When 'Being Rushed;' Don't Rush!

Please don't forget that first and foremost nearly all evidence says don't consolidate schools because it harms academics, student sense of well-being, student participation, and that it increases costs. Having said that, the site is receiving such attention because outside of perhaps Chernobyl, it would be difficult to find a worse spot to build a school.

In 2015, the best message to the WB Area School Board was:

"When 'Being Rushed' Is the Problem . . . Rushing Is Never the Solution."

Details
Written by Brian W. Kelly
Date: May 29, 2015

None of this is verified as correct for 2019 as things have changed since this was written. After four years, there are anachronisms. However it does give the perspective as to what the board scenario looked like four years ago.

****** PRESS RELEASE ******

Note to Press: You may use all or part of this press release in a report or column. It was written by Brian W. Kelly.

Bill Crawford writes: when 'Being Rushed' is the problem . . . rushing is never the solution." Just because officials think they have done enough planning does not mean they have a workable plan.

And so, here we are again with a more pressing high school building crisis. With a few thousand people at the LCCC graduation at the same time as the meeting on the schools (great timing) on May28, 2015, I am sure there would have been at least one more person in attendance (me) than the 100 who thankfully cared enough to make the meeting. I was at the graduation with good reason—my daughter, who graduated that day, and I would not have missed it for the world.

What I get out of it is a sense that Governor Tom Wolfe is now running our school board. The Governor has decided that Wilkes-Barre must play by his rules or else no money. This bullying from a foreign power makes this whole thing a charade and not a community decision. It does not matter what the board president suggests.

The people are getting forced into a rush mentality so somebody can please Tom Wolfe. I would prefer to sue the Governor for whatever we think we are due for whatever we choose to do --repair or build, rather than have Harrisburg dictate what happens in NEPA.

This is a ram a new school down the public's throat approach because of money and because even with a zillion maintenance [custodial] personnel, our school district leaders have not maintained the school properties appropriately. Will they maintain a new school any better? Can we trust them with a new school? What will they do differently that we should invest over $100 million to their good nature? Worse yet, to their competence?

By the way, do we send our children to school to learn about subjects and life in general or do we send them to school so that we can afford the school buildings? Is money the only consideration? Where is the will to do the right thing? Sean Walker [my opinion in 2015 but not in 2019] is the smartest guy on the School board. His question is the only one that counts: "if money was not an issue, what would we do for the kids?" [Has anybody answered that question yet?]

Dr. Mark Schiowitz, who was once on the board, [His wife Terry is one of my five recommendations for election to the board in November by SOS] and who should be on the school board, at this 2015 meeting, urged the board to keep the three smaller schools as "students learn best in high schools of less than 1000 students." Why did Walker's and Schiowitz's ideas not get more traction? Why are we in such a rush to do the wrong thing?

Never let a good crisis go to waste! The public may not always be willing to pay for good planning but if politicians can create a crisis— real or perceived, a good-hearted public can more easily be manipulated into rushing into bad decisions. Often power brokers make their decisions and then shape the facts to support their choices—not necessarily for the good of the public.

Did the board make a decision to rip down the schools before all of the analyses even began? I surely don't know the answer but it appears that there is no will to reevaluate this destructive idea. Who are we kidding here? Why does the board want to build before it even knows what it will build?

How did WB Area come from deciding what to do about the three existing high schools to almost definitely preparing to build a new consolidated high school—*the Big Toxic School.* And, by the way, all of us know that if a new school were to be built, the best locale would be the Murray Complex. And so, this site was summarily eliminated from consideration. Hah! Nice Job Harpo!

[BTW, the Luzerne Country Transportation gobbled up the Murray Complex while the WBA board was sitting on its hands.]

The reality is that anybody not staring greedily at Tom Wolfe's big pocketbook would conclude that building a new Plasticville model 25-year duration school is not the answer. Hey for young officials, in 25 years, they would get to create a new crisis and build a new school again!

In December, I spelled out the best plan for the School District. It would cost one to two million dollars per year. Yet, not one person asked me about it in the six months since it was published. I even made "Save our Schools," one of my campaign initiatives in my losing bid for Mayor of Wilkes-Barre to again bring it to the minds of the public and the school officials. Yet, nobody asked me about it one time during the duration of the campaign.

When nobody seeks real input from those with opposing views it typically means the fix is in. This fix will fix it real good for Wilkes-Barre once again. Real good! Does anybody really care? Taxpayers and parents ought to be incensed at what is happening. It is our money and our children's lives these presbyopic leaders are toying with.

One thing we should not do is let Tom Wolfe bully us into making a decision too quickly. We know that haste makes waste; and we are about to waste some wonderful and historically significant school traditions and school buildings. Moreover, in the process it seems we are willing to sacrifice the opportunity for our children to attend smaller and better run schools and be better educated and be happier than in bully-prone mega schools.

Think of all of the kids from Larksville, and Newport, and Swoyersville, and Plymouth, who because of the huge Wyoming Valley West jointure formed in 1971, two years after I graduated from King's College, never got to play high school sports or who never got to be a big fish in a little pond or get to see how their voice matters in a setting of their peers. Is this what we really want?

By the way. Do we really know what we want? Where is the education plan? Where is the quality of life plan for the school students? Where is the best option plan?

Where there's a will, there is a way. We can surely build anything we want. We must first know what we want. Don't let them kid you? It starts with dreams, and then ideas, and then plans, and then, and only then does it move to action. Why is nobody dreaming about the ideal situation for Wilkes-Barre Area, the School Children, and the Taxpayers?

For now, we must decide what our will is in this debacle? My suggestion is that we had better stop this poorly planned project and do some real planning before we take another step in any direction. No immediate decision is always better than a bad decision. Let's not be bullied by the big bad Wolf!

[Let's not rush!]

*** End of Press Release ***

Chapter 16 Sometimes Your First Plan Is Your Best Plan

Please don't forget that first and foremost nearly all evidence says don't consolidate schools because it harms academics, student sense of well-being, student participation, and that it increases costs. Having said that, the site is receiving such attention because outside of perhaps Chernobyl, it would be difficult to find a worse spot to build a school.

PLANNING
Still a good thing to do first.

Brian W. Kelly wrote a solution to the high school crisis in WBASD way back in 2014. He submitted it to the local papers. Here it is as written with an update from December 2014

Why would we not save what we can and destroy only that which we must?

After this was submitted to the papers, it ran in Wilkes-Barre's Citizens Voice on Dec 31--New Year's Eve—2014 under this title

Special landmarks do not have to be destroyed.

So, why does the WBASD want to destroy them? What is in it for the board? We do not have an answer to that but it is a conundrum.

The fixes required for WBA School District high schools have been depicted as un-affordable by taxpayers regardless of the approach--fix it or demolish and build it again cheaper. I don't think so. I don't buy it. It would have been interesting if the numbers and "plans" had been presented at Wednesday's meeting [In December 2014] along with the impact on millage. Truth is hard to find with WBASD board members in charge.

We all know the school district has not been a tax bargain for local taxpayers. [Build or not the board plans another big millage increase this year.] More importantly for all of us living in Wilkes-Barre Area, the question should be, "Do we really want to destroy historically important well-built school buildings and replace them with cheap quality twenty-five-year plasticville models?"

Wilkes-Barre High was established in 1890. It later was renamed Coughlin High after GAR opened in 1925. This old Coughlin school building is in fact the oldest public high school building in Pennsylvania. Can you believe some people want to tear down the oldest public-school building in the State of Pennsylvania? The Coughlin Annex structure was built in 1952. The original Coughlin building was occupied in 1909 though construction had begun much earlier.

Citizens of Wilkes-Barre Area need to get involved and think about what is being proposed [now under construction] and we must ask ourselves if there are not better ways to solve this problem without doubling our already un-affordable school tax burden, and without erasing our parents' history.

In March, 2005 Cliff Greim wrote an excellent piece titled *New Construction vs. Renovation for Older School Facilities*. Though fourteen years old, it still covers the issue quite well. It is available for all to read at http://www.facilitiesnet.com/educationalfacilities/article/School-Choice-Build-New-or-Not--2639#

Greim offers readable counsel on the big decision for WBASD:

"Generally, schools built in the 1950s or earlier have impressive architectural character and often are fixtures in their neighborhoods. They are structurally sound and can accommodate new systems. In addition, there is often strong sentiment to keep them in some form."

"Newer schools built in the 1960s and '70s generally lack architectural character, are not energy-efficient and are constructed of cheaper materials. These get torn down more often or become hand-me-down conversions from high schools to junior highs or from junior highs to elementary schools."

All of the school buildings in question were built post 1950 other than the Coughlin Annex, which was built in 1952. I think it is safe to say that the same logic Greim discusses for pre-1950 buildings applies to the Coughlin Annex. It was built to last and has been around 67 years which is lots longer than the requisite 40 years. It is still being used.

I admit I was taken back by board members at a most recent meeting who said, "It's going to cost a lot but it's something we have to do." I would ask whether they would vote to tear down historic Independence Hall if it were within their responsibility back in 1860 when it was just over 100 years old. It helps to know that at that time, this famous Philadelphia structure was about the same age as Coughlin is right now?

We all know that Independence Hall is the birthplace of America. We also know that the Declaration of Independence and the U.S. Constitution were both debated and signed inside this remarkable building. Independence Hall was built between 1732 and 1756 to be the Pennsylvania State House. It served as the capitol for the Province and Commonwealth of Pennsylvania until the state capital moved to Lancaster in 1799.It still stands and thrives. Why can Philadelphia preserve a monument and Wilkes-Barre cannot?

Originally, this building housed all three branches of Pennsylvania's colonial government. Yes, it was built (1753) even before the USA became the USA. It is now two and a half times older than the old Coughlin High School and it still has a lot of life left.

[Why does the WBASD want to kill the most precious school building in the state, especially when it is a "forever" building.]

Think of the famous graduates of Coughlin, GAR, and Meyers, and think of all the memorable events at those schools. These buildings are special landmarks in our home area, and they do not have to be destroyed.

GAR is well over ninety years old and Meyers is the baby at over 85 years of age. Why would we give up these historically significant well-built structures and replace them with thirty-year throwaway plasticville-square one-story buildings made of sheet metal, plastic, and other cheap materials?

We have great historical buildings with grand designs, granite and limestone interiors, and exquisite stained-glass auditoriums. Why are we supposed to cast this all away so that in twenty years another study like this can be done as the next generation is asked to rip out the el-cheapo structures to be built and go with even cheaper buildings with twenty-year lifetimes or perhaps a modular school or a few trailers. Who wants anything like that? [We can stop it.]

Where there is a will, there is a way. Somehow we lost our will with the Hotel Sterling after spending $6 million without fixing the roof. Let's keep our will and our wits as the board tries to shove a huge millage increase our way... for a less desirable outcome than the status quo.

One off-hand suggestion I have is to allocate about a million dollars or two or perhaps three if we can afford it each year on maintenance and refurbishing. We can bring in a great building contractor from our area to allocate five or ten artisans just for WBA, to begin work on these buildings, one year at a time, one objective at a time.

Let's get the hazards out of the way first. When real emergencies occur in the other district buildings, we can dispatch this crew of experts along with WBA custodial/maintenance personnel, which we also need, to fix the problems post haste.

I would also use our political representatives to get waivers for the Meyers beams that can withstand lateral forces. This is a very costly undertaking and should be ruled out immediately. Clearly all of the WBA buildings in question have not been blown over by big puffs of wind in the 90 to 110 years in which they have been standing and they are not going to be blown over tomorrow or any time soon.

I would also try to get waivers for increasing the physical size of the classrooms. They seem big enough to have been able to be used for conducting classes for so many years and surely they could continue to be used. Waivers would save a lot of money for a poor district and they are practical and safe.

I would bet that the local and state historical societies would help in gaining the waivers. How can we consider destroying such history for a promise we know will be broken thirty years from now. After all, citizens make the laws. If the laws do not fit, waivers are a good way to save money and still have the benefits of a safe school.

When all the emergencies are fixed, I would put the new team of artisans to work on one floor at a time of one building at a time. I would use as many vocational students to help in the effort as possible.

Think of the training our technical students would get. Additionally, Wilkes-Barre Area also has a lot of custodial personnel, who I bet would love to learn new skills working with the best artisans in the valley in building, plumbing, electrical, carpentry and other endeavors.

Where there is a will, there is a way. Nothing in life truly worth having is easy. Why should our school district give up the best for a solution that may not even be good enough to be second-best?

Submitted by Brian Kelly, December 31, 2014

Chapter 17 Mine Shaft High Students— Little Fish in a Big Pond

Please don't forget that first and foremost nearly all evidence says don't consolidate schools because it harms academics, student sense of well-being, student participation, and that it increases costs. Having said that, the site is receiving such attention because outside of perhaps Chernobyl, it would be difficult to find a worse spot to build a school.

Brian Kelly May 24, 2018 with updates

I sent this in to both local papers. The CV published it. citydesk@citizensvoice.com or yourvoice@citizensvoice.com, and mailbag@timesleader.com. The local papers need to help SOS with this issue. They make their money in this community. This is a community issue. Somehow the papers have taken a neutral stance sometimes but they are too pro-board and anti-residents.

The Citizens Voice published a shortened version of this as a LETTER TO THE EDITOR / PUBLISHED: JUNE 2, 2018

There is a lot more room for bullying when there are small fish in a huge school. Kids are not necessarily kind to each other. The bigger the school, the bigger the opportunity for bullies to practice their trade.

Here is what I sent:

The recent WBASD decision to consolidate to one team for each
sport in one pseudo high school, may help the board's longing and
determination to create one big high school to replace the three city
schools but it does not help Wilkes-Barre as a City and it does not
help WB Area residents.

Board members saying this move gives our kids more of an
opportunity is a lot of hooey. Perhaps these members did not finish
high school as simple math says that three teams from three schools
in any sport enables three times as many students to play on the
varsity than one team per sport. Folks, if it smells rotten, chances are,
it is rotten.

This board does not represent students or parents or citizens. It
comes up with one bad decision after another. If they cannot do
simple math, it is no wonder they think they can spend over $100
million to build a new super high school on top of a toxic mine shaft
in Plains Twp. and somehow Wilkes-Barre will pay less in taxes and
be better off without neighborhood schools-- hooey again. It's plain
bull sh_t and we all know it.

Does it not bother the people of Wilkes-Barre that the Mayor of WB
and the WB Council are silent on the matter? [What does the winner
of the Democratic primary think? He too is silent.]. What do the
elected leaders think of the impact of eliminating major schools in
Wilkes-Barre neighborhoods? Is this a good thing, Mr. Mayor?
Three neighborhoods in Wilkes-Barre City are impacted by this bad
decision. The people in these neighborhoods have no reason to be
happy.

There have been a lot of answers for how to improve the schools but
none of them are being proposed by the WB Area School Board,
much to the chagrin of city taxpayers and parents with students in
our high schools. I have concluded and a number of people on the
Save our Schools Forum available on Facebook, have agreed with
me that at this point for those paying taxes to the WBASD, there is
only one good answer left.

If the question is school consolidation to one big high school and/or cutting the # of student varsity athletes to 33% of today, there is only one good answer left. It does not take a genius to know 66% less kids will be playing on sports teams in the future and that is not good for morale or for a good academic environment. e

The SOS Group and most of Wilkes-Barre Area know we need to find a replacement board of directors. The Save Our Schools Group (forum is on Facebook) needs to help find people who love Wilkes-Barre, who would be willing to serve on the school board so that we can arrest control from a tyrannical dictatorial board and return governance of this important body to the people.

Regular non-political people tune out when there appears to be no hope. They still care but they do tune out when tyrants rule. A slate of candidates from the Save Our Schools Group would be the perfect answer.

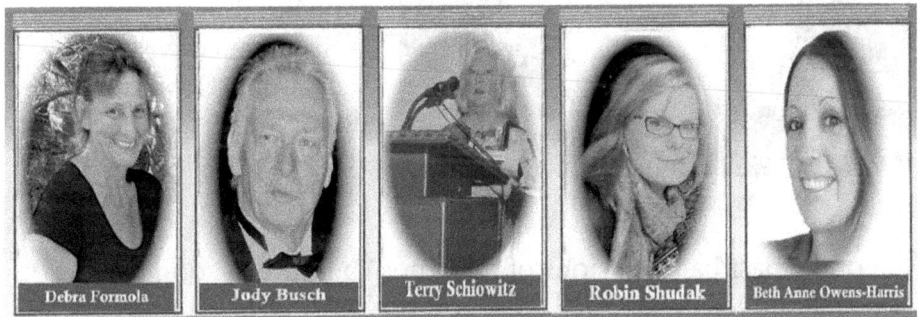

Debra Formola   Jody Busch   Terry Schiowitz   Robin Shudak   Beth Anne Owens-Harris

The good news for Wilkes-Barre and surrounds is that the SOS Group sought out and found five exceptional candidates from the community to run for the Wilkes-Barre School Board. Four of them already ran in the Primary Election and two won the opportunity to run on as Democrats and Republicans in the November General Election and one won a Republican Party nomination. The other two dis well and two candidates from SOS will be running as write-ins. Check the spelling of their names please: JODY BUSCH & DEBRA FORMOLA.

The remaining two, Bob Holden & Debra Formola barely lost party nominations but there is great news regarding these two dedicated members of the SOS Group. SOS is sponsoring Jody Busch and Debra Formola to be write-in candidates for November. B

<<< Bob Holden SOS Vice President had to step down as a write-in but Jody Busch is Bob's choice for a replacement.

When you vote to get the best people for our school board, pick Robin Shudak, Beth Ann Owens-Harris, and Terry Schiowitz, and then please write-in Jody Busch and Debra Formola. Check the spelling ahead of time but don't worry, your well-intended write-in vote will count. Have fun on doing the write-in. It is not scary. It is a unique experience.

All of the past bad decisions of the school board will soon be be reversed in December 2019 (Election is Nov 5, 2019) when we vote in this new board of directors of WBASD. Instead of board choice the decisions will be based on the people's choice.

This group will not only go back to neighborhood schools, but they also will pay attention to bring up the academic scores of the students within a proper educational setting. There is no reason for Wilkes-Barre Area to be ranked 443rd of 501 school districts in PA. Don't you think we can do better?

With new board members supported by SOS, our children will be able to learn enough to be ranked much higher in the state of Pennsylvania. Isn't that what education is all about—student learning? Who cares whether the board's greed is satisfied?

Don't forget to vote and don't forget to bring a sheet of paper with you to the polls with the names of these five candidates with the proper spelling of Jody Busch and Debra Orlando Formola as write-ins.

It is too bad that there is no such thing available as a law to enable the impeachment of a school board as this board deserves impeachment for not serving its constituency. Short of impeachment, besides voting as noted above, I would suggest WB residents join the SOS forum and post often and also that we write one letter after another to the local papers demanding that the entire school board, including the paid superintendent step down to force a special election. Another great idea is to call Frank Andrews at WILK and tell him what you think. Frank is a voice of reason in a sometimes savage land.

Call in to all the local talk shows please as this is the biggest issue Wilkes-Barre will see in future years. Wilkes-Barre is doomed without neighborhood schools. The people must speak up. The citizens of Wilkes-Barre deserve more than what the current board chooses to provide.

Hopefully the Mayor of Wilkes-Barre and the Council, after this book is published and they read it, will help the citizens in this matter. We also need help from George Brown, who will more than likely be our Mayor for the next four years.

Three athletic teams from three high schools give three chances instead of one for prospective athletes to get a starting position on a varsity team. That's the math folks no matter what the board has up its sleeve.

Hopefully Frank Andrews from WILK will hear our plea as he is always for the little guy who is being pushed around by government bullies like the WBASB.

Here is the shortened fine-tuned version that ran in the Citizens Voice

School consolidation doesn't help city

Letter to the Editor / Published: June 2, 2018

Editor: The recent Wilkes-Barre Area School Board decision to consolidate to one team for each sport in one pseudo high school, may help the board's longing and determination to create one big high school to replace the three city schools but it does not help Wilkes-Barre as a city and it does not help Wilkes-Barre residents. Board members saying this move gives our kids more of an opportunity is a lot of hooey. Perhaps these members did not finish high school as simple math says that three teams from three schools in any sport enable three times as many students to play on the varsity than one team per sport. This board does not represent students or parents or citizens. We need to find a replacement board of directors.

The Save Our Schools forum on Facebook needs to help find people who love Wilkes-Barre, who would be willing to serve on the school board so that we can wrest control from a tyrannical dictatorial board and return governance of this important body to the people. Too bad there is no such thing as the impeachment of a school board as this board deserves impeachment for not serving its constituency. Short of impeachment, I would suggest Wilkes-Barre residents join the forum and post often and also that we write one letter after another to the local papers demanding that the entire school board and the superintendent step down to force a special election. Wilkes-Barre is doomed without neighborhood schools. The people must speak up. The citizens of Wilkes-Barre deserve more than what the current board chooses to provide. Hopefully the mayor of Wilkes-Barre and the council will help the citizens in this matter.

Brian Kelly
WILKES-BARRE

Five people from SOS ran for school board in Primary
Brian Kelly
April 30 , 2019

I am so pleased that five people who think like I do got out of their shells and decided to run to take-over the corrupt anti-people Wilkes-Barre Area School Board known as the WBASD. Please ask for yard signs and provide places for these candidates and the SOS group to speak. Please!

We all know that all the buildings can be restored over time by craftsmen and it would not cost us a quarter a million and we know that our kids would not suffer from anthracosilicosis or who knows what, from attending school on top of a poisonous dump. We must support these brave candidates. I thank you all so much for taking on the scourge of this school board. God bless you all.

Request for PR from Frank Andrews

Hi Frank, I sent this to the SOS group as a post less than a year ago. This group had several people make the primary and those of the five that ran who did not gain a party nomination (plus one endorsed substitute) will be running as write-in candidates in the general election. I hope you can help us as the Wilkes-Barre Area School Board is a tyrannical ruling body and they are not effective caretakers of the people's assets.

They should not get another shot at building a school when all the real estate they manage is in such a state of disrepair. Rebuilding is not a good maintenance strategy. BTW, I am writing a book about this matter, which you may now be reading, and I would love you to write an opinion piece that can be used as a chapter. Thank you. More than likely this note to you will be in the book.

Brian Kelly shared a group.
September 1, 2018

Frank Andrews is a people's person and he is a major asset to the folks in NEPA. His show from 3 to 6 every day is very good and he touches on topics that matter to a lot of people. I asked him to look into the situation with a Board of Directors that knows more than its constituency to help us out in having WB residents know what a sham this is and how much it will cost taxpayers in the future even if 76 passes. Since the newspapers and the TV stations seem to be disinterested in the plight of the City of Wilkes-Barre, and WBASD, and their interlinked nature, perhaps WILK and specifically Frank Andrews can help us. I am sure Frank would be happy to hear from you.

https://www.facebook.com/groups/826594454122549/

Note from BK to Frank Andrews: The people of Wilkes-Barre are about to get whacked with a $100 million or more for a school consolidation v neighborhood schools' approach. The Save Our Schools group is calling this project Mineshaft High because of the fact that it will be built on an expensive and perhaps unsafe toxic ash mineshaft in Plains at a cost per acre substantially more than the Bear Creek Charter School.

As you know, Wilkes-Barre was just denied its application for distressed city status. Having no high schools in the City will make WB a Ghost Town. Why would anybody stay and face the coming tax burden. The board is recalcitrant in that it does not care what the people think. Most people in the City are not awake yet on this issue—just like the RAIN TAX you are championing, but they will come awake when their homes are taken from them. It would be great if your show would help the City of Wilkes-Barre fight a board that does not care about the people's ability to pay.

Thank you.
Wilkes-Barre Area Save Our Schools
1,938 Members

Chapter 18 Where is the WB Mayor & WB Council?

Please don't forget that first and foremost nearly all evidence says don't consolidate schools because it harms academics, student sense of well-being, student participation, and that it increases costs. Having said that, the site is receiving such attention because outside of perhaps Chernobyl, it would be difficult to find a worse spot to build a school.

In July, 2019, I wrote the Mayor and posted to the SOS Forum hoping to move Council and the Mayor to take action on behalf of the Citizens of Wilkes-Barre and the surrounding area. The objective of my note was to induce Wilkes-Barre officials— Mayor, Council, and George Brown, the winner in the primary, to unequivocally endorse the save our schools candidates and write a contribution to the book expressing positive opinions about the goals of SOS.

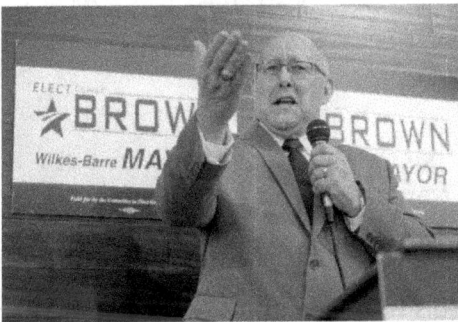

Saving Grace for Mayor George

Tony George offered a few comments but no solution.

Sorry I didn't get back to you.
I agree with everything you wrote. Actually I stated several years'ago when the decision to move out of the city was made' that I feared it would be the end of secondary education in the city.
Unfortunately I can't interfere with their decision.
The taxpayers have the right to vote and decide what happens. I can't change their minds. I think SOS stated their objections numerous times.
Thank you
Tony

Here is Tony George's last response.

From: "Tony George" <tgeorge@Wilkes-Barre.pa.us>
To: "Brian W. Kelly" <bkelly@ptd.net>
Subject: Re: I think you made a big mistake Tony
Date: Mon, 29 Jul 2019 23:23:23 +0000

I said at the time they announced that they were going to build in Plains, that I feared it would be the end of secondary education in Wilkes-Barre. That is what happened. I don't agree with their decision, however. I have no authority to change that.

I don't agree with Tony's position that the city has no power, but I thank him for his response and his frankness.

Note re Elimination of City High Schools to Mayor Tony George

July 21, 2019

Dear Mayor George,

One of the purposes of this note is to remind you that I sent an extensive letter to your office on July 5, in care of Ms. Linda Sanfillipo, Administrative Assistant to Mayor. I have received no reply or acknowledgment of receipt. I have already posted this July 21 note to the Save Our Schools Web site.

The multi-page letter that I sent requested that the Mayor's office contact all the present council members and other candidates who may prevail in the general election – including write-ins that you may expect. I asked your office to provide all with a copy of the letter I sent on July 5. Additionally, I asked if you would notify the campaign of George C. Brown and candidates for council (on the ballot or write-in) so that all Wilkes-Barre officials, both current and future would be aware.

The specific request I made to WB Officials is regarding a contribution to the book, which I am in the process of writing. It is as follows:

The new school building is held in such antipathy, it is referred to as Mine Shaft High. The Save Our Schools Group opposes the building over a toxic waste dump in Plains Twp. and the elimination of three Wilkes-Barre City High Schools in the process. We are very concerned about the inaction of Wilkes-Barre officials, including your office and Council.

The City seems preoccupied with other matters and has chosen not to be involved at all in this important issue. Yet Wilkes-Barre City has a lot to lose if its three high schools are torn down. Don't you think? Personally, I would like to see the City sue the School District on behalf of the residents of the City who will not be able to handle the expected tax burden.

I asked that each official and candidates for the general election write a brief paper to be included within this information book. The audience for the book is intended to be all the citizens of Wilkes-Barre and Wilkes-Barre Area. Those who do not obtain the book in paperback form from Amazon will be able to download it for free from a link on the SOS site or **[savewbschools.com/toxicschool.pdf]** . The book will also be available from Amazon and Kindle.

Additionally, I asked that Council Chambers be opened once a week [or bi-weekly until the election] for the Save Our Schools Group and City Officials for a press conference and presentations of the issue to the public. Since the City and SOS are on the same side, we anticipate this will not be an issue. Mr. Mayor, I would like your answer as soon as possible so we can plan accordingly.

Clearly the interests of Wilkes-Barre City and the SOS Group are aligned perfectly. That is why it has been such a surprise to find the City's team not raising hell about what may turn out to be the biggest nail in the City's Coffin. If Wilkes-Barre cannot keep its own high schools in the City, Mr. Mayor, can you explain why any business would locate here and why you would expect any new residents to come to live in our City?

I ask your positive response and your positive action in this matter.

Kindest Regards,
Brian W. Kelly
WB Council Person Beth Gilbert responded to my letter, which was posted on the SOS forum and I sent her a note back

Here they are

Beth Gilbert Council Chambers cannot be used for political purposes; however, I am sure there are other places in the city that would allow you to do this. You may be able to present in front of Council what the SOS group has found, and formally ask for action from Council. This would go through the City Clerk, Jim Ryan.

Melissa Etzle Beth Gilbert thank you!

Brian Kelly Beth, if Council, the Mayor, the Citizens of Wilkes-Barre and the SOS group are all on the same page for the good of Wilkes-Barre, why can chambers not be used to inform the public of what is happening in Wilkes-Barre? The School Board is clearly against the interests of Wilke-Barre City residents in this action and it will hurt the City. Have you gotten the City attorney's legal position on this? Should we see what Atty Borland has to say. If there is a way to do this to show that Council and the Mayor are for Wilke-Barre residents, then it is worth looking under every rock. I wonder what the penalty would be for Wilkes-Barre City Council and the mayor taking action in Chambers for the benefit of the City--if Council and the Mayor believe it to be so. Perhaps the City should pay the fine. Thank you for your response. Will you help us try to accomplish this? Don't give up the ship.

Beth Gilbert promised to write a note to the people of Wilkes-Barre about the fact that there will be no high schools soon within the City of Wilkes-Barre. Thank you Beth for giving it a try.

No other Council member nor Mayor George nor prospective Mayor Brown have chosen to offer their comments on this issue. As a Wilkes-Barre resident with the destruction of neighborhoods because of the destruction planned by WBASD of the only three public high schools in the City, like many other residents, I am appalled. If our officials were fighting for Wilkes-Barre, you bet we would know about it. They are not. It is as if they live in a different city but their lack of interest will result in higher taxes and no industry for sure—I regret to say.

Thanks to Council person Beth Gilbert for working with SOS. However, one WB official is not enough.

That is it for July. We are getting close to having a book available.

Chapter continues

Brian Kelly
April 13, 2018

My concern in this note is about Wilkes-Barre City officials sitting back and letting the WBASD decide to abandon our City.

Wilkes-Barre City is blessed with a Mayor and a Council that from my observations recently seem to have a hands-off policy about the school board that chooses not to care about what its constituents or WB students think. The board uses the Superintendent, a paid employee of the people of the district, not an elected representative, as the spokesman for the folly of building a super school with a 40-year cost of a THIRD to a HALF BILLION dollars in another municipality, when refurbishing, not ripping down, is the right solution.

And, so, Wilkes-Barre City officials are MIA in helping the City on the biggest issue that any of them will ever face in their political careers. Dear Council and Dear Mayor. Would you consider taking a stance on this issue? Would you consider pushing Wilkes-Barre City as the solution using a renovate rather than a destroy philosophy. Unless I am missing something, it is what WB residents want. Why don't City officials want what WB residents and taxpayers want? I know that I would like to know that answer.

If the super-school is built, WB residents will all have to pony up for a big School Tax increase so even if residents are quiet now, the roar will be heard when the first tax bill comes. All residents care that WBASD has mishandled this issue but that does not mean that the citizenry needs to bend over and take it on the chin.

Residents will have long memories that the officials did nothing to help bring residents a solution other than no high schools in Wilkes-Barre. My recommendation for City Officials is to present to the board a compendium of reasons why it is important for Wilkes-Barre to remain the focal point of Wyoming Valley, and not by becoming the biggest exporter of high school kids to another municipality for education. We can do better.

I would suspect those residents who do not have the good fortune to be able to move out of town from a city with no high schools and high taxes, will not be pleased that WBASD has blighted our city by removing three grand sets of buildings / schools. WB Citizens will not be happy if it is perceived that elected WB City officials sat on their duffs and left this travesty happen.

Again, I would ask City officials to tell the citizens of the City why they have no time to take to continue to fight the school board's decision to blight Wilkes-Barre and build up Plains? I would ask City officials to defend Wilkes-Barre from losing all of its High schools from actions taken by the school board. Take them to court, please.

Why not take a stance?

Wilkes-Barre residents are not at war with Plains. Plains has a lot going for it. Wilkes-Barre wants to have a lot going for it also such as the three high schools we already have. God bless Plains. Let Plains people work for what is best for Plains while WB people work for what's best for Wilkes-Barre. Let's not fight against each other.

Let me make my point one more time, please. WB officials need to know who they represent. Nobody said they have to be nice to the WBASD board of directors who are delivering a death blow to the city. Why be nice to a group that is trying to destroy our City? Fight them! This issue is important enough that it should be adjudicated with WBASD as a defendant and WB City as the Plaintiff. Your constituency, the residents of the City of Wilkes-Barre will love you for it.

I presume City Officials want to get reelected and will be running again for their current offices. Fighting to help the city of Wilkes-Barre should help you get reelected. I urge you to join the fight. Don't let the school board bully the City. This should not happen on your watch in a City that you all are sworn to protect?

Go to Court. Get the papers involved, the radio stations, the TV stations, the network news, etc. The WBASD will back down when and only when the power of the entire City is against them. The City's officials need to be on their citizens' side and not on Plains' side in this matter. Certainly, WB officials should not be on the Wilkes-Barre Area School Board's (WBASD) side.. This is the fight everybody in Wilkes-Barre will always remember. All city officials that permit Wilkes-Barre to be a city without a high school despite the pleas of its residents will be remembered in infamy.

Shortened version was sent as letter to Times Leader and Citizens Voice

Letter to the Editor submitted July 1, 2019

I am writing this note to make Wilkes-Barre citizens aware that our elected officials have been sitting back and letting the Wilkes-Barre Area School Board (WBASD) decide to abandon our City.

Re: Council & Mayor
Brian Kelly
June 9 at 12:09 PM

Why don't we formally ask City Council and the new Mayor whether they advocate having no High Schools in the City? Do we have open channels of communication between our group and the City? City officials ought to be enraged. If they are not, perhaps we need to find some write in candidates to run against them in the fall. It is a fair statement that you are either for us or against us. There is no other way.

Chapter 19 Neighborhood Schools vs. Consolidated Schools

Please don't forget that first and foremost nearly all evidence says don't consolidate schools because it harms academics, student sense of well-being, student participation, and that it increases costs. Having said that, the site is receiving such attention because outside of perhaps Chernobyl, it would be difficult to find a worse spot to build a school.

Mine Shaft High Is a Monster High School

Introduction

Prior to deciding to build Mine Shaft High, the big environmentally-challenged consolidated monstrosity to be built on top of toxic coal ash on land that no real estate developer would build on, the Wilkes-Barre Area School Board was on record in their opinion that Neighborhood schools resulted in far better performance for students than large consolidated schools. What happened to this once totally honest board?

Then as if it were nothing more than a change in the direction of the wind, something happened and the board changed directions 180 degrees. They are now opposed to neighborhood schools such as Coughlin, GAR, and Meyers High Schools. And, so they must be replaced by community minded people who think like the rest of the people.

Something changed that caused this board almost unanimously, other than Melissa Etzle Patla, to begin thinking incorrectly that bigger is better. The fact is as you have seen in this book that the period in US history for building huge consolidated schools where kids get lost going from one class to another has passed. However, this board among many other faults has decided that student outcomes and a positive learning environment no longer matter to them.

More and more information is learned daily that the consolidated form of a monster school v neighborhood is being discarded by school districts across the country. WBASD was right when it favored the neighborhoods. Who is responsible for changing that approach. Here is a post to the forum from August 10, 2019 showing what Philadelphia things. They are putting their money where their plans are:

Gabby Richards shared a link.
Admin · Yesterday at 11:36 AM

An interesting report on Pennsylvania's school districts. A major takeaway? We are ranked 24th out of 496 in diversity. Only 24% of students are proficient in math & 40% in reading. 94.5% of our students receive free or reduced lunch. Another major grade? The Administration was given a D+.

For comparison, Philadelphia is ranked 44th in diversity and there has been a major push to save neighborhood schools, including a $40M commitment from the Mayor to rehabilitate 25 public schools.

Why?

Because it is proven that community schools generate better outcomes for students and foster an inclusive learning environment. Our challenges as a district start from the top down, with an administration that has grossly mismanaged funds, mislead the public, and time and time again failed our students.

Numbers don't lie — our students, teachers, and community deserve better.

To help present the case for neighborhood schools in this chapter, I have chosen three selections. The first is an article by Diane Weaver from Education World entitled *"Are Smaller Schools Better Schools?"* The second is *"Small Schools vs. Big Schools,"* by ILSR (The Institute for Local Self Reliance). Finally, to wrap up this topic, I have selected a short piece titled—*"W-B Area School Board's ideas on school consolidation defy reason,"* by Dr. Richard Holodick, one time WBASD Official and a school administrator with national credentials. He currently serves as the President of the Save Our Schools Committee.

Clearly as you will see, the building of Mine Shaft High in Plains Twp. as a super school for Wilkes-Barre Area students is not good for Wilkes-Barre or Plains Twp., or any of the other communities forced to live with the anti-student and anti-resident decisions of this incompetent board. Our children who opt to stay and live in Wyoming Valley will be paying for our mistakes until they die.

As we have suggested throughout this book, there is only one solution to this travesty and we get to do it on November 5, 2019. Vote them out! Replace them with a slate of pro-people board members that are sponsored by Save Our Schools.

Can Help Keep Older Communities Vibrant and unmistakable.
By Jeri E. Stumpf
President, Jeri E. Stumpf and Associates Inc.
Retired Director, Urban Affairs Committee,
Pennsylvania House of Representatives

Many schools are activity centers, where adults play basketball outdoors or in the gym and where local programs can be conducted.

The presence of a neighborhood school functions much like a major retail store in a shopping center or mall; it is the anchor that attracts and retains the other stores. An abandoned school, much like a closed and abandoned store or factory building, adversely affects a community's morale even more than the loss of jobs. A closed building soon begins to deteriorate, and that adversely impacts the values of neighboring homes. People looking to buy a home in the neighborhood get the feeling that nobody cares.

ON SCHOOL CLOSURES

Are Smaller Schools Better Schools?

By Diane Weaver Dunne from Education World

Reforming public education may be as simple as creating smaller schools. The results of two recent studies indicate that small schools may be the remedy for lots of what is wrong with public education. Small schools can reduce the negative effects of poverty, reduce violence, and increase parent involvement and student accountability.

Creating a better school may be as simple as creating a smaller one. The results of two recent studies indicate that small schools may be the remedy for lots of things that are wrong with public education, especially for the nation's poor children. The separate studies credit small schools with reducing the negative effects of poverty on student achievement, reducing student violence, increasing parent involvement, and making students feel accountable for their behavior and grades.

Educators have long known that poverty hurts student achievement. Researchers Craig Howley, of Ohio University and the Appalachia Educational Laboratory, and Robert Bickel, of Marshall University, set out to find out whether smaller schools could reduce the negative effects of poverty on student achievement.

In four separate studies of seven states, they repeatedly found that poor kids do better if they attend a small school. In fact, in the most recent four-state study, the correlation between poverty and low achievement was ten times stronger in larger schools than in smaller ones in all four states. Howley and Bickel found that the benefit of smaller schools was particularly important in the middle grades, when children are most at risk of dropping out.

The researchers initially evaluated schools in California. Howley then replicated the research in schools in West Virginia and Alaska.

More recently, the Rural School and Community Trust, a national nonprofit organization, asked Bickel and Howley to study School Size, Poverty, and Student Achievement in Montana, Ohio, Georgia, and Texas. The study included 13,600 urban, suburban, and rural schools in 2,290 school districts.

They found that at least one-fourth of the schools serving moderate-to low-income communities in Texas, one-third in Georgia, and two-fifths in Ohio are too large for students to achieve top performance. In Montana, among kids in grade 8 in larger districts, the power of poverty over achievement was 2.5 times greater than in smaller districts overall and three times greater in elementary-only districts.

SIZE MATTERS

"Everyone knows that there is a strong association between social class and achievement and that this association works very much to the disadvantage of economically disadvantaged students," Bickel told Education World. "The California research, however, had the virtue of demonstrating that this disadvantage was exaggerated as school size increased."

Each time Bickel and Howley conducted another study, the results were very similar. "It's very unusual in education research to find this degree of consistency," Bickel said.

Howley and Bickel did not base their findings on a definition of what constitutes a large or small school but looked at school size on a continuum. They found that poor students from relatively smaller schools outperform poor students from larger schools.

TEST SCORES DROP IN LARGE SCHOOLS

In Georgia, achievement scores in schools serving children from poorer communities fell on 27 of 29 test scores as the school size increased. In Texas, scores dropped on eight of ten tests. In Ohio, at all grade levels, students in both smaller schools and smaller school districts that served poorer communities had a higher achievement rate.

The researchers also found all students benefited from attending small schools, regardless of the levels of community poverty. That was especially true in Montana. In fact, groups of less-affluent students out-performed groups of more-affluent students on standardized tests in the eighth grade if they attended a smaller school

[Who would build a huge school wit these facts at their disposal. Only a politically active board who cares nothing about its constituency. What a shame that is what we have in the Wilkes-Barre Area. Would it not be nice if we did not.]

SMALL SCHOOLS MAKE 'CENTS'

"A common argument for making schools larger is expressed in terms of economics of scale: Large schools save money," Bickel said. "Recently, however, using the Texas data set, we have found that 116 districts that have only one school for all grades have an expenditure per pupil that averages about $389 lower than the more conventionally modern schools. These schools tend to be small, they have at least 13 grade levels from kindergarten to grade 12, and the students are distributed more or less evenly across grade levels.

"Hardly sounds like a modern consolidated school," Bickel continued. "So perhaps cost in dollar terms is not a barrier to making schools more equitable places."

TEACHER SATISFACTION WENT WAY UP!'

Another study also linked student achievement with small schools. The two-year study, Small Schools: Great Strides, was conducted by Bank Street College of Education and funded by the Joyce Foundation.

A team of seven researchers took a close look at 150 small schools in Chicago, many created as part of education reform that started in the city during the past decade. The schools had enrollments between 200 to 400 students, far below the national average of 741, said Pat Wasley, one of the principal co-investigators of the study.

The researchers found that student achievement was greater in the small schools than in the larger schools. Students, parents, teachers, and community volunteers reported greater satisfaction because they felt more connected to one another, Wasley told Education World.

"Teacher satisfaction went way up!" Wasley added. "[Teachers] thought teaching was more fun, satisfying, and that they were more effective teachers, that they could get the kids moving in a positive direction." Many teachers told the researchers that teaching at a small school reminded them why they became teachers in the first place.

GREATER EXPECTATIONS

The report found that teachers expected more from their students because they knew them better and cared about what happened to them; students acknowledged this to researchers.

Teachers reported more collaboration with colleagues and more-regular professional development activities at their schools. They also had greater contact with parents and understood them as an important element in student success. Lack of parental involvement in schools is often a problem in poor communities.

Like the Howley and Bickel studies linking small schools to reducing the impact of poverty on student achievement, the Chicago study also found the connection. "Some of our schools in the study were among the most disadvantaged neighborhoods in Chicago," Wasley said. However, the study found that those students still outperformed their peers in large schools in many areas.

"We actually do think that urban school districts should create smaller schools because it's doing so much for the students," Wasley explained. "If we had our druthers, we really would want to see large schools the exception, not the rule."

WHERE EVERYONE KNOWS YOUR NAME

Although a variety of factors affect student achievement, the greatest factor was the reduction of anonymity -- going to a school where someone knows you and your name. Being known by your teachers and peers makes a difference, Wasley noted.

The study found that small schools are also safer for this reason. "We really think that size does have to do with the reduction of anonymity and isolation of students, which reduces fighting and violence," Wasley explained.

Students took more responsibility for their behavior and the behavior of their classmates in small schools. They told researchers they fought less because they knew one another.

SMALL SCHOOLS NOT ENOUGH

The researchers warn other school districts that simply creating small schools isn't enough. They advise the following key considerations for districts that want to create small schools.

Small schools need support from within and outside the system to flourish. All the schools in the Chicago study had outside partners that supported the school. The central administration also needs to support the creation of small schools.

Small schools succeed only when teachers and administrators have enough time to plan the vision and mission of the school. They must act as a unified team to build the school's structure, rules, and consequences for parents and students.

School systems must supply ongoing staff development to help teachers identify and use best practices. Schools do better if they rely on data rather than educational trends.

Being small isn't enough to improve student achievement. Small schools are a key ingredient, not a panacea for improvement. Understand that small schools are fragile and need commitment from staff members to hang in there when times get tough.

SCHOOLS WITHIN SCHOOLS

One way of creating smaller schools is redesigning large schools to house schools within schools, Wasley said. "I think we are going to have to have some of these great big buildings refitted for a bunch of small schools."

Wasley has support from the nation's top educator. Last fall, Richard W. Riley told the U.S. House of Representatives Committee on the Budget:

"And both new and renovated schools should be designed for the kind of education we know works best: smaller schools that create a sense of community and small classrooms in which teachers can provide lots of individual attention."

https://www.educationworld.com/a_issues/issues108.shtml

Diane Weaver Dunne
Education World®
Copyright © 2000 Education World

Thank you for permitting this in this book.

Small Schools vs. Big Schools

by ILSR (Institute for Local Self Reliance) | Date: 19 Mar 2012 |

One of the most effective ways to improve student achievement and curb school violence is to reduce the size of the nation's schools. Hundreds of studies have found that students who attend small schools outperform those in large schools on every academic measure from grades to test scores. They are less likely to dropout and more likely to attend college.

Small schools also build strong communities. Parents and neighbors are more likely to be actively involved in the school. The students benefit from community support and the school in turn fosters connections among neighbors and encourages civic participation. (For more information on the benefits of small schools, see Stacy Mitchell's article "Jack and the Giant School" in the Summer 2000 issue of the New Rules Journal.)

Although the empirical research in support of smaller schools is extensive, the trend toward ever larger schools continues.

[Wilkes-Barre Area for example, has the advantage of knowing these studies but they are a very proud board and, though they produce failing students consistently, they believe their ideas are better than even the experts and so they find no fault in making big mistakes.] They think the experts have a problem. What a shame for WB Area.

Over the last decade, the number of high schools with more than 1,500 students doubled. Two-fifths of the nation's secondary schools now enroll more than 1,000 students. This trend has largely been driven by public policy.

Operational Funding

State and local policymakers often prefer large schools, because they are less expensive to operate on an annual per pupil basis. In many states, education funding formulas provide a flat rate per pupil and make no adjustment for the higher costs of running a small school.

This favors larger schools and pressures smaller ones to close. Such policies are short-sighted. Small schools may require higher levels of annual per pupil funding, but they are far more cost-effective. Small schools have higher graduation rates and, on a per graduate basis, they cost about the same or less than large schools. Vermont is one of a few states that recognize the effectiveness of small schools and provide additional financial support to maintain them.

[Are the kids important or is saving the last dime?]

Construction / Renovation Policies

State and local policies often favor the construction of new, sprawling schools on the outskirts of town over renovating smaller, more centrally located schools. Examples of these policies include minimum acreage requirements (national guidelines call for at least 50 acres for a high school); state funding programs that support new construction and limit funding for renovation; and inflexible building codes designed for modern construction methods. For more information , see "Why Johnny Can't Walk to School," a report from the National Trust for Historic Preservation.

[Go back in this book's pages if you would to see that the Zoning Board of WB actually had better insights into the favored school philosophy than the school board that wanted every student to lose weight to go to a WB high school. OK, maybe it was not this bad but then again, maybe it was!]

Dr. Schiowitz: more notes on the impact of consolidation

The last major report to argue for larger sizes for districts or schools.... appeared in 1970. ...contemporary research does not support claims about the widespread benefits of consolidation because there are none.

Research on the effects of contemporary consolidation suggests that new consolidation is likely to result in neither greater efficiency nor better instructional outcomes. ...The contemporary research, as a body and almost to a study, has not recommended consolidation either to save tax dollars or to improve the outcomes or quality of schooling."

They add, "Contemporary school consolidation efforts often fail to deliver the promised enhancement of academic offerings." (Citing statewide school consolidations in W. Virginia)

"After the school consolidation (closures), students attended larger schools where they received less individual attention, endured longer bus rides to and from school…and had fewer opportunities to participate in co-curricular and extracurricular activities (a result of both increased competition for limited spots and transportation issues). Families' experiences included fewer opportunities to participate in formal school governance roles (as members of site based leadership teams, for example) and increased barriers to participating informally in their children's education."

"Large school and district size negatively affects desirable academic outcomes. A sizable body of research investigating school size has consistently found larger size… to be associated with….. more dangerous school environments, lower graduation rates, lower achievement levels for impoverished students, and larger achievement gaps related to poverty, race, and gender."

ON SCHOOL SIZE

For standardization mavens, students in small schools were reported to outperform students in large schools on standardized achievement tests, and significantly so (Bryk & Driscoll, 1988; Gladden, 2000; Howley & Bickel, 2000; Husbands and Beese, 2004; Lee & Smith, 1997; Raywid, 1980). Students in small schools also were getting more units before graduating high school.

Research consistently reveals that in small schools, students of all "types" feel they can connect with one another much more readily and openly, and also with caring adults whom they know quite personally. The true small school offers a greater sense of relationship connectedness and opportunity among virtually all stakeholders, such as are both implicit and proven in small organizations and communities.

Small schools demonstrate great achievement equity. Smaller, more "communal" learning environments reduce both student and teacher alienation commonly identified in larger school systems, and enhance student engagement in learning. For instance, Nathan &

Thao's 2001 study showed that "Students at large schools are more prone to be alienated from their peers..." In small schools, respectful relationships prevail, as do high expectations for behavior and achievement.

The percentage of high school students engaged in co-curricular and extra-curricular activities is higher in small schools, possibly far higher. For illustration, at small schools there may not be as many teams or honors courses to pick from, but a greater percentage of students are on a team or in an honors course; also, a greater percentage of students are in multiples of such activities. Small size also makes it easier for teachers to organize hands-

Large school increased costs include:

- Increased drop out rates
- Increased violence
- Decreased sense of social safety and connectedness
- Lower teacher satisfaction and higher teacher turnover
- Lower achievement in college
- Less happiness
-

W-B Area School Board's ideas on school consolidation defy reason
PUBLISHED: JANUARY 2, 2016

Prologue

Among many advantages, neighborhood schools deliver a sense of belonging. Students are not going to schools in somebody else's big neighborhood. The only touted advantage of large schools where students get lost has been that they cost less to build and maintain. Even this no longer is true.

Large schools are like waking up one day in school and finding you are in some big corporate structure where nobody seems to count. They function like bureaucracies and are hard to like.

Neighborhood schools are smaller schools that are more like communities. Students in such smaller schools are less likely to feel alienated and more likely to report a strong sense of belonging. Teachers in large schools might have 150 students each semester. Students tend to be relatively anonymous and easily slip through the cracks. Some graduate never having been noticed by anybody.

Small schools enable teachers to work more closely with a smaller number of students. This encourages teachers to go the extra mile and enables them to respond to individual needs. The result is that both students and teachers have a more positive attitude about school. I want to send my children to a small neighborhood school where among many other great things, it is student-friendly

The following article is written by Richard A. Holodick, Ph.D.

Eleven years in the private sector, construction electrician IBEW local #163. Degrees from Temple, Penn State, and Colorado State universities. The Ph.D. earned through a U.S. Department of Education Scholarship. Completed professional goals to work at the secondary, community college, and university levels. Assistant superintendent in Oklahoma City SD, 5000 employees, 40,000 students; Director of Planning, City Colleges of Chicago, one of the largest community college systems in the US; the Pennsylvania State University, main campus. Twenty years part time consulting for an international master curriculum/facility firm, Grand Rapids Mi.

Coughlin   Meyers   G.A.R.

It's long past due to say whoa Wilkes-Barre school board. This board has been all over the place spewing out ideas that defy reason. Two examples are the trailer park high school and the Makin split schedule.

1. We start with the most significant statistic, our student's rank near the bottom of 500 school districts in the state achievement scores. But the rank and file reason that test scores aren't everything; test scores are everything when you are this far behind 400 school districts!

There is just no excuse for this; there is a reason, the curriculum directors over the years may have ignored the demographic changes in the student population. Operative word to keep in mind, ignored!

All students can learn. Best stated, if students are not learning what we teach, we might need to teach the way students learn. There are just too many examples of successful programs for the academically challenged across this nation that prove that all students can learn, in fact excel. Stop with the excuses. Stop the consolidated school design, and design neighborhood high schools that meet the needs of students not board members.

This board is ignoring data that clearly show that students with our demographics do not do well in consolidated schools. Ignoring the research that documents districts that consolidated are returning to the neighborhood school concept.

2. Problem number two: facilities — not one school building of nine purportedly meets state standards. There is no excuse; there is a reason, the preventive maintenance and upkeep was ignored. Three historical and architecturally significant buildings; Coughlin must be demolished? The second, Meyers High shuttered with only five years shelf life remaining? Then there is a third school, GAR, to remain as a high school for undetermined years. As reported by the "team" who's background in restoration is minimal.

There are just too many examples across this country, private and public sector, where restoration was successful, preferred and cost effective. In the overall picture four architectural local firms did a near half million-dollar study of all district facilities and made recommendations. The board established two task force committees that provided "conclusions on facilities." Citizens also provided recommendations on facilities.

All the aforementioned apparently ignored as the board's facility committee recommended on a Friday a "plan" and voted on that plan the following Monday in the face of many citizens opposition and two board members opposed. The plan to consolidate Meyers and Coughlin high schools at Coughlin's Washington Street location is seriously flawed educationally and physically. The site has 2.7 acres when state and national and state recommendations are 35 to 40 acres for a school over 2,000 students.

The consolidation is in opposition to research that states that the academically disadvantaged do poorly in large consolidated schools as opposed to the neighborhood schools. Scoring 422nd out of 500 school districts may validate that we are academically disadvantaged. Having declared a potential $8 million dollar shortfall we may be financially disadvantaged. Without question our facilities are disadvantaged. The senior citizens are fiscally disadvantaged. In consideration of all the aforementioned, the "team" and this board have ignored the research.

3. Problem number three is planning and leadership. At the bottom in student achievement, at the bottom financially, at the bottom of quality facilities, there is no curriculum or facility master plan to phase a $300 million price tag to make the district whole and affordable for taxpayers.

The district is in a crisis with the potential of putting a city in crisis. As for the leadership question with the present superintendent nearing retirement, what the district does not need is a superintendent who must learn on the job. A national search must be conducted to employ a proven change agent with documented experience in fiscal, facility and student achievement master planning and implementation. The Wilkes-Barre Area School District has hired internally for 50 years; how has that worked?

-- End of article

Besides the negative impact on students of closing small schools and moving education to huge monster schools. The blight caused by school closures has a detrimental effect on PA neighborhoods.

ON SCHOOL CLOSURES

PUBLIC SCHOOLS HAVE ALWAYS impacted communities in ways that go beyond just educating young people. Well-maintained school facilities can help revitalize struggling neighborhoods, just as decrepit buildings can hurt them. And whether it's attracting businesses and workers into the area, directly affecting local property values, or just generally enhancing neighborhood vitality by creating centralized spaces for civic life, research has long demonstrated the influential role schools play within communities.

Rachel M. Cohen (the American Prospect 4/22/2016) The Devastating Impact of School Closures on Students and Communities

Final Comments

This article by Dr. Schiowitz, was written two and a half years ago and things have gotten worse. Check out this post and a few post comments written right before this book went to print:

Dr. Mark Schiowitz Admin July 23, 2019

OK Times Leader, Mr. Costello, Mr Krzwicki: In a way you and the board majority and the solicitor have staked your reputation to this project. You have much to lose with an admission of error. I won't ever hear that. I don't know how much if anything you might gain.

You refuse to entertain the legitimate issues and cannot refute that education generally bombs in large consolidated schools and costs increase. It's statistically the case throughout the literature.

Opportunities fall, class offerings seldom increase, dropouts increase, security issues increase, busing increases, students who are uprooted face adjustment difficulties. The academic decline is most prevalent among the impoverished student group, or about 70%.

Salvageable neighborhoods in the county seat will see their chances to rebuild go down the drain. Shame, too, to city leaders who have not stepped forward to address this.

Coal ash is the 2nd largest toxic waste stream in the country and 40 acres of your property have had it dumped there. Shame on you. 21 states would discourage or prohibit a school on this site. You ignore Plancon's schools siting suggestions and make a mockery of those specified by the EPA, not to mention the process. What process? I want to scream.

EPA says living near a coal ash pond equates with the health risk of smoking. "Pediatric Health" noted children living near coal ash suffered a higher rate of cognitive, sleep and respiratory illnesses than children elsewhere. Duke University warns of substantial radioactivity in coal ash from anthracite.

A cancer cluster has been seen at Fayette prison attributed to a nearby coal ash landfill. Of 900 clean-up workers at a wet coal ash spill in 2008 in Tenn. (who had daily close contact with ash) 34 have died and 300 others are ill or dying from lung cancer, respiratory or hematologic illnesses. No problem, says the solicitor, just like mega-sued Jacobs Engineering in Tenn. : "You would have to eat this stuff to be harmed."

Cap it they say. Well, in the Carolinas, Duke Energy has been ordered to stand down from closing coal ash landfills with a cap:

They have been ordered to remove the ash to remote, lined, landfills away from rivers. We are capping near an American Heritage River. EPA says don't close a coal ash landfill by capping if the land is unstable.

What do you think of this land's stability with ground compacted for months? Coal ash in contact with contaminated ground water is said to be a contraindication to capping. It's been a little tough to prove recent contamination because it hasn't been checked, but it was contaminated in the past.

Representatives of Environmental Integrity Project have labeled this site "unprecedented" and "dangerous." Makes sense.

Does this plan make sense? What is an acceptable future rate of cancer or respiratory disease among teachers, staff and future students?

I'll just mention air pollution, traffic, subsidence, and lack of infrastructure as other ecological ills. Congratulations WBASD. Hard to get anything this poorly planned, this irregular, this friendly to the coal industry, this costly, this unpopular and this unhealthy in 1 package. God help you if the worst should happen.

The above article by Dr. Mark Schiowitz drew a lot of attention Here are a number of comments from the Save Our Schools Website

Sharon Koter:
Very well said and informative! Very concerning

Marilyn Jones: Besides being very toxic what about when this toxic high school caves into a sink hole. Those in charge need to get some professional help before going any further with the building of this toxic poisoned high school. Maybe they will help you stop this deadly mistake!!!! 💀 💀 💀 😠 😠 😠 😠 😠 😠 😠 MAYBE ITS Time you listen to the taxpayers 😠 😠 😠 😠 😠

Susan Bavitz Kosloski:

I definitely wouldn't and don't trust the so called wisdom of any of the people involved in that mess. I think they have their own personal agendas that have nothing to do with education or our children's well-being. To add to that they aren't concerned one bit with the preservation of historical buildings or the people who live in WB.

Ruth VanWhy Hagenbaugh:
Very well stated Mark. I do hope this will be in the editorials of both papers. More people that will have children going to this dump they are calling a school need to be informed of the truth. A lot of parents have no clue it is this bad.

James Edward: . . . .get em' Doc !!👍😊

James Edward:
It s all about money, "kick-backs", giving the construction (bids)jobs to friends/relatives etc . . . .the last thing they're worried about, is the students !!😠

Brian Psolka: Does anybody think that the state attorney general needs to get involved plus the FBI to go through all of this? Something doesn't sit right with this since it began. The longer this waits it means another brick is being added to the new building. I believe a lawsuit needs to be issued and a ruling by a judge to stop any building until a full investigation by the state AG. Folks, there has to be some good lawyers out there and a fund could be set up to pay attorney fees. Complaining will not get the job done totally .It's time to get some legal help along with demanding the state attorney get involved ..

Mark Schiowitz: replied

Mark Schiowitz⭐ Since this post is a bit of a summary, please share with those that haven't seen it all. And don't forget to bother officials about a moratorium on construction.

A few more notes:

In the literature, we found little disagreement that small schools do better than large in the areas of safety, teaching conditions, and academic performance. The cases for these are overwhelming, not difficult to make. Indeed, the historical rationale for consolidated, comprehensive schools were based on other factors: (1) economies of scale, (2) social equality, and (3) increased program offerings—these presumed benefits had outweighed the other educational attributes. The alarming part of our research was that these large school benefits had virtually never been verified and, as we weighed large schools in the balance against small schools we found them—all three of them—to be either questionable or outright false. - See more at: http://www.communityworksinstitute.org/cwjonline/essays/a_essa ystext/grauer_smallsch1.html#sthash.HJRotRIN.dpuf

Big Myth: Large Schools Provide an Economy of Scale

Myth Buster: "The 'cost savings' of larger schools are only apparent if the results are ignored." -- The New Rules Project.

If large schools were cheaper to operate in the long run, perhaps we might have some rationale for their overwhelming prevalence—we could simply say we cannot afford smaller schools; but there is great uncertainty in knowing if they really cost less. Research is still scattered and unreliable, but our own studies indicate that larger schools with enrollments in excess of 1,200 have not produced expected economies of scale that result in better lower per-pupil costs when compared to true small schools - See more at: http://www.communityworksinstitute.org/cwjonline/essays/a_essa ystext/grauer_smallsch1.html#sthash.HJRotRIN.dpuf

Mark Schiowitz The Crazy Numbers

A lot of the cost estimates given by the board et al over the years are not necessarily without some rounding. We must remember the board wants its solution to look good and others to look bad so we get numbers that make their case. Here are some numbers that may help those who like looking at numbers to sort this out

Life of a new school: (with maintenance) 45years
Restored 1930's school: Indefinite

District cost to restore GAR: It's in good shape
(then) $39 million (facility study)
(now) $51 Million

District cost to restore structurally sound Meyers:	$113 million
District cost to restore older unsound CHS:	$85 million
Actual cost at (same age/size as Meyers) Dupont in De.	$44 million
District cost for a 1200 student school on Biscontini land	$72 million
(+ land acquisition, mining concerns, and environmental abatement)	
Actual cost of 1200 student Dallas High School (no inflation)	$39 million
(just) Bringing Kistler up to code (feasibility study)	$25 million
Kistler Addition for Meyers (meeting design team) (also)	$25 million
(just) Bringing Heights up to code (feasibility study)	$19 million
Heights addition (meeting from design team)	$25 million

Sometimes learning about things we do not really want to believe is the toughest learning of all.

Dear Wilkes-Barre Area School District:

Prior to making this monumental decision to consolidate schools, I invite you to visit the Hazleton area school system and witness first hand the after affects of consolidation. Years ago, our school district was faced with the same decision. Aging schools, limited income, and overwhelming enrollment numbers spiraling.

Our educational numbers for testing have plummeted, safety issues are paramount, parents are electing to cyber school their children instead of sending them to the behemoth high school. When dealing with children from poverty, something our both districts face, it's not just the education that the teachers must face-hunger, clothing, lack of school supplies, suicide attempts, gangs, fights, lack of parental attention also balloon. The issues our children face today are something all of us cannot imagine. The teachers are overwhelmed with having to play the role of surrogate parents-on a grand scale.

I beseech all of you on behalf of the children you represent, come to Hazleton. I will be more than happy to set up meeting and a tour of Hazleton's school district.

If I could have had the ability to foretell what the consolidation would result in, I would have been vehemently against it. You have this ability.

Thank you for taking the time to research this matter fully.

Lorine Angelo Ogurkis, Esq.

http://www.times-news.com/news/new-school-construction-costs-skyrocket-across-region/article_e5da0348-5cbf-11e5-8cd7-

Chapter 20 The Auditor General Is Coming to Town!!!

Please don't forget that first and foremost nearly all evidence says don't consolidate schools because it harms academics, student sense of well-being, student participation, and that it increases costs. Having said that, the site is receiving such attention because outside of perhaps Chernobyl, it would be difficult to find a worse spot to build a school.

Let's begin this chapter on the Wilkes-Barre audit with an August 5, 2019 post to the Save Our Schools Forum by SOS President Richard Holodick. It crisply tells the gist of why the Auditor General is now studying The Big Toxic School currently under construction. School Groundbreaking picture below followed by site picture

You can see the mine waste in this picture taken before most of the digging

Post by Richard A Holodick
August 5 at 3:41 AM

There is a need to inform this board where they govern, or better stated TO govern in a responsible manner. No one better to explain that than, The Honorable Eugene DePasquale, Auditor General and he cometh soon.

The where they govern is in a poverty-ridden district (76%), underfunded (so they claim) $33 million; with many home foreclosures, city blight; many seniors desperately trying to stay in the homes; and numerous low-income single families.

To govern in a responsible manner was to utilize all available resources (historic schools?). To prioritize board actions, i.e. students' academic needs, finances, facilities. Not sports, facilities and ignore, academics and finances!!!

The board's first actually completed action was to (prematurely) consolidate all sports, select a mascot, school colors, for a high school that doesn't exist. All in the face of students ranked **443rdout of 501** school districts in academics, **dead last** in SAT's.

The school design included a library too small to hold adequate book volumes; first, change order, expand the swimming pool and upgrade flooring; cost $1 million. Presently the students lack adequate books, teachers' need teaching supplies; and in the new school a too small library, but we have eight coaches' offices and an Olympic sized pool.

We, are at $20 million, own a coal ash dump, with known subsidence and contamination problems, that the taxpayer's paid 4 x the assessed value; three renderings at a Rembrandt cost. The site prep alone exceeds $10 million, and not complete. Oh and please bring a friend; Josh Shapiro. [*Pennsylvania Attorney General (Since 2017*]

Auditor General and Attorney General are asked to hear the people's cry for HELP!

Letter sent from Dr. Richard Holodick to Executive Editor of TL. This has to do with the Times Leader writing in their Diamonds and Coal section about the Attorney General's inquiry into Wilkes-Barre Area School District

Mr. Joe Soprano;

I agree with your "Diamonds to" on the visit of DePasquale, both sides need to agree following an unbiased review of the Pagnotti project finance review. As President of Save Our Schools I am troubled by "both sides;" not with the TL implication but with the school board's implying SOS as adversaries. You see their own mission statement, " to collaborate with the community," coupled with the Plan Con requirement to involve the community. Then we add the former superintendent's requests in a public meeting, "we can't do it alone we need your help."

SOS were formed and incorporated to meet the aforementioned. SOS membership are not a bunch of gadflies; they are professionals, covering the public and private sectors in leadership positions, parents, grandparents, and graduates. As important, we have WBASD volunteers, some exceeding 20 years with the district in sports and extracurricular activities. A retired University of Scranton architect, a retired superintendent, an environmental expert; and four outstanding attorneys that have hosted monthly meetings, provided positive advice for four years. Attorney's that care about children to the extent that they volunteered for 20 years as Meyers' Speech and Debate coaches.

Most certainly the district's agreement to pay 4 times the lowest assessed value, and $3.2 million for mineral rights for a mine shut down 40 years prior, and no professional assessment got the attention of DePasquale. But there is more; serious concerns, contamination and the assurance it can be 100% capped; five states out right forbid public schools on or even near contaminated sites. The research clearly describes large consolidated schools, dropped in the 70's, as educationally un-sound.

The WBA study lists closing the neighborhood schools as a "disadvantage." And what about the impact of moving the schools out of the city? Consider not doing due diligence to establish restoration of the historic high schools as recommended by PDE, PSBA, AIA and the historical society as irresponsible. The third to a quarter of a BILLION dollar project, to serve only a third of the students, in a poverty-ridden district is beyond irresponsible. A determination established by DePasquale in the Penn Hills District.

The district faces an Auditor General project review, a pending Plan Con hearing; and a future federal environmental review. "Diamonds," to all agencies that are listening and responding and the public for making the requests. SOS has done considerable research and developed a plan that restores two historic high schools, maintains the neighborhood schools, and saves a hundred million dollars over the traditional life span of a school; 40 years.

Regular folks in Wilkes-Barre Area are smiling!

For years, the public in the Wilkes-Barre Area School District have felt that life has been dealing bad cards to students and taxpayers alike. Many have been looking forward to the day when there would be a corruption probe of the school board. After all, right up the road for the last several years there has been an ongoing probe of the Scranton School District which was hot and cold and hot again as law enforcement agents were raiding the offices of the school board secretary and transportation director. They left with documents and computers. Scranton's board can no longer hide like ours has been hiding.

Then, in Scranton in September, this was followed by the arrest of the former fleet manager. Then, the state audit (investigation) of the financially struggling school district appeared to expand, as more than a dozen agents from the state police and the attorney general's office spent six hours in the administration building. Sometimes the Auditor General's investigation brings about an Attorney General's investigation and the public patience is rewarded when the knaves get to spend time in the Big House.

The scrutiny has been intense and it intensified further when Auditor General Eugene DePasquale issued a scathing report last fall, criticizing district leadership and operations. The Auditor General also questioned the costs of the district's no-bid contracts with DeNaples Transportation, and some school directors later questioned whether prior contracts were even legal.

From living in Wilkes-Barre in an area just south of Scranton, I can say that many residents are pleased with Scranton's results. Wilkes-Barre are is looking forward to similar results for the coming inquiry into the WBASD, which AG Eugene DePasquale initiated last week. Maybe our "friends" in Scranton will have some "good company" with whom to share their stories in the lockup.

It was on August 1, 2019, late last week, that Auditor General Eugene DePasquale asked the Wilkes-Barre Area School District in Luzerne County to provide him with details of its school construction and consolidation plan. Many residents of the area think there are a lot more skunks and rats to find than just those under the footers of Mine Shaft High, the euphemism for the big boondoggle monster school, which the district is building.

The Auditor General noted that *"more than 30 residents of the Wilkes-Barre Area School District have contacted my office to express concerns about the district's consolidation and building project," DePasquale said. "I take these concerns very seriously."* Thank God for large favors.

As you know from this book, the district plans to consolidate its three high schools into one new huge building on top of a toxic mine waste dump. DePasquale asked the district to provide copies of feasibility studies, appraisal documents, financial and debt service plans, lists of vendors and details on project costs. Residents of our area would surely enjoy to be flies on the wall watching the bags of evidence be unopened.

DePasquale said his interest in the Wilkes-Barre project is driven by public concern and his 2016 audit of the Penn Hills School District in Allegheny County, where a consolidation and building project left that district's taxpayers saddled with $167 million in long-term debt. Surely no taxpayer in this area can afford even small increases in taxes. That is why we see the whole monster school idea as something that will hurt the area and cause a lot of taxpayer exodus, and then, worse than even that, the elderly, already well overtaxed, will be losing their homes.

You can learn more about the Department of the Auditor General online at www.PaAuditor.gov. The Save our Schools group is opposed to the actions of the WBASD school boards for many of the reasons outlined in this book and many more.

It is no surprise that the officials of the board would immediately promise cooperation with the audit as let's face it, they have no choice. The lies are about to get bigger and bigger as this story gets spun to keep the board and the district's officials out of the Big House.

Covering their tracks, the Wilkes-Barre Area School District responded to the Auditor General in a written statement to Eyewitness News. Dr, Brian J. Costello, Superintendent, said the following:

The Wilkes-Barre Area School District has been contacted by the Auditor General's office in response to complaints of approximately 30 residents over the new high school project. The district has proactively contacted the Auditor General's office to pledge its full cooperation and support of this project.

The district looks forward to sharing our pathway to the future with the Auditor General.

DR. BRIAN COSTELLO

FYI, NOW THAT 30 RESIDENTS HAVE PRESENTED THEIR LETTERS TO THE AG,, I KNOW FOR FACT THAT MANY MORE LETTERS ARE COMING AS THIS IS SOMETHING THE RESIDENTS OF THIS AREA HAVE BEEN HOPING FOR. HAVE YOU SENT YOUR LETTER YET?

Auditor General seeks details of WB Area high school consolidation project

Times Leader reporter Mark Guydish wrote a piece in the August 1 edition of the paper titled: Auditor General seeks details of WB Area high school consolidation project. Your fans in the Wilkes-Barre Area wish you well, Mr. Auditor General.

State Auditor General Eugene DePasquale

Guydish wrote" "Along with responding to the complaints, the release said DePasquale is reviewing the Wilkes-Barre Area project in light of a 2016 audit of the Penn Hills School District in Allegheny County, "where a consolidation and building project left that district's taxpayers saddled with $167 million in long-term debt."

"That audit did cite Penn Hills for borrowing $135 million for a construction consolidation project without "adequately" budgeting for debt service payments, but it also cited a broad range of failures involved transportation contracts, fuel purchases, sporting event ticket sales, and having a single board member serve as both secretary and treasurer.

"Pathway to the future" refers to a multi-pronged approach the school board adopted in dealing with long-standing problems of budget shortfalls, low student scores on standardized tests, and chronic building problems.

A spokesman for the Auditor General's office said the specific complaints filed by residents regarding the project are not public record, and Board Solicitor Wendolowski said the district has not been provided detailed information on the complaints. Wendolowski, listed the documentation requested by DePasquale, some of which is also available on the district website:

• A copy of the "Pathways to the future" plan. An overview of the plan, labeled "Pathway to success," is on the district website.

• The district-wide feasibility study, first adopted by the board in December 2014, with two later revisions, one in June 2015 and one in May 2016. This is also on the district website.

• The total amount paid to prep the original planned site for a new high school. The board initially voted to consolidate grades 9-12 at Coughlin and Meyers high schools into a new building at the Coughlin site, but the Wilkes-Barre City Zoning Hearing Board denied a needed zoning variance. The board later voted to add GAR Memorial to the plan and build a new school in Plains Township. Before making that change, the district had spent considerable money gutting the main building of Coughlin and removing asbestos in anticipation of demolition.
• A copy of the Zoning Hearing Board decision on Coughlin. Two of the five board members recused themselves due to connections to the district, and the remaining members voted 2-1 to reject the plans for the new high school.

• Appraisal documents for the purchase of the construction site. The board agreed to pay $4.25 million for about 73 acres of a former mining site, and critics have argued it was assessed at no more than $800,o00, with no assessment for mineral rights. Wendolowski has staunchly defended the price as fair, comparing it to recent purchases of similar properties.

• Evidence of mining rights. Shortly after the purchase, Tom Dombroski contended the deeds did not convey mineral rights. Wendolowski insisted it was an oversight that was then corrected.

• The state Department of Environmental Protection conditional approval for the land use. Critics have repeatedly attacked the safety of the property because some coal ash was dumped there, and core samples found high levels of some hazardous materials. The district has countered that it is working with DEP to assure safety.

• A report from the PFM Group on a financial review of the district. That 2016 report, which projected potentially tens of millions in deficits if changes weren't made, is available on the district website. Wendolowski and others have noted the district has since made changes that led to improvement in the district's credit rating and a gradual increase in the district fund balance.

• Projected annual savings from the consolidation. The district has argued savings will offset the additional debt service taken on to complete the building. Critics have vigorously argued the savings will not materialize.

• List of vendor names and approved amounts of the contracts. In March the school board awarded 11 contracts totaling $88.8 million for most of the construction work on the school. Costello and Wendolowski have repeatedly insisted the contracts came in well under the projected costs, allowing the board to approve additions and to pay extra to assure the school is completed in time to open in fall of 2021.

The President of the Save Our Schools Committee, Dr. Richard Holodick took the opportunity to respond to the Guydish TL article cited above and his response follows:

When the AG report is complete, your author will change the book appropriately and add the results of the audit to this chapter.

A note from Dr. Holodick precedes his response:

"I attached a response to the Guydish story which contained spins on their actions and what the Auditor General will be looking at. I did this for the candidates but may send it on to Mike Burnell, Governor Wolf's Chief of Staff. who will give it directly to AG DePasquale. I will hold off on that until Tuesday to see what input you may have. I apologize for the length but I wanted to hit all the bullet points."

Auditor General seeks details of WB Area high school consolidation project

My (Holodick) replies to each of the bullet points in Guydish piece.

• The district-wide feasibility study, first adopted by the board in December 2014, with two later revisions, one in June 2015 and one in May 2016. This is also on the district website.

But not the total study, original and revisions appear on their web site. This half million-dollar study is interesting to see how many of the findings the board ignored. Prime example the study lists closing the high schools and creating a middle school as "disadvantage." We close the high schools and convert GAR into a middle school.

• The total amount paid to prep the original planned site for a new high school. The board initially voted to consolidate grades 9-12 at Coughlin and Meyers high schools into a new building at the Coughlin site, but the Wilkes-Barre City Zoning Hearing Board denied a needed zoning variance. The board later voted to add GAR Memorial to the plan and build a new school in Plains Township. Before making that change, the district had spent considerable money gutting the main building of Coughlin and removing asbestos in anticipation of demolition.

The first attempt, weak at best; not mentioned is paying the architect to design a school and do a rendering of a school they did not yet have approval to build. If the intent was to demolish the building then removal of asbestos was not needed in a poverty-ridden district. It may be a million for the architect and two million to remove the asbestos. That would be included in the demolition contract.

• A copy of the "Pathways to the future" plan. An overview of the plan, labeled "Pathway to success," is on the district website.

Considering a potential quarter of a billion dollar project this "plan" falls seriously short. A detailed long-range curricular/master plan is mandated. The board was offered an RFP from Harrisburg Community College for a master plan.

• The district-wide feasibility study, first adopted by the board in December 2014, with two later revisions, one in June 2015 and one in May 2016. This is also on the district website.

What should be posted is the total original study and the revisions; just one example of poor transparency/communications with the residents.

• The total amount paid to prep the original planned site for a new high school. The board initially voted to consolidate grades 9-12 at Coughlin and Meyers high schools into a new building at the Coughlin site, but the Wilkes-Barre City Zoning Hearing Board denied a needed zoning variance. The board later voted to add GAR Memorial to the plan and build a new school in Plains Township. Before making that change, the district had spent considerable money gutting the main building of Coughlin and removing asbestos in anticipation of demolition.

This paragraph should get the spin award. The total amount $4.9 million on demolition, asbestos removal, school design and a rendering of the building. The board was told by the solicitor that there was no way the zoning board could deny the request, hence the extensive costly work. Yes an official vote was taken to add 800 students to the new school. It was done at the end of the meeting under new business; the board not only did not provide what the additional cost would be; the public had no say at all on the decision.

The June 2015 board meeting was the worst, most arrogant; irresponsible (at a loss for adjectives) I have ever attended. There was a blatant disregard for children, sound education principals, the disregard of community input, and even discrimination. The plan voted on was illegal due to the segregation of the GAR students from the new school. Callous as the action was, it was done at the GAR High School, while the students sang their alma mater. Sixty people spoke to the board expressing their concerns. The board ignored them to the point of not responding to their concerns. It was this behavior, coupled with a rushed plan and not listening that cost the taxpayers $4.9 million dollars.

• A copy of the Zoning Hearing Board decision on Coughlin. Two of the five board members recused themselves due to connections to the district, and the remaining members voted 2-1 to reject the plans for the new high school.

The abstentions made no difference in the outcome. It was a huge school on a postage sized lot of 2.7 acres. State recommendation is 35 acres. It was to be built on a one way narrow street. What made the plan more irresponsible and potentially illegal, was that it segregated an entire high school, with the highest percentage of minorities and economically disadvantaged children. When asked about the GAR students the superintendent under oath told the zoning board, "GAR will not be included in this school." It is my professional opinion this plan was out right negligence and should have never been submitted to PDE.

• Appraisal documents for the purchase of the construction site. The board agreed to pay $4.25 million for about 73 acres of a former mining site, and critics have argued it was assessed at no more than $800,000, with no assessment for mineral rights. Wendolowski has staunchly defended the price as fair, comparing it to recent purchases of similar properties.

It was far from fair considering the fact that the charter school paid $3000 an acre for pristine land. Agreeing to pay over three million dollars, in a poverty-ridden district, mandated an appraisal, not a "that's what every body else paid conclusion." It is my understanding that this is not like "other similar properties," because it was not just mined but also, an unlined coal ash dump.

• Evidence of mining rights. Shortly after the purchase, Tom Dombroski contended the deeds did not convey mineral rights. Wendolowski insisted it was an oversight that was then corrected.

A $3.2 million dollar mistake was far beyond an "oversight." Was the deed read before the sales agreement was signed? It wasn't. The question was raised; why wasn't there two actions at this time—a vote for the land and a vote for the purchase of the mineral rights?

• The state Department of Environmental Protection's conditional approval for the land use. Critics have repeatedly attacked the safety of the property because some coal ash was dumped there, and core samples found high levels of some hazardous materials. The district has countered that it is working with DEP to assure safety.

Conditional approval a red flag? Yes "critics" have attacked the safety because a lot of coal ash, (not some) has been dumped on an unlined site. It is good they are working with DEP; will they give us a 100% assurance the site is safe for children? I say that because deaths have occurred from just being close to a contaminated site; this is very serious as we are building directly on top of a contaminated site! A disgrace when so many other safer and less costly sites are available.

• Projected annual savings from the consolidation. The district has argued savings will offset the additional debt service taken on to complete the building. Critics have vigorously argued the savings will not materialize.

Site purchase, $4.2 million; site prep, $9.5 million; Washington St, $4.9 million; Kistler, $1.3 million; additional bussing $1.5 million; interest $180 million; the incumbents said do the math and we did. It will not be possible to pay the debt over a 40-year period, which at that time we start over with a new school. The past history of building maintenance is a predictor that the new school will not last forty years. At a board meeting a "critic" (give professional courtesy attorney Borland critic) stated the library was too small to hold the volumes recommended by the library association. At the next meeting the board voted for a $1 million dollar change to expand the library? No to expand the swimming pool and better flooring.

• List of vendor names and approved amounts of the contracts. In March the school board awarded 11 contracts totaling $88.8 million for most of the construction work on the school. Costello and Wendolowski have repeatedly insisted the contracts came in well under the projected costs, allowing the board to approve additions and to pay extra to assure the school is completed in time to open in fall of 2021.

As stated throughout this response, this is a poverty-ridden district; we got a break on the bidding that came in well below what was anticipated. Board says lets blow the savings and first pays an extra $1 million dollars to "rush" the project;" a precursor to an increase in change orders. Then votes a change order to add two additional lanes to a not needed swimming pool and better flooring at a cost of over a million dollars. We are in excess of $20 million, we have three renderings:

Kistler $ 1 million lost   Washington Street $5 million lost   A pending loss $15 million?

and a coal ash dump:

At a location that may be land locked for getting 58 busses and 200 cars in and out at early morning and mid afternoon; with a hospital right up the road. River; Maffet; Cross Valley.

*They do not have a busing plan; another prime example of not conducting impact studies prior to taking official board action. This board has not demonstrated the ability to govern this school district. **Richard A. Holodick, Ph.D.***

Chapter 21 What Happens to the People? Does Anybody Care?

When all said and is done with the Big Toxic School on the Big Toxic Mountain, where will the people of Wilkes-Barre Area find themselves. The facts on the table indicate that if this Taj Mahal project is not halted soon, the project will scar the people and the area for a long time to come. The smart people will be the ones who are long gone.

What can we expect?

1. A school complex that puts children and adults at a major health risk.
2. Lower student achievement
3. Wilkes-Barre—major neighborhood blight
4. Huge public debt and high taxation
5. Minimal relief from **HB 76** and **SB 76**,

Major Health Risk

On November 18, 2018, the Times Leader's Mark Guydish made the most out of what will go down in history as The Big Toxic Mountain where the Big Toxic school will be built. The toxicity of the site and the runoff should worry the people of Plains as well as those in Wilkes-Barre Area who must expose their children daily to these poisons. Does anybody care if things don't go well for the people here?

Guydish writes that "Up an old industrial access road riddled with cracks, just over a ridge, the view becomes both old and new: Heavy earth vehicles scattered across a blackened landscape so common in coal country. A high hill of what looks like culm refuse. A fresh hole dug deep into the ebon turf, all surrounded by scrubby vegetation turning brown with the bitter cold. [Kinda gives you a warm feeling about building a new school there, don't you think?]

In the article Guydish discusses Area Super, Brian Costello pointing to one large hill in the distance. He notes that , "the "new" pile, it turns out, correlates directly with a large hole that has been excavated…That's where they found a soft spot, according to Costello so it had to be remade by either compacting or excavating so the ground will not shift when the school is occupied. Nice thought!

The truck in the distance sits roughly to the right of what is to be the main entrance of Wilkes-Barre Area's new consolidated high school. - Aimee Dilger | Times Leader

The "grassy areas" of the Pagnotti site in Plains Twp on Big Toxic Mountain, mark large swaths that were 'capped' years ago with top soil and vegetation to seal coal ash dumped as fill. I see no grass anywhere in the "grassy area;" do you? Considering the "capping" project is years old, would it be too much to ask for there to be some signs of life? Would you build your new home here if you could have all the land around it for free and tax free for years to come. Maybe they can dump green dirt for your landscaping needs since it sure seems that even weeds won't grow on Big Toxic Mountain where the Big Toxic school is being built.

A year 200 mining study by Wilkes University tells the obvious:

Summary

"The extraction and processing of anthracite coal caused an enormous environmental impact to nearly 100,000 acres of terrestrial and aquatic habitat throughout northeastern and east-central Pennsylvania. Original terrestrial forests were destroyed by strip mining and the deposition of culm material. Due to those activities, thousands of acres are marred by steep slopes and coarse substrates characterized by low fertility, toxic levels of certain elements, extreme drought, and high summertime temperatures. Natural revegetation has proceeded slowly on mine-impacted sites, resulting in sparse communities of low-value scrubby species. Ecological productivity, biological diversity, and recreation values are substantially lower on mined sites than on forested unmined areas. Animal life is also impaired due to insufficient food and water, and to extreme physical conditions."

"Corrective measures can be taken to address the ecological damage of mining. The methodologies employed are improving thanks to new research findings…" Reclamation typically involves planting and fertilizing to prevent erosion. The study suggests a nice use would be as a pasture. It says nothing about putting schools on top of these waste areas.

The verdict on how to reclaim land is not completed science and there is no study of which I am aware that offers a solution for the ultimate building of a facility that houses children and adults for over eight hours a day, every day. Solving the environmental problems of mining will require the collaboration of federal and state agency officials, scientists, and the private sector. Sufficient funding will be needed to pay for the expertise, labor, and materials needed to develop and execute a successful plan. The American Heritage River initiative should play a central role in coordinating the effort and securing funding. What has the WBASD done to assure safety. That answer is nothing and the people should be concerned about their health.

Lower student achievement

In many areas of this book, we have noted and proven conclusively that large schools produce lower student achievement. This is a summary of that finding taken from a Harvard study

Between 1930 and 1970, average school size in the United States increased from 87 to 440 and average district size increased from 170 to 2,300 students, as over 120,000 schools and 100,000 districts were eliminated via consolidation.

We exploit variation in the timing of consolidation across states to estimate the effects of changing school and district size on student outcomes using data from the Public-Use Micro-Sample of the 1980 U.S. census.

Students educated in states with smaller schools obtained higher returns to education and completed more years of schooling. While larger districts were associated with modestly higher returns to education and increased educational attainment in most specifications, any gains from the consolidation of districts were far outweighed by the harmful effects of larger schools. Reduced form estimates of the effects of consolidation on labor-market outcomes confirm that students from states with larger schools earned significantly lower wages later in life.

Neighborhood Blight in Wilkes-Barre

Throughout the book, we cautioned that the lack of Wilkes-Barre official's involvement in the fight to retain neighborhood schools, would create major issues or Wilkes-Barre neighborhoods in which the schools are destroyed.

Neighborhood blight refers to the deterioration and decay of neighborhoods in many cities across the country due to neglect, crime or lack of economic support. This can also be referred to as urban decay. As homes or properties fall further into disrepair, they can negatively affect other properties around them.

Some suggest that Neighborhood blight and urban decay and urban blight are either the same or similar. Urban blight for example is the process where a city, or a part of it, such as the areas around GAR High School or Meyers High School deteriorat and are abandoned for several reasons including unemployment, depopulation, outmigration, ethnic clashes, high level of crime. Without GAR or Meyers High Schools, think about what happens to the city. Neighborhood blight can also be known as Urban Decay. It is a stage where any prior economic growth comes to a halt. There is hardly any development seen in the region. In many ways Wilkes-Barre is already there and eliminating high schools as centers of communities and large employers in specific areas dooms those sections of the city.

The U.S. Department of Housing and Urban Development defines a "blighted structure" as: "A structure is blighted when it exhibits objectively determinable signs of deterioration sufficient to constitute a threat to human health, safety, and public welfare." Expect more of them when the high schools are torn down.

Poor Urban Planning is a cause. Considering that there is little to no urban planning in Wilkes-Barre, the officials seemingly have been indifferent to losing all the high schools in the city. If the city were doing its job, it would consider the needs and issues of the local area to make meaningful use of a vast space. It would not be standing by permitting buildings to be torn down with no replacement in mind.

Huge public debt and high taxation

Nobody is contesting the probable out right debt package to be paid by taxpayers in Wilkes-Barre area will be about $137 million. This is an awful lot when repairing the buildings is all we needed. The long term cost over 40 years is calculated with interest at being between a third and a half BILLION dollars. The financial complexion of the area cannot afford such a huge cost. Taxes will continually go up at the max allowed by the state while social security check increases lag behind as always. The elderly will be forced to give up their long held homesteads.

This year the District could have upped the taxes by another percentage but they did not. Speculation is that they did not do this because they are up for election and if they succeed this time, by the time the next election comes along. It will be too late. Mine Shaft High will be operating and 55 busses a day will be asking for the roads to be paved. By then, more and more people will be packing up and leaving rather than pay the max tax increase by law to sustain the Taj Mahal.

Minimal relief from HB 76 and SB 76

Many residents of Pennsylvania are longingly expecting good news soon. The fiscal provisions of HB 76 and SB 76, The Property Tax Independence Act, were developed using actual and projected revenue and school district expenditure figures provided by the House Appropriations Committee staff and the Governor's 2012-2013 Budget Book. It is no joke ladies and gentlemen, this could really help the people, especially the elderly and others on fixed incomes.

Many Pennsylvanians lose their homes and a lifetime's work to sheriff's sales each year because they can no longer afford to pay their property taxes. Senior citizens on fixed incomes are increasingly forced to sell their homes because of unrelenting increases in their tax burden. Young families cannot afford to purchase a home because the per month property tax escrow is simply too high.

Multigenerational family farms are being sold piece by piece to pay property taxes, devastating Pennsylvania agriculture. School districts in areas of the state with limited population and no commercial tax base are in distress and are unable to afford to give their children a quality education. Job losses, outmigration, and abysmal state economic performance caused by burdensome property taxes are devastating Pennsylvania's economy.

Home foreclosures and tax sales are occurring at an expanding rate and the home market is at a standstill. The opportunity to fund education from a statewide source is rapidly vanishing as relentlessly rising property taxes outpace available revenue. This will have major implications for school districts statewide. It can no longer be ignored or diminished. Replacement of the school property tax must be accomplished now.

Wilkes-Barre Area taxpayers expect that when Bill # 76 is passed, they will no longer pay any property taxes to the school district. That may be true for some other school districts but not for districts that have built huge schools. It looks like our area will be paying property taxes forever to pay off the Taj Mahal school in Plains Twp. Thank your local school board. Better yet, complain and get them to stop construction and then replace them.

Here is what it is all about folks Should Act 76, property tax relief pass or any version of property tax relief, it should be noted that the Wilkes-Barre Area homeowners would still have to pay 20% (could be higher) until the debt service is paid. But as for the increased tax on goods, we will have to pay that full amount. Figuring the cost of land, land prep, interest over forty years, increased bussing costs and so on, we are close to a HALF BILLION DOLLARS. There are bean counters that say this district cannot pay off that debt in 40 years. One would think that a board would do everything possible to maintain reachable goals; this board has done the opposite. Poor us! But we can still fire them. Pardon the humorous cartoon but what is,is!

TAXPAYER'S

Worth re-stating: "There is a wider lesson here also for the voting public: character matters when placing people in office and choosing un-trustworthy leaders at any level of government can have dire, real-life consequences." Citizens Voice

Appendix A—Many SOS Posts

Please don't forget that first and foremost nearly all evidence says don't consolidate schools because it harms academics, student sense of well-being, student participation, and that it increases costs. Having said that, the site is receiving such attention because outside of perhaps Chernobyl, it would be difficult to find a worse spot to build a school.

GAR High School (Grand Army of the Republic)

Purpose of this chapter

Because there are so many active Save Our Schools Forum members who make exceptional posts, I have collected a number of very recent ones and they are in this chapter for your reading pleasure. Remember the immediate goal is to replace the school board so Wilkes-Barre Area can finally have a competent board that serves the people. The current board chooses not to hear the people though they may in fact hear, but choose not to consider. Experience shows that the opinions of residents who make their opinions known at such times as during the five minutes one gets to speak at a board meeting, are given minimal respect.

Why do the people want the board replaced? Come to a meeting and you too will see that this board is self-centered, uncaring , ignorant, bullying, arrogant, biased, bigoted, prejudiced, unreasonable, fanatical, foolish, ignorant, and quite often plain old stupid. There are even other negative adjectives that describe the current board but we need space for other matters in this battle against the board.

Yes, believe it or not, there are other reasons why the people desire to fire all of the board members except for Melissa "Missi" Etzle, Patla, our one representative of the nine.

Thank you for reading so far. From this book, you now know the issues this board has caused for the people of the Wilkes-Barre Area. Rest assured that they are not done. They will continue to cause trouble for us until we fire them.

Let me go on just a bit longer and then I will turn this chapter over to the posts from the people's forum on Save Our Schools, a Facebook site designed to get the best government possible from the Wilkes-Barre Area School Board.

The precepts in this section below were extracted from "BULLIES on the Board" by Carol Humphries

Carol Humphries

Carol Humphries knows how to lead. She is the Principal of Ideal Consulting Ltd, and she works with a lot of the types of boards that run small and large organizations. She is passionate about lifelong learning, and loves working for boards who use learning to be the best they can be. She is creator of *Good Governance and Great Policies*. I regret that Carol Humphries would not be happy with our Wilkes-Barre Area School Board.

Melissa "Missi" Etzle Patla is the kind of director any board, especially a school board would be delighted to have as a member. She comes prepared for every meeting. She takes up jobs that fit her specific skills and experience and she thinks no job is too unimportant if it helps the students in the Wilkes-Barre Area. She works well with staff and students and teachers and whoever she can to further the progress of the students in this school district. Melissa, would not tell you this but we see it.

This school board as well as the officials in the district including the board chairman choose to treat her as a renegade because she represents only the people's interests and not the interests of the school board. Melissa is working hard with the SOS group to help bring in five new School Directors so that the board can begin to work for the people for a change. Of course she needs your help in getting them elected.

The natural reaction and one preferred by this board would be for anybody who is for the people and not for the board should not be encouraged to remain on the board and the objective is for them to depart more sooner than later. How surprised this board had to be when not only did Missy not choose to leave but she helped recruit others to take the slots of the bully board members who made life so difficult for her to do her job, which by the way, the people elected her to do.

Others would have left a long time ago but not Missy. The problem, folks, is that the Wilkes-Barre Area School Board is suffering from what Carol Humphries would call a *Bully on the Board*. In fact, the disease in this board is so rampant that eight members including the chairman suffer from this same malady. Melissa is a surprise to their nasty style of governance. She is person who, though small in stature, is huge in courage and determination. She fights back against the bullies and I think she is going to win in the final analysis. That means of course that the people will win because of "Missy.".

Carol Humphries notes that psychologists define bullying as a negative power relationship carried on by one individual or a group of individuals toward another person. Bullying does not necessarily need to be brutal or involve physical violence. Rumors, threats or hurtful words or scheduling group meetings with all people with an opposite opinion—meet with just one person such as Melissa to discuss matters privately. Think of how uncomfortable that would make you feel.

The fact is that bullying occurs everywhere to all kinds of people where a culture of respect and kindness is missing. Go to a WBASD board meeting and you will see that there are few people who get much respect from our esteemed board. Our board's bullying is more blatant than the norm in which a board likes situations when `no one is watching' or `no one will stand out and stand up." Our board does not seem to care about the norm. As a group, they are so self-assured and cocky that they don't seem to care who they push around and offend. Bullying is very prevalent in the manner in which this board conducts its business.

The notion that bullying only happens to a few people on poorly supervised schoolyards or in abusive family situations no longer holds true. We've seen it ourselves. Bullying is found where there are people with a propensity to be abusive. Thanks to Melissa Etzle Patla, this board does not get away with it as much anymore.

You might enjoy reading more about Carol Humphries and her take on "Bullies on the Board." For now, lets move on with the rest of this chapter. The members and friends of Save Our Schools have a lot to say about what is good for Wilkes-Barre Area and we do not reflect the thinking or the bullying of the Wilkes-Barre Area School Board.

Linda Metzger Teberio shared a link. 51 mins
It's pretty sad when your info sheet on Wilkes Barre area school district highlights the past 4 board members corruption arrested for accepting kickbacks for teacher jobs—bribes, bribes, no jail time, influencing contractors etc. That's the info sheet. And a D- rating with the Sunshine Board on financials and accountability. They are in charge of $137 million dollar new school . That's accepted? Why? I don't have a warm and fuzzy feeling

Robin Shudak 1 hr
Plains residents: If you live near the site, you should have received
the letter below. If you haven't, please PM me and call DEP 570-621-
2522 you can say "I'd like to file a formal complaint," and tell them
you didn't get the letter. It goes an record. If you have run-off or any
other problems from the site, you can list it, too.

Ruth VanWhy Hagenbaugh I can't understand why the teachers of
this new high school don't stand up and demand a better place for a
new school. Why are they letting this sh_tty school board build on
contaminated land that will, in time give them and the students
cancer? All teachers should take a stand. Or don't you care if you get
cancer? I know I wouldn't want to teach there. No way. This school
board is getting away with murder and it shouldn't be allowed.

Richard A Holodick: I am most encouraged on what looks like
teachers speaking up on social media. You see your posts is talk the
talk,; who better than you who walk the walk. Common theme,
parental or grandparent involvement, small learning communities.
We need more teachers...See More

Marilyn Jones: Why can't we the TAX PAYERS PUT THIS ON
THE BALLOT AND LET US VOTE ON WHETHER TO
RENOVATE OR BUILD ON TOXIC LAND. IT SHOULD BE
OUR RIGHT AS TAXPAYERS—SAVE OUR BEAUTIFUL
HISTORICAL HIGH SCHOOLS

Mark Schiowitz   Admin · Yesterday at 5:28 PM
For those who may be new to the discussion...the careful manner in
which district funds were nurtured in obtaining a school construction
site:

The land alone is a story: The land value was $200,000-$800,000
when assessed. Mineral right were never assessed and one would
expect no value there. That assessment would have cost about
$10,000.

The solicitor publicly stated that if they tried to take the land by
eminent domain at assessed value, they would be sued for the
mineral rights. Since Pagnotti wanted $8 million for land that laid

fallow for years, the solicitor reasoned, "This is a great buy. at a mere $4.2 million.

Then, the deed left the mineral rights with Pagnotti. When the district was sued in magistrate's court, a "revised deed," was produced showing after all, the district held the mineral rights. None of that sounds dishonest or fiscally irresponsible, right?
Then, there is the continuing chapter on reclamation.....

Gordon Williams: We attended the hearing where Mr Dombrowski pointed out that the deeds did not include mineral rights. This meant that Council did not read the deeds that were conveyed. But earned an increase in their law firm fee anyway.

Mark Schiowitz edited a doc.
Admin · Yesterday at 2:15 PM

Coal Ash Concerns
https://pilotonline.com/news/article_c204fb59-ad38-5f9c-94c0-75f29392f0d4.html
sierra-club-and-a-small-tribe-sue-the-blm-to-stop-the-expansion-of-a-coal-ash-landfill
https://www.readfrontier.org/stories/environmental-groups-file-suit-seeking-to-overturn-epas-transfer-of-coal-ash-disposal-regulation-to-state/
http://www.herald-dispatch.com/news/lawsuit-affected-by-chemical-exposure/article_d47784b4-84f0-5a8e-870a-313889f8a668.html
https://www.charlotteobserver.com/news/local/article40650402.html
See More

Richard A Holodick: We (SOS) have provided so many examples of the serious health hazards, including deaths of adults and children that are near coal ash dumps; despite that, we build on top of a coal ash dump. Thirteen inmates in a Pa. prison got a death sentence, not for a crime but for incarnation NEAR, not on top of a contaminated site. Apparently our residents of the WBA school district are 100% sure the WBASD will do due diligence to make sure the toxics are 100% capped (Impossible you know). The same WBASD that did such a great job maintaining three historic high schools. Clarification, if this site was donated and there was no other possible site maybe it would be worth the gamble. But it was not donated and we paid 5 x the lowest assessed value; and there are 123 square miles of land available, not to mention the district owned sites.

Marilyn Jones: That school board sucks. There is no care about anyone's life just money in their pocket-- death money at that☠☠☠😠😠😠

Richard A Holodick July 15 at 4:04 PM
Not intended to be funny; intention, pathetic!

WBA has 117 sq. miles and district owned property to select a site. They select a coal-mine, coal ash toxic dump. Little concern for the safety of the children and staff. They pay 5 x the lowest assessed value, & $3.2 M for un-assesed mineral rights that could be worth zero. They purchased un-reclaimed land and are building on un-reclaimed land. No concern for the taxpayers and so irresponsible there needs to be an investigation.

What a steal? Pun intended

Rear Creek Charter: $3,000 a green acre   Coal Shaft High: $55,000 a lifeless grey acre.

To quote the solicitor, *we do not have the "wisdom" (Oxymoron?) to question the decisions of the board.* When a board pays 5 x the lowest assed value for a toxic dump, with subsidence issues; and pays $3.2 million for mineral rights without a licensed appraisal someone with WISDOM better have the right to "question!"
The Federal Bureau of Investigation?

 Mark Schiowitz, Bob Holden and 20 others   65 Comments 6 Shares

Gordon Williams: Big problem is the few folks that vote—pull for the buddy system. Look at the board. Educators with pensions. They have a one-way mind set. New school good, old schools bad. And I'm worried that the registered voters will step up and vote these folks See More

Richard A Holodick: You are correct my friend. The same people will vote the same way. Our only hope is to get more people out to vote and that will take work. I believe that we must get the feds involved and I think the latest board actions may get their attention.

Kryssy Prula: We need to keep calling the FBI or the Atty Generals .
1
Richard A Holodick: [Pic BELOW] Groundbreaking shot as you can see it is a color shot by the yellow caution tape, but your right it sure looks like a black and white. Am I still a fake in your mind? But I have to thank you for proving the dismal appearance of the site not to mention the toxic material that creates that look.

Jessica Kelly Stork: Richard A Holodick this photo is so very ominous.... 😊

Robert M. Dohman: It's a toxic waste dump with an extremely high content of hazardous waste materials that make it unbuildable and still hasn't changed, dead land is dead land.

Mark Schiowitz: 🛡️ Everyone likes to see scarred mining land re-purposed and beautified. However, this plan has 3 huge flaws:
1. The vast store of educational literature says large consolidated schools result in educational decline. The district has been unable to refute this.
2. That same body of written evidence says operational costs usually increase and don't consolidate to save money.
3. This particular site was deep and surface mined and then was used as an unlined coal ash landfill for years when a power plant transported the toxic waste from burning coal and culm to this site. It hasn't even been checked for 2 of the more worrisome toxins that can be found. Add the admitted "moderate " risk of subsidence (10 episodes were reported at the site in the past) and already-noted toxic levels of arsenic in the soil, and a plan that potentially can increase river pollution, it is fair to say this is an inappropriate site for a school. 21 states limit the use of such sites for school construction. Several groups and EPA outline how you pick school sites and it has

no resemblance to this haphazard process. A representative of Environmental Integrity Project has called this site, "unprecedented."

Joseph Zakarauskas: Is it toxic? Isn't it toxic? Why take a chance with the health of "Our" people Think about where we have built things over mine shafts, over old landfills, So I think if it was worth anything for developing someone would have sucked it up.

Joan Finn: I'm curious....was that land ever really listed "For Sale", or was it just offered to the school district (for a steep price, of course)?

Robert M. Dohman: That land was not ever listed for sale due to its hazardous waste materials and use, it can't be sold in the state it's in. It is all an under the table deal.

Richard A Holodick: July 8 at 8:47 AM
I am confused. There is a law that requires the owner to reclaim coal mine sites before the land can be sold, showing vegetation growing. At the ground-breaking ceremony the appearance of a moon shot, nearly all black or grey did not appear to be reclaimed land. So we bought un-reclaimed land. We not only bought the un-reclaimed land we are building on the un-reclaimed land.

A FB post revealed paperwork that the district will pay nearly $10 million to "reclaim" the 78 acres, that is the responsibility of the Pagnotti Enterprise. If you take the purchase price of $4.2 million, add $9,500,000 for reclaiming the land, the add on swimming pool at $17 million +$1 million change order to expand the pool $18 million; equals over $35 million the cost to build the Bear Creek Charter School. The $88 million awarded bids, plus the change orders/upgrades have the project over a $100 million dollars. They have a budget figure of $121 million and trust me they will get to that figure shortly.

Richard A Holodick: July 14 at 7:33 AM
This form (outdated?) is difficult to read; board meetings are held at times difficult to attend; when attending it is difficult to hear board members speak (a blessing?).

It is difficult to understand millions upon millions of voted on expenditures because there are no discussions. What is understandable is there is a pattern; avoid transparency at all cost and I do mean ALL COSTS!

Joe Molitoris: Even in NJ which is easily as corrupt as PA to build a high school is either 50 M$ in central jersey (where the super pads the contractors) or 25 M$ in south Jersey (same school less contractor padding). So it's amazing that it costs 100 M$ in Wilkes-Barre. It's sad to see such corruption tolerated and tax dollars wasted.

Linda Metzger Teberio shared a link. July 11 at 8:07 PM
F- rating Pashinski. Vote him out F- rating in state reps. Pashinski. How embarrassing. Isn't he a former teacher? Pitiful. Here's a bit of humor for a Thursday evening. This worthless slug defeated a terrific

candidate last November and we lost a vote for HB 76. He is an "F-" and is at the VERY BOTTOM of the list of effective Representatives. Thanks, Luzerne voters. Keep pressing the big button at the top and putting this jerk back in office. We have you to thank for the lost vote. Enjoy the polkas from Eddie Day and the Starfires when the sheriff comes to toss your family from your home.

Eddie Day Pashinski --- NOT ONE OF THE Good Guys for the AREA!

Linda Metzger Teberio: July 9 at 10:00 PM
Demand a board recall. Does anyone know why this new school was not on a voter referendum or the ballot like 100% of other school districts? It appears the majority board misrepresented school enrollment numbers and used 2011 numbers and added the middle school to the total school costs when in fact they knew they weren't adding the middle school at this location. They are required by law to have this school on a voter referendum and let all vote yay or nay

E is maximum bldg cost per state $97,185,264. D20 c is $116,965,141 contract the contracts they signed. Since they're over by $19,779,877 it needs to be on a referendum. They got around it by saying middle school going in plan but is that the case? That's why they are lying 😔. And the 1973 forms they are using are outdated.

Richard A Holodick   July 11 at 7:48 AM
The Moving Forward group running for re-election posted, "SOS plan? SOS plan? Thank you for asking. Educationally and financially sound; maintains the neighborhood schools preferred by this board, PFM and the board's feasibility study. Restores historic GAR & Meyers, recommended by, PDE, PSBA, AIA, and Pa. Historical Society. Builds a right-sized high school for the dissected Coughlin High School. Refurnishes and maintains the Kistler swimming pool as the previous board committed to when removing the Miner Park Pool to build Kistler. Refurbishes the Memorial stadium using donated funds and naming rights. Saves a million a year on busing alone. Does not place students and employees in potential harm's way due to contamination; I said potential. Does not pay 5 times assessed value of seriously scared land; or $3.2 million for mineral rights that un-assessed could be worth zero.

Linda Metzger Teberio 100% of school funding comes from the PA state revenue sources. That's been the case for 15 years under all administrations. What I do applaud Betsy Devos is the architect of dismantling the US dept of education and promoting charter schools and vouchers so kids don't get stuck in the PA Dept of education teacher union discriminatory hot mess with taking students hostage with contracts and strikes.

Robin Shudak shared a post. July 11 at 9:32 AM

[NICE Note Robin – REAL NICE] July 11, 2015
Think you are too young, insignificant, or unknown to make a difference?

If you are my age or older, you probably grew up with a healthy fear of The Soviet Union, a nuclear WWIII, and mutually-assured destruction. The now-faded navy and yellow "Fallout Shelter" sign and bullhorn atop Meyers High School meant something very imposing: "If that horn went off, could I make it here in time?"
But times CAN change. One of the biggest symbols of the Cold War was the Berlin Wall. For 28 years, it cemented the imposing reality of the war & its two immovable sides. And then on Nov 9, 1989, nine days before my birthday - it came down. Progress! Peace! A chance to see family members I only knew from pictures!
How did it start?

"Mr. Gorbachev, tear down this wall."
President Reagan delivered those words like gunshots at Berlin's Brandenburg Gate two years earlier, effectively telling the world the US was going to take a more active role in helping the people living under Communism. The speech goes down as one of the most popular & significant given by an American President.
But did he write it?
No.

Richard A Holodick: July 9 at 5:20 PM
Does anyone disagree that the W-B school district is in dire straits educationally, financially? Has it been established that with the exception of Mackin all school facilities do not meet state standards? Estimated cost $300 million! Is it true the district is suing the state

because the district is underfunded by $33 million dollars a year? Is it a fact that programs were closed and libraries, teachers released, and students lack textbooks and teachers buy their own to teach...More

Linda Metzger Teberio Everyone needs to call or email our auditor and state buildings and grounds offices to stop the madness.

Joan Finn: And there's the problem - it looks like a school district has to be in multi-million dollar debt before an audit is done. It doesn't look like an audit will STOP this train wreck in the WB district!

Linda Metzger Teberio · July 6 at 9:36 PM
Did you know that the majority WBASD school board members knew, at least as of April the primary, they were going to be increasing "real estate increased at maximum cap rate" yet misled all with a public forum wherein they publicly stated taxes would decrease. And showed $65,650,021 as cash assets available for the school. Once again, this alleged official document is all marked up. Without seeing bank account statements I don't see cash available assets of $65 million. Cash assets readily available for use seems unrealistic considering they had a negative $3.7 million starting cash balance.

Linda Metzger Teberio · July 7 at 2:18 AM
Aggregate building expenditure standards put this school at $97,185,364. They went with the pool option of $17,000,000 million. Plus many school upgrades such as a Solariums and major flooring upgrades. . So it's $123,548,000 million. They are using 2010-2011 enrollment numbers. Not current Enrollment which are much lower. Once again these docs are all marked up and changed so I am not sure what we are buying. It's like a car. Everything should be on the sticker marketing info. Not the case here WBASD has us buying a full Cadillac with all upgrades.

Richard A Holodick July 7 at 10:02 AM
Pictured is the rendering of a consolidated high school, sitting on what looks like a moonscape, ill-planned by the WBA school board/superintendent/the Team, and legitimized by the solicitor. Consolidation of schools ceased in the 70's. The school is placed on a former coalmine, deep and stripped mined, used as a coal ash dumping ground. A site near impossible to build homes on and so

contaminated that five other states will not allow public schools on or even near. The 78 acres resting between River/Maffet Streets and North Main is land-locked as it relates to having 58 buses, 200 cars enter and exit early morning and mid-afternoon; in an area with a major hospital. One would conclude enough said to negate this selection; no there is more.

Bob Holden and 12 others   6 Comments 7 Shares

Ruth VanWhy Hagenbaugh What kind of land scaping will they have around the school? You can't grow anything on that soil. This is the most corrupt school board ever. They just don't care how much money they have to spend. They are being taken advantage of and we have to pay for it. If I could sell my house, I would get out as fast as I could.

Robert M. Dohman They are still segregating in the middle school, Coughlin 7th to 9th stay at the Solomon school instead of the new remodeled GAR middle school. So their intentions are still as clear as day.

Richard A Holodick: July 2 at 1:06 PM
Five districts-Greater Nanticoke Area, Hanover Area, Hazleton Area, Scranton and Wilkes-Barre Area-PERFORMED THE WORST, missing state averages on all 18 tests.

I am not an advocate of testing due to many possible variables that test validity. But when you are at the bottom, labeled the worst, a validity test is not needed to draw realistic conclusions. It's a fact we have serious academic achievement problems; what is our board's "master plan?"

The first priority, consolidate all sports reducing student's opportunities to participate; activities are known to keep students in school and maintain passing grades. Move all high schools out of the city's neighborhoods to an isolated potentially toxic site, adding to the burden of economically disadvantaged parents and students to be active in school events. Convert GAR High School to a middle school, where our own studies and the research say contributes to academic decline and attendance problems. Build a consolidated school that our own study and PFM list as a "disadvantage," and research established shows it is not conducive to low achieving students, adds to discipline and attendance problems.

We are number one in the state for truancy and the number of students fleeing the district. Oh, then we bus 2400 students adding hours to some student's day, a haven for bullying, and then getting 58 buses in and out of the isolated site; pick-up of 2400 students at 7 am, over 117 square miles will be a real challenge.

Dorothy Price-Knorr: The problem here is you all keep voting the same old buffoons back to the school board. They taxed me out of my house so I don't have to worry about that ginormous bill anymore. Have fun people...

Linda Metzger Teberio: · July 6 at 1:08 AM
We were all told there would be no new borrowings for Wilkes Barre Area School construction and we would have a perpetual 40 year tax increase. Guess what? They lied. Here's the new borrowing note proposal and fees at $137,318,879 million. This is insane. This district put all of us in a $137 million dollar debt with no input.

Linda Metzger Teberio · July 4 at 3:13 AM
Wondering why WBASD has $3,004,101.94 million in a Food Service checking account at Landmark Bank marked as "proprietary funds" Do parents deposit funds in a cafeteria account? Would it amount to $3 million? Is this free lunch money that wasn't used and is now being fraudulently used by majority board to inflate assets and increase borrowing power? Free lunch money being diverted?????

DID you all know there is $517,000 in a elementary and secondary activity fund? Line 23 n 24. So why do they make you fundraise?

Mark Schiowitz shared a link. Admin · July 4 at 9:49 AM
The EPA on schools in neighborhoods like W-B City:
"Policies that encourage the renovation of existing schools, with appropriate mitigation of environmental hazards if necessary and the siting of new facilities within existing neighborhoods can contribute to solving multiple challenges in older communities. Conversely, policies that discourage renovating existing schools or siting schools within the community can lead to a disinvestment in the community that may contribute to physical, social and economic decline in the community. Siting schools in the communities they serve— particularly in urban areas where disinvestment in neighborhoods has led to chronic environmental, economic and public health disparities—can be part of a revitalization strategy aimed at a wide range of improved community outcomes.

Mark Schiowitz And you should read the section on how to site a new school if you must build one. It is totally different from what went on here. We are supposed to accept whatever the board majority says is best, like sheep. All we need to do is pay up. Meanwhile our children will potentially bear the cost: impaired education, fewer opportunities, horrific debt, and hazards to health. Return no incumbent to the board in the fall. Fight this senseless, dangerous and worthless site.

Bob Holden shared a link. July 1 at 7:23 AM
Interesting. The board spent $7.5 million already on the new school. I will have to assume that is not including other money wasted on the Coughlin site and the Kistler "expansion". On top of the $127 million they estimate us paying, the INTEREST will cost $162 MILLION. With the expenditures on the lost projects that puts this project at over $300 million right now. Wow!!!!

Debbie Orlando Formola July 2 at 12:55 PM
I challenge anyone to call the DEP in Pottsville and ask them if they did ANY groundwater testing at the prospect site Ever !!

This is a public notification...

The Pennsylvania Department of Environmental Protection (DEP) was responsible for issuing the surface mining permit and renewals. In addition to monitoring the surface mining and ash placement activity ,DEP also conducted groundwater monitoring g prior to ,during and after the ash was placed . In accordance with the regulations (5 years of groundwater monitoring), the sampling concluded in 2010. Results of the sampling were compared to DEP drinking water standards. In general the trends for the parameters tested did not show potential risk for contamination. The mining permit will be closed within several weeks.

Mark Schiowitz ⭐ EPA has no jurisdiction over mining land and is the only major agency with a coal ash rule. They generally defer to the state and DEP is, I think, pretty mining-friendly. Other thing is that they and all of us like to see ugly mining land brought back, but this site is inappropriate for a school. Staff from Environmental Integrity Project have labeled it. "unprecedented" and "dangerous."

Lois Ann: July 1 at 9:45 AM
I would like to understand more about the environmental issues at the Pagnotti site. I know several of you, namely Debbie, have done tons of research on this issue. I'll be honest, I've tried to follow along but I am completely dense when it comes to this topic. Would anyone be willing to write out the issues in laymen's terms so we can get a grasp on it?

Linda Metzger Teberio shared a post.

Visual Storyteller · June 29 at 11:17 AM

Jason Carr ▶ Greater Wilkes Barre Taxpayers Coalition
June 29 at 10:40 AM

Because SHAWN WALKER, MARK ATHERTON and JOHN QUINN voted to raise your property taxes last week caused by a new school, that the residents overwhelmingly do not want, your Wilkes-Barre School District Tax is calculated $18.43 per $1000.00 as of July 1 2019 of your assessed property's value.

Karen Delaney Komorek and 16 others   20 Comments 3 Shares

Richard A Holodick: Joseph, Joseph, Joseph, the June 24, 2019 board meeting was a disgrace, but I must admit your consistent as most board meetings are an ignominy; inconsistent times and dates, inconvenient times (9 am). There was as usual a complete lack of concern for the comfort of attendees (seating), especially the elder (me) and handicapped. Then there is the hearing impaired as a microphone, one, must be shared with 11 people. But $14,000 is spent on a camera for the superintendent to remain on his buttocks in his office? Seriously? My opinion the speakers were treated crudely, and unprofessionally as board members chatted with each other; the super played on his computer. Repeating a past very costly action item that was done at the end of the meeting, under new business, awarding a contract valued at nearly a million and a half dollars for the solicitor. The taxpayers that must pay for the costly board actions had no possibility to speak to the issues they must pay for. You just don't care counselor Caffery…you just don't care!

Richard A Holodick:
Elected officials can be fined and removed from office by state law for maleficence or miss-administration of duties. It does not take an illegal activity. Do any of the following apply?

1. An official board vote to send a discriminatory plan to PDE's Plan Con Division that segregated and entire high school from the proposed two high school consolidation. It was the high school with the highest % of minority and socially disadvantaged students. Local CEO of NAACP; "Racism is alive and well. She blasted the consolidation. The board under "new business" added the segregated high school with a motion that did not include public discussion, board discussion and no cost for adding 800 students to the "new high school."

2. Spending $4.9 million on demolition, site work, and school design prior to receiving zoning approvals to build; and the zoning was denied.

3. Paying 5 x the lowest assessed value for 78 acres of seriously scared land; then paying $3.2 million dollars for mineral rights without a professional assessment. Bear Creek Charter board paid $3000 an acre for pristine land;

4. The purchase of a 78-acre mining site, which was still an active mining site, before the land was declared, reclaimed; the law states that mining land cannot be sold prior to being reclaimed by the owner, with clear evidence of vegetation. Construction started on land possibly not completely reclaimed.

Mark Schiowitz shared a link. Admin · July 4 at 9:58 AM
From "Renovate or Replace?" by the Pa. School Board Association and Pa. Dept. of Education

"The presence of a neighborhood school functions much like a major retail store in a shopping center or mall; it is the anchor that attracts and retains the other stores. An abandoned school, much like a closed and abandoned store or factory building, adversely affects a community's morale even more than the loss of job."

Referring to classic schools:

"Many were over designed in load-bearing capacity by today's structural standards. Most of these older schools are easier and less costly to renovate than schools built in the postwar suburban era, when cheap materials and inferior construction techniques became common. Most older schools are well-suited for renovation as "green" buildings. Their compact, multi-story layout is more efficient to heat in the winter and cool in the summer than sprawling one story buildings. High ceilings provide plenty of room for wiring, duct work, and piping."

NEPOTISM???

Richard A Holodick June 25 at 8:58 AM
On June 24, 2019, the query of nepotism in the WBASD may have been answered. A citizen concerned with the harm done to senior citizens and low-income residents, by the perpetual property tax increases, suggested furloughing teachers. The truth arose as board member Evans blurted out; " Yes you stand there and recommend laying off teachers; what if you were on the board and it was your wife to be laid off?" The nerve of this guy wanting board members to furlough family members; heartless I say. Bet that hit home with Walker, Atherton and Caffery, all have their spouses working in the WBASD. But it pales in consideration of past quotes; at least this was humorous as opposed to morally offensive.

Mark Schiowitz ⬡ My opinion for what it's worth? Cheer is a sport. If the district has sports programs, cheer deserves support. Probably all activities should and almost all do, however, contribute to program support.

But..... look at us expending energy, anger, frustration on the crazy sports consolidation. The big issue is that smaller schools in residential neighborhoods are far more likely to rescue the kids and teach them well than a consolidated school. That's based on evidence. Anyone wants it, I have it. Placing a school on the worst site this side of Chernobyl should be a huge red flag to this whole community, too. I am (oops was) a volunteer football coach for 10 years. Love MHS football, but let's battle for better education and better governance.

In the meantime, get these kids safely to practices and conditioning if anyone really cares.

Richard Holodick: June 22 at 1:40 PM
There are 117 square miles in the WBASD, the board selects a site that all things considered cost the taxpayers $55,000 an acre for an isolated coal ash dump. As compared to Bear Creek paying $3000 an acre for pristine land. No hidden agendas here?

Mark Schiowitz: Admin · June 21 at 10:14 AM
In the educational literature there hasn't been a major article supporting consolidation in 50 years.

There is recent consensus that middle schools with their additional transition year cause some academic and social setbacks. Consolidation articles: educational demise, higher costs, more dropouts, poorer security, less school participation.
Is the leadership illiterate or is it just tunnel vision?

Schiowitz add'l notes on middle schools:

Middle Schools are not the way to go. For example, Public middle schools in New York City have fallen behind their peers in K–8 schools. This is true both for math and English achievement. Even more troubling, the middle-school disadvantage grows larger over the course of the middle-school years. With the transition into a middle school, students set out on a trajectory of lower achievement gains.

Moreover, parent evaluations of school safety, academic rigor, and overall educational quality was much lower among those whose children attended middle schools than among parents with children in K–5, K–6, and K–8 schools.

There is substantial evidence that middle schools' systems have lower on-time high school completion rates. Since graduation rates are best interpreted as a measure of the success of weaker students, our results therefore suggest that middle schools are failing less able students or the group they were supposed to help the most.

Several researchers have raised concerns about the lack of personal attention and monitoring in middle schools. Although we know of no systematic evidence, prior to this study, to either validate or refute these concerns, some researchers have pointed to the decline in sixth grade math and science scores as evidence that middle schools are failing. Maybe more convincing is the very recent decision of one of the largest school districts in the country, New York City, to eliminate as many as two-thirds of their middle schools and replace them with K-8 grammar schools in an attempt to improve the quality of education and increase student-teacher connectedness (New York Times March 3, 2004)

Research on the 6-12 model's effectiveness is almost nonexistent, but other urban districts that have used it have touted the benefits for retention and academic enrichment.

After four years and 15 new 6-12 schools, the dropout rate improved by 60 percent and enrollment that had been falling for years leveled, One expert said that "students were coming in behind in terms of their academics and they were beginning to face extreme challenges around having to work, they had problems around transportation and teachers didn't have enough time to sort of hook them.

Richard Holodick: I made some corrections:
Location, Location, location, shout the realtors when marketing land. The Luzerne County Transit Authority (LCTA) just secured the Murray site, ideal location for $1.5 million, $130,000 an acre.

The site contains 11 acres and a large restorable brick structure (not sure it was included). It does not need a reclamation. LCTA vs. WBASD, no contest; the WBA school board paid $55,000 an acre for and isolated location, toxic, requiring (so far), $9 million in site work, and an additional $35,000 to fill what appears to be a sinkhole.

This site is known for subsidence problems. Social media and the word on the street favored this site for a WBA high school. The site was rejected by the WBA board, due to safety concerns of children crossing a busy street, and railroad tracks. So, they selected an isolated site near railroad tracks, seriously contaminated with subsidence problems, and next to the very busy Cross Valley expressway.

Educationally unsound, a potential health catastrophe; and all that was needed, 5 votes to put 3000 students and employees in way, and 67,000 district residents in debt. Does the aforementioned validate the need for a referendum? Does the aforementioned support the need in Pa. for a recall or impeachment provision for elected officials?

Robin Shudak tagged you (BK) and 19 others in a post:

"PLAINS RESIDENTS:

If you've seen this orange-yellow run-off in your neighborhood, please know you can file a complaint. Contact DEP at 570-621-3118 or http://www.depgreenport.state.pa.us/EnvironmentalComplaintForm/ I ADVISE ALL - DO NOT TOUCH.

A chemist familiar with the site and fossil fuels said it could be arsenic sulfide, a water-soluble form of arsenic. Arsenic sulfide can be absorbed through the skin, causing irritation and a painful headache.

OTHERS: DEP has opened a comment period about this site. To put yourself on record, write: Pennsylvania Dept of Environmental Protection Pottsville District Mining Office 5 West Laurel Blvd. Pottsville, PA 17901 Include your contact info &reference: SMP #40840206 (Jeddo-Highland Coal Company, Prospect Bank Operation) Questions? Call 570-621-3474 A template for the letter is available at https://docs.google.com/document/d/1zOgqbx8bcoKgH6jjVffQ9k vrRZUHGNXSMNyghd9UFVw/edit?usp=drivesdk".

Other Books by Brian W. Kelly: (amazon.com, and Kindle)

Hope for Wilkes-Barre-John Q. Doe Next Mayor of Wilkes-Barre PA: John Doe Plan,to help create better city!
Democrat Secret for Power & Winning Elections: Open borders, amnesty, millions of new Democrat Voters
The Cowardly Congress Whatever happened to Congress doing the work of the people?
Help for Mayor George and Next Mayor of Wilkes-Barre How to vote for the next Mayor &Council
Ghost of Wilkes-Barre Future: Spirit's advice for residents about how to pick the next Mayor and Council
Great Players in Air Force Football: Air Force's best players of all time
Great Coaches in Air Force Football: From Coach 1 to Coach Troy Calhoun
Great Moments in Sir Force Football: From day 1 to today
Great Players in Navy Football: Navy's best including Bellino & Staubach
Great Coaches in Navy Football: From Coach 1 to Coach #39 Ken Niumatalolo
Great Moments in Navy Football: From day 1 to coach Ken Niumatalolo l
No Tree! No Toys! No Toot Toot! Heartwarming story. Christmas gone while 19 month old napped
How to End DACA, Sanctuary Cities, & Resident Illegal Aliens . best solution to wipe shadows in America.
Government Must Stop Ripping Off Seniors' Social Security!: Hey buddy, seniors can no longer spare a dime?
Special Report: Solving America's Student Debt Crisis!: The only real solution to the $1.52 Trillion debt
How to End DACA, Sanctuary Cities, & Resident Illegal Aliens . best solution to wipe shadows in America.
The Winning Political Platform for America Unique winning approach to solve the big problems in America.
Lou Barletta v Bob Casey for US Senate Barletta's unique approach to solving the big problems in America.
John Chrin v Matt Cartwright for Congress Chrin has a unique approach to solving big problems in America.
The Cure for Hate !!! Can the cure be any worse than this disease that is crippling America?
Andrew Cuomo's Time to Go? "He Was Never that Great!": Cuomo says America never that great
White People Are Bad! Bad! Bad! Whoever thought a popular slogan in 2018 would be It's OK to be White!
The Fake News Media Is Also Corrupt !!!: Fake press / media today is not worthy to be 4th Estate.
God Gave US Donald Trump?   Trump was sent from God as the people's answer
Millennials Say America Was "Never That Great": Too many pleased days of political chumps not over!
White People Are Bad! Bad! Bad! In 2018, too many people find race as a non-equalizer.
It's Time for The John Doe Party… Don't you think? By By Elephants.
Great Players in Florida Gators Football… Tim Tebow and a ton of other great players
Great Coaches in Florida Gators Football… The best coaches in Gator history.
The Constitution by Hamilton, Jefferson, Madison, et al. The Real Constitution
The Constitution Companion. Will help you learn and understand the Constitution
Great Coaches in Clemson Football The best Clemson Coaches right to Dabo Swinney
Great Players in Clemson Football The best Clemson players in history
Winning Back America. America's been stolen and can be won back completely
The Founding of America… Great book to pick up a lot of great facts
Defeating America's Career Politicians. The scoundrels need to go.
Midnight Mass by Jack Lammers… You remember what it was like Great story
The Bike by Jack Lammers… Great heartwarming Story by Jack
Wipe Out All Student Loan Debt--Now! Watch the economy go boom!
No Free Lunch Pay Back Welfare! Why not pay it back?
Deport All Millennials Now!!! Why they deserve to be deported and/or saved
DELETE the EPA, Please! The worst decisions to hurt America
Taxation Without Representation 4th Edition Should we throw the TEA overboard again?
Four Great Political Essays by Thomas Dawson
Top Ten Political Books for 2018… Cliffnotes Version of 10 Political Books
Top Six Patriotic Books for 2018… Cliffnotes version of 6 Patriotic Boosk
Why Trump Got Elected!.. It's great to hear about a great milestone in America!
The Day the Free Press Died. Corrupt Press Lives on!
Solved (Immigration) The best solutions for 2018
Solved II (Obamacare, Social Security, Student Debt) Check it out; They're solved.
Great Moments in Pittsburgh Steelers Football… Six Super Bowls and more.
Great Players in Pittsburgh Steelers Football ,,,Chuck Noll, Bill Cowher, Mike Tomin, etc.
Great Coaches in New England Patriots Football,,, Bill Belichick the one and only plus others
Great Players in New England Patriots Football… Tom Brady, Drew Bledsoe et al.
Great Coaches in Philadelphia Eagles Football..Andy Reid, Doug Pederson & Lots more
Great Players in Philadelphia Eagles Football Great players such as Sonny Jurgenson
Great Coaches in Syracuse Football All the greats including Ben Schwartzwalder
Great Players in Syracuse Football. Highlights best players such as Jim Brown & Donovan McNabb
Millennials are People Too !!! Give US millennials help to live American Dream
Brian Kelly for the United States Senate from PA: Fresh Face for US Senate
The Candidate's Bible. Don't pray for your campaign without this bible
Rush Limbaugh's Platform for Americans… Rush will love it

Sean Hannity's Platform for Americans… Sean will love it
Donald Trump's New Platform for Americans. Make Trump unbeatable in 2020
Tariffs Are Good for America! One of the best tools a president can have
Great Coaches in Pittsburgh Steelers Football Sixteen of the best coaches ever to coach in pro football.
Great Moments in New England Patriots Football Great football moments from Boston to New England
Great Moments in Philadelphia Eagles Football. The best from the Eagles from the beginning of football.
Great Moments in Syracuse Football The great moments, coaches & players in Syracuse Football
Boost Social Security Now! Hey Buddy Can You Spare a Dime?
The Birth of American Football. From the first college game in 1869 to the last Super Bowl
Obamacare: A One-Line Repeal Congress must get this done.
A Wilkes-Barre Christmas Story A wonderful town makes Christmas all the better
A Boy, A Bike, A Train, and a Christmas Miracle A Christmas story that will melt your heart
Pay-to-Go America-First Immigration Fix
Legalizing Illegal Aliens Via Resident Visas Americans-first plan saves $Trillions. Learn how!
60 Million Illegal Aliens in America!!! A simple, America-first solution.
The Bill of Rights By Founder James Madison Refresh *your knowledge of the specific rights for all*
Great Players in Army Football Great Army Football played by great players..
Great Coaches in Army Football Army's coaches are all great.
Great Moments in Army Football Army Football at its best.
Great Moments in Florida Gators Football Gators Football from the start. This is the book.
Great Moments in Clemson Football CU Football at its best. This is the book.
Great Moments in Florida Gators Football Gators Football from the start. This is the book.
The Constitution Companion. A Guide to Reading and Comprehending the Constitution
The Constitution by Hamilton, Jefferson, & Madison – Big type and in English
PATERNO: The Dark Days After Win # 409. Sky began to fall within days of win # 409.
JoePa 409 Victories: Say No More! Winningest Division I-A football coach ever
American College Football: The Beginning From before day one football was played.
Great Coaches in Alabama Football Challenging the coaches of every other program!
Great Coaches in Penn State Football the Best Coaches in PSU's football program
Great Players in Penn State Football The best players in PSU's football program
Great Players in Notre Dame Football The best players in ND's football program
Great Coaches in Notre Dame Football The best coaches in any football program
Great Players in Alabama Football from Quarterbacks to offensive Linemen Greats!
Great Moments in Alabama Football AU Football from the start. This is the book.
Great Moments in Penn State Football PSU Football, start--games, coaches, players,
Great Moments in Notre Dame Football ND Football, start, games, coaches, players
Cross Country with the Parents A great trip from East Coast to West with the kids
Seniors, Social Security & the Minimum Wage. Things seniors need to know.
How to Write Your First Book and Publish It with CreateSpace. You too can be an author.
The US Immigration Fix--It's all in here. Finally, an answer.
I had a Dream IBM Could be #1 Again The title is self-explanatory
WineDiets.Com Presents The Wine Diet Learn how to lose weight while having fun.
Wilkes-Barre, PA; Return to Glory Wilkes-Barre City's return to glory
Geoffrey Parsons' Epoch… The Land of Fair Play Better than the original.
The Bill of Rights 4 Dummmies! This is the best book to learn about your rights.
Sol Bloom's Epoch …Story of the Constitution The best book to learn the Constitution
America 4 Dummmies! All Americans should read to learn about this great country.
The Electoral College 4 Dummmies! How does it really work?
The All-Everything Machine Story about IBM's finest computer server.
ThankYou IBM! This book explains how IBM was beaten in the computer marketplace by neophytes

Amazon.com/author/brianwkelly
Brian W. Kelly has written 199 books. Thank you for buying this one.
Other Kelly books can be found at amazon.com/author/brianwkelly